W9-AZM-254

Trends and Issues in Distance Education

International Perspectives

A Volume in
**Perspectives in Instructional Technology
and Distance Education**

Series Editors: Charles Schlosser and Michael Simonson
Nova Southeaster University

Perspectives in Instructional Technology and Distance Education

Charles Schlosser and Michael Simonson, Series Editors

Research on Enhancing the Interactivity of Online Learning (2005)
  edited by Vivian H. Wright, Cynthia Szymanski Sunal, and
  Elizabeth K. Wilson

Towards the Virtual University: International On-Line Learning Perspectives
(2003)
  edited by Nicolae Nistor, Susan English, and Steve Wheeler

Learning from Media: Arguments, Analysis and Evidence (2003)
  edited by Richard E. Clark

Trends and Issues in Distance Education

International Perspectives

edited by

Yusra Laila Visser
Wayne State University

Lya Visser
Learning Development Institute

Michael Simonson
Nova Southeastern University

Ray Amirault
Wayne State University

INFORMATION AGE
PUBLISHING

Greenwich, Connecticut • www.infoagepub.com

Library of Congress Cataloging-in-Publication Data

Trends and issues in distance education : international perspectives
  / edited by Yusra Laila Visser, Lya Visser, Michael Simonson.
     p. cm. — (Perspectives in instructional technology and distance
  learning)
     Includes bibliographical references and index.
     ISBN 1-59311-212-2 (pbk.) — ISBN 1-59311-213-0 (hardcover)
     1. Distance education.   I. Visser, Yusra Laila. II. Visser,
  Lya.
     III. Simonson, Michael R. IV. Series.
     LC5800.T74 2005
     371.35—dc22

                                                    2005020174

Printed in the United States of America

CONTENTS

PART II:
INTERVIEWS WITH LEADERS IN
INTERNATIONAL DISTANCE EDUCATION

PART III:
NATIONAL AND REGIONAL CASE STUDIES IN
DISTANCE EDUCATION

FROM COVER TO COVER

The World in Your Hands

INTRODUCTION

The term "distance education" conjures up in many minds the image of modern, computer-enabled technology that has blossomed in only the last 20 years. But in fact, distance education has had a surprisingly long history that stretches all the way back to the correspondence education programs of the 1800s. In spite of, or some might contend, *because* of, the strongly heterogeneous characteristic of the group we refer to as "distance learners," distance education practitioners and researchers have made great strides in responding to the learning needs of all types of learners in virtually every part of the globe. Many of the lessons learned over the last century of distance education research and practice have been implemented in a wide variety of distance education programs worldwide, from higher education online learning programs in the United States to rural, radio-based instructional programs in developing countries. Yet, there remains little question that there is a growing base of intellectual capital within the field that desperately requires collection and codification.

Distance education is a truly international discipline. While it is true that the term "distance education" has a universal definition, local distance education experiences are often quite idiosyncratic. This idiosyncratic nature emerges from the need to integrate distance education within the constraints, opportunities, and realities of specific cultural and geographic contexts. From these local distance education experiences, educators are developing new understandings of the broader field of distance education, including the trends and issues present in the field.

In spite of the international nature of distance education, the field itself has not always been successful in offering an integrated representation of the experiences of distance educators around the world. When such international perspectives *have* been brought together in the past, they have rarely been analyzed from the standpoint of the state of the discipline *per se*. This limitation is of note because it denies people in the global distance education community the opportunity to capitalize on the experiences of others who have faced similar challenges while working in the distance education arena.

This book seeks to make a contribution to the discipline of distance education by presenting international perspectives on the state of the field, and by examining and discussing specific current trends and issues faced by the distance learning community. To this end, 24 authors from five continents have contributed their viewpoints on a wide array of distance education themes, including conceptual perspectives, local case studies, interviews, and "nuts-and-bolts" considerations for the design and implementation of international distance education programs. The result is a wide-ranging text that offers insight into the multi-faceted world of international distance education.

ABOUT THIS BOOK

To provide a coherent structure for presenting such material, this book has been organized by thematic content into four main sections (labeled *Parts I-IV*). Each of these sections represents a unique level of analysis for trends and issues in distance education. Part I presents five distinct perspectives on the state of distance education and the trends and issues of the field. The chapters in this section are the broadest within the text, addressing themes and topics that are applicable for analysis of distance education at a global, international level. Further, these chapters are conceptual in nature, integrating research findings and theories to make general observations about phenomena in relationship to distance learning, such as international human development, international research, and the relationship between trends in education and trends in distance education.

Part II contains a series of interviews that were conducted with international distance education leaders. The individuals interviewed in this section were selected because they have played a significant role in the development of distance education theory, research, and/or practice. Each interview presents a different structure with a different focus, reflecting the specific manner in which each individual has contributed to the distance education field. For example, in Chapter 6, Visser and Gagnon present an interview with Don Ely, a pioneer in distance education as well as a key contributor to defining concepts and terms in the field of instructional technology. In this interview, Ely is asked to elaborate on how the terms "trend" and "issue" might be defined, and how these terms are to be distinguished from one another. On the other hand, in Chapter 8, Amirault and Sievert interview Robert Morgan, founder and director emeritus of the Learning Systems Institute. Morgan has dedicated a significant part of his professional career to designing large-scale educational systems and, thus, this chapter focuses on Morgan's experiences as one of the lead architects of Florida State University's centralized distance learning initiative. The individualized nature of these interviews, therefore, makes reading each one of them a unique experience in distance education literature.

Part III of the book presents a fascinating array of case studies in distance education. The chapters in this section of the book cover experiences with programs and initiatives in places as diverse as South Africa, Brazil, and Turkey. Some of these case studies report on experiences within a specific nation (e.g., Chapter 8, which is concerned with British distance education), while others discuss *regional* distance education experiences (e.g., Chapter 11, which concerns the use of information and communication technologies for distance education in Africa). These case studies speak to both the successes and the shortcomings of distance education in various regions of the world. Through these case studies we at once feel great optimism about the role of distance education programs in overcoming the barriers to learning and human development, while also feeling disheartened by some of the disappointments experienced in spite of often noble intentions. Taken individually, each of the chapters in this section presents a contextualized look at trends and issues for distance education in a particular region of the world. Collectively the case studies in this section of the book reflect a rich array of both overlapping and, sometimes, contradictory trends and issues.

The last part of the book, Part IV, focuses on practical issues in distance education. In this section, chapter contributors discuss some of the key trends in the design and development of distance education for international audiences and settings. One author in this section discusses the wide array of technologies and strategies that can be used for distance education, while giving special consideration to the impact of human and environmental differences on the selection of appropriate approaches. Another author presents an analysis of how mentoring roles evolve as the technologies enabling distance learning become increasingly interactive and accommodating of student-to-student and student-to-instructor interaction. Still yet another author discusses experiences with learning management systems at higher education institutions in a variety of different countries. These chapters draw general conclusions about distance education program design and development for consumption by practitioners throughout the world.

From our standpoint as editors, one of the most appealing attributes of this book is the sheer diversity the text represents. While the text indeed threads together chapters under the common theme of international perspectives on trends and issues in distance education, the individual chapters are nevertheless quite distinct in terms of the specific trends and issues they discuss. Further, the diversity that characterizes the book is also evident in the writing styles of the individual authors. We, as editors, feel so strongly that this helps communicate the richness of experiences reflected by the authors that we have minimized "standardizing" the writing style to a common format or structure. Finally, some contributors provide analyses of general trends and issues, while other contributors present specific case studies from which the reader may deduce what trends and issues are at play in local contexts, and how these compare to other, localized trends and issues as well as discipline-wide trends and issues.

While this book indeed contains a great deal of diversity within between its covers, we make no pretense that the text represents an exhaustive review of *all* the international perspectives that might come to bear on trends and issues in distance education. Rather, our view is that the text represents a "moment-in-time" snapshot of the breadth of perspectives on trends and issues in today's distance education. As editors of this unique collection of chapters, it is our sincere wish that you, the reader, will have your horizons extended through the many interesting contributions represented in this book.

Yusra Laila Visser
Lya Visser
Michael Simonson
Ray Amirault

PART I

PERSPECTIVES ON GLOBAL TRENDS AND ISSUES IN DISTANCE EDUCATION

CHAPTER 1

A SURVEY OF PROGRESSIVE AND CONSERVATIVE TRENDS IN EDUCATION WITH IMPLICATIONS FOR DISTANCE EDUCATION PRACTICE

Brent G. Wilson

A number of trends currently shaping educational practice are reviewed for purposes of developing an understanding of the likely context of distance education practices today and in the near future. Focus is given both to trends within the instructional design community and to public-school learning in the United States. Various trends are identified as having either a *progressive* or *conservative* impact on distance education practice. *Progressive* practices encourage re-envisioning education through change, risk-taking, innovation, and new tools and strategies. *Conservative* influences seek established gains in productivity, efficiency, quality control, and accountability. Distance educators preparing new distance learning programs are encouraged to consider both the need for change, as well as the mandate to demonstrate quality outcomes.

Trends and Issues in Distance Education: International Perspectives, 3–21
Copyright © 2005 by Information Age Publishing

Distance education has been described as a disruptive technology. Disruptive technologies are innovations that, while initially posing no threat to established institutions, over time challenge conventional practices and contribute to new ways of thinking (Archer, Garrison, & Anderson, 1999). Many people reflexively assume that distance education will play a greater role in our future. Indeed, a future without more flexible delivery of learning resources is hard to contemplate, as technologies and expectations continue to evolve.

In many settings, distance education has already moved from marginalized status to a mainstream method of learning. This is true, for example, of higher education in the United States and other developed countries, particularly those with scattered populations. Virtually every American university now offers some form of distance-based courses, with a steady increase of comprehensive degree programs offered at a distance at both the undergraduate and graduate levels. Businesses and governments of developed countries are also increasing the use of distance-based training materials. The teaching of children has seen slower overall adoption of distance education methods, but growth is happening at all levels, including public schools.

At times of rapid change, assessing progress and determining needs can be challenging. Assessing progress and determining current needs for the distance context can be challenging. Regardless of the difficulties involved, it is wise for instructional designers and distance providers to step back, review the broad trends in the distance learning world, and reflect on what those trends mean for future distance learning practice. That is the purpose of this chapter.

To help facilitate the review and reflection process, this chapter outlines a number of current trends and also considers their likely impact on distance education. Some brief pointers toward the future are also presented. My hope is to allow the reader to more fully consider, reflect, and properly react to these salient issues from the distance context.

Current trends do not determine the future, but they can certainly be used as the basis for understanding what the future may potentially hold, as well as provide a basis for present action. The trends depicted in Table 1.1 are "pulling" in different directions: some fostering change, others reinforcing the status quo; some using technology to control, others using technology to empower, and so on. Largely for reasons of keeping the table of manageable length, the presentation of these trends is broad and inclusive of different viewpoints, but limited in depth. I leave it largely to the reader to reflect on how various trends might compete or combine together to create entirely new scenarios for the future.

Table 1.1.   Key Trends Relating to Education, Distance Education, and Learning Technologies

Technologizing of School Systems
- Standardized competencies
- System-side assessments and accountability
- Incentivization of funding
- Regulated processes and methods
- Alignment of outcomes, assessments, and methods
- De-professionalizing the teacher's role

Learner- and User-Centered Philosophies
- Convenient, anytime/anywhere access
- Constructivism
- Field-based and informal learning
- High-touch connectivity

Moves to Automate Instructional Design
- Standardized taxonomies for learning outcomes and instructional strategies
- Data-driven generation of rule-based instruction
- More flexible, adaptable authoring tools
- More modular, re-usable design

The Digital Shift: Advances in Information Technologies
- Archivability
- Searchability
- Replicability
- Hypertext linkability
- Communication tools
- Representation and modeling tools

Global Marketplace
- Economies of scale
- Globally distributed labor pool
- Disaggregating of products and services
- Commoditization of instruction
- Mixing of commerce and education

Radical Forces Inspired by Global Connectivity
- Web as democratizing, emancipating, empowering force
- Open Source
- Self-publishing and knowledge sharing
- Peer-to-peer networking
- Self-organized learning- and performance-support groups
- Threats to credentialing, degree-granting institutions
- Global education as an alternative to a national curriculum

Changing Paradigms of Thought in Instructional Design
- From strategy to activity
- From individual to social
- From social to value
- From multiple scales to integration of scale
- From linear causality to systemic impact

TECHNOLOGIZING OF SCHOOL SYSTEMS

School systems throughout the world (and increasingly in the United States) are facing pressures to modernize and "technologize" their processes by establishing more predictable outputs and methods (Tyack & Cuban, 1995). Although American public schools are the immediate point of discussion for this section, the principles extend to any schooling or educational system.

Standardized Competencies

The standards movement seeks to establish a common set of learning outcomes that can be shared across districts, states, or an entire nation. These standards may be set by a professional organization or by government, or both. Curriculum standards are presented in quasi-behavioral language, but with a fairly high level of generality to accommodate different teaching methods and adaptation by local units.

System-side Assessments for Accountability

Standardized assessments are now being mandated throughout the United States and in other countries with nationalized curricula. These assessments are part of an overall move towards making schools more accountable to the public and to the government. Test scores are thus indicators of tax dollars and government resources being well spent.

Incentivization of Funding

Increasingly, operational funds and other privileges are being tied to compliance with specific mandates and regulations. These mandates are made at levels beyond individual schools, intended to bring schools into line with desired teaching and assessment practices. This centralized control of rewards and incentives is in marked contrast to earlier notions of site-based management, wherein schools were empowered to take risks, set goals, and allocate resources to accomplish local goals.

Regulated Processes and Methods

Traditionally, teachers have enjoyed considerable autonomy in their classrooms, choosing teaching methods that fit their style while meeting curriculum expectations. Now, with increased emphasis on high-stakes testing, teachers are being asked to fit their teaching methods more closely to the larger system of goals and assessments. In many cases, specific methods are established and prescribed by schools, districts, and even states and federal governments, leaving less room for professional judgment and variations in teaching style. This can also constrain teachers' efforts to meet unique needs of diverse learners.

Just as teachers are facing constraints, educational researchers are likewise directed to pursue particular research agendas, employing a more constrained set of research methods. In both cases, the direction is more centralized and controlled at higher levels, leaving less room for innovation or local variation.

Alignment of Outcomes, Assessments, and Methods

In a well-coordinated schooling system, an alignment exists between processes and outputs. Specifically, this alignment is made between standardized outcomes, assessment measures, and acceptable teaching methods. The notion of alignment is well established as an instructional design principle, but until recently, has not been the norm within the American public-school system.

De-Professionalizing the Teacher's Role

Tighter alignment of processes and outputs has a definite impact on the teacher's role in an educational system. As suggested above, the teacher often assumes a *technician's* role of implementing prescribed rules, as opposed to a *professional's* role of exercising judgment.

Businesses and governments are facing similar pressures to standardize and technologize training curricula, also for reasons of accountability. Managers need better evidence that training investments are contributing to the company's mission and core processes.

The overall effect of the trends in this section is a move toward standardization, conformity, and efficiency. This is consistent with a factory or industrial model of education, i.e., given known inputs, the system applies predictable rules and processes, resulting in fairly standard and controllable outputs. I use the term *technologize* because it suggests the application of knowledge and technologies to the solution of a practical problem: in this case, the education of children and adults in a responsible and efficient manner.

Learner- and User-Centered Philosophies

At the same time schools are moving toward efficiency and control, the mood among many educators is definitely more learner-centric in orientation. The constructivist movement in education stresses individual and collaborative construction of meaning. While many teachers wish they could teach in more learner-centered ways, the system can make it difficult. Teachers and trainers thus face a certain tension between efficiency and control on the one hand, and learner-centered flexibility on the other. The trends below relate to the treatment of learners, but also to teachers and managers themselves. Both instructors and students are thus seen as end-users of learning resources.

Convenient Anytime/Anywhere Access

Instead of students going to class, learning is coming to the student, in the workplace or at home. Just-in-time, just-in-place learning resources are increasingly available to learners in their normal living settings. This has always been a defining advantage of distance education; the Web has only continued and improved upon this trend. Adult learners are typically seeking specific skills as opposed to general educational outcomes. The result is that many adult learners are starting to look first to the Web and to locally available resources before committing to formal programs of study. Significantly, those without access to distance learning resources are finding themselves at an increasing disadvantage.

Constructivism

Constructivism is a psychologically-oriented approach to learning that emphasizes individual and collaborative meaning construction. While early theorists Vygotsky, Dewey, and Piaget paved the way for constructivism's foundation 60-70 years ago, constructivism moved to the mainstream only in the 1990s. Constructivist teaching strategies give students complex and engaging projects and tasks to perform, with scaffolding and support from peers or a teacher/facilitator. Learning happens via meaningful experiences and direct encounters. Examples include guided inquiry activities such as Webquests, or problem-based learning cases. Constructivist approaches stand in contrast to traditional lecture-and-test methods common in schools and colleges, as well as traditional correspondence courses.

Field-Based and Informal Learning

Many educators have become conscious of the limits of learning in courses, because it happens outside of the natural and authentic contexts where students spend considerable time and energy. This has led to greater appreciation for informal and field-based learning opportunities. Informal learning happens by virtue of participation in some other valued activity, e.g., work or play. Field-based learning refers to semi-structured activities, such as internships, practicum experiences, expeditions and trips, etc. These informal and field-based experiences are compatible with constructivist values and are learner-centered in the same sense: the emphasis on individuals' meaningful encounters with the world, as opposed to direct instruction in controlled settings. Of course, loss of course control carries a number of risks, including erratic or variable experiences leading to non-standardized outcomes.

High-Touch Connectivity

Ironically, some of the strongest resistance to technology innovation comes from the technology community itself (Ryder, 2005). People who know technology best are often sensitized to the need for the human touch. Thus, many technology innovators maintain a dual focus in their dissemination efforts, providing advanced information tools coupled with high levels of personal support and connectivity among individuals (Naisbitt, 1982; Spitzer, 2001). The commitment to both high-tech and high-touch suggests a need to make tools people-centered rather than the reverse (Norman, 1993).

Thus we see something of a conflict or tension between standardization and learner-centered values. How does distance education fit within these conflicting forces? Interestingly, distance education can be seen to support both movements. A well-conceived distance education program can fit comfortably within a strictly controlled standards-based curriculum. Indeed, materials offered at a distance are nearly always more fully developed and tested than classroom materials. At the same time, some aspects of the distance learning experience are more learner-centered, especially the factors of access and convenience. If constructivist methods of teaching are intentionally adopted within a distributed delivery environment, then a curriculum, at least potentially, can address both of these seemingly conflicting trends.

MOVES TO AUTOMATE INSTRUCTIONAL DESIGN

The field of instructional design has a long tradition of research aimed to improve and standardize methods for developing sound instruction. The research agenda of M. David Merrill, for example, has focused on how to make high-quality instruction happen more regularly and consistently. One way to do this is to create intelligent tools that will ensure adequate instructional quality, based on a defined theory of instruction. In this section, several trends are outlined that relate to making instructional design processes more efficient and effective, either through improved tools or improved theories.

Standardized Taxonomies for Learning Outcomes and Instructional Strategies

A basic precept of instructional design is known as the "conditions of learning" assumption (Ragan & Smith, 2004). Before producing instruction, an instructional designer determines what is needed to teach, as well as the specific audience and situation for the instruction. These initial determinations are required before good instructional strategies can be determined. To make this assumption workable, instructional designers use specific *taxonomies* of learning outcomes, matched up with instructional strategies. Examples of this strategy-outcome coupling include Robert Gagné's Nine Events of Instruction and Dave Merrill's Component Display Theory. According to this view, the connection of learning outcomes with instructional strategies becomes essential to the systematic practice of instructional design.

Data-Driven Generation of Rule-Based Instruction

An automated version of this line of thinking seeks to make instructional development largely a data-driven activity. In theory, automated instructional design is an ambitious concept: one simply plugs in data concerning learning outcomes, learners, and situation, and the automated rule system spits out not only recommended strategies, but even the draft materials themselves. A major advantage of an automated system like this would be the efficiency gains achieved through re-usability of data. For example, investment in content representation (depicting the facts, procedures, principles, and examples in a subject area) could yield some quickly-developed instruction for different learners in different situations, according to the rules of the system. Learning objects are based on a similar idea, although perhaps not as theory-driven (Parrish, 2004; Wiley, 2002). While research on automating instruction has continued over two decades, the agenda is still in its infancy, and may prove increasingly viable in coming years. I consider this an empirical, rather than ideological question. That is, building a successful automated program may be the best way to respond to ideological opponents to this research agenda, for example, certain constructivists who view any automated attempt doomed from the start.

More Flexible, Adaptable Authoring Tools

In addition to rule-based taxonomies and instructional prescriptions, authoring tools have become more flexible and powerful. Rather than force designers into linear, top-down ways of thinking, powerful authoring tools allow late and iterative changes in design, more in keeping with the natural design process. An example might be a software-based authoring tool that allows prototyping and creation of "dummy" interfaces to test out concepts at early stages before investing in full-design development. These powerful tools are useful, not just to instructional design professionals, but to nonprofessionals seeking to engage in design activities.

More Modular, Re-Usable Design

The learning objects movement is about reusing content to make efficiency gains in the instructional development process. Because digital content is "non-rival" in nature (i.e., copies of equal quality can easily be made from originals), reusability for various purposes, media, and occasions becomes an inviting possibility (Wiley, 2002).

But the learning-objects movement is only one line of an overall effort to allow for modular reusability of design components. The idea is that good instructional design is based on a very finite number of models, templates, and solutions, which were created while addressing earlier problems. The task is to adopt these available resources, reusing and appropriating wherever possible, to address the problem at hand (Parrish, 2004). This modular attitude seems to draw from a workshop metaphor that sees designers as craftspersons reusing ideas and content for different clients and purposes, somewhere between factory or pure-artist metaphors of production. The IMMEX environment for problem-based learning lessons (http://www.immex.ucla.edu/) is a Web example of template use.

Like the standards-and-accountability movement, I see efforts to automate ID processes as essentially conservative in nature. The end result will be greater standardization of product and reliability of outcome. Until now, instructional strategies have been fairly traditional, and the theory base has relied solidly on information-processing models of cognition and behavior. Combined with more progressive strategies, however, these efforts may again satisfy progressive educators looking for more substantive change in instructional methods.

THE DIGITAL SHIFT:
ADVANCES IN INFORMATION TECHNOLOGIES

New technologies serve a number of functions: they empower people and open up new possibilities for action. They serve as metaphors for new ways of thinking about problems. They eventually come to constrain our thinking and actions, especially after heavy investment in their use. Advances in information technologies over the last 20 years are so profound that they are affecting every area of our professional lives. I term this condition the "digital shift" because, as we convert our thinking, knowledge, and communication to digital and informational form, a whole new set of possibilities opens up (Brown, 2000; Brown & Duguid, 1996).

As information undergoes digital transformation, it changes in a number of ways, including:

- *Archivability*—Digitized information is traceable and archivable. Exchanges and interactions are more easily captured, at least on a digital level.
- *Searchability*—Digital databases are searchable to a degree that we can often retrieve needed resources when solving problems in real time.
- *Replicability*—Because of their non-rival nature, digital resources can be copied and distributed an infinite number of times at zero or extremely low cost.

In addition to these changes in information, the digital shift is marked by these additional trends:

Hypertext Linkability

The hypertext structures of the Web draw heavily on the associative structures conceived by behaviorists and systems thinkers in the 1940s and 1950s (Hebb, 1949). Using webs of interconnecting information has become commonplace in the problem-solving practices of information workers.

Communication Tools

We have learned more about how to navigate rich information structures, and then to communicate with other people within those structures.

Online communications tools will increasingly allow higher resolution, more modalities, more choice, and more fidelity to everyday and face-to-face encounters.

Representation and Modeling Tools

Representation tools—everything from lecturing aids to 3D animation to digital TV and beyond—are changing our notion of reality. These tools, coupled with sophisticated communications, have led to virtual worlds that, increasingly, allow for rich experience and interaction. We now need to match this growth with a better understanding of how to use the tools for good learning effect.

Viewing the digital shift as an overall trend, there is no question that education is being affected. In fact, theoretical progress is often stimulated by technological developments such as hypertext and the Web. At the same time, we are careful to avoid the kind of technological determinist thinking that attributes change simplistically to new technologies. Instead, technology interacts with culture, theory, and existing practices in the creation of new practices.

GLOBAL MARKETPLACE

In recent years, economies worldwide have moved toward greater linkages and interdependencies. This move is called the global economy or the global marketplace. I discuss below several aspects of this global trend as it relates to the delivery of educational and learning resources (see also Collis & Gommer, 2001a, 2001b for a helpful analysis on this general issue).

Economies of Scale

By virtue of the Web and the shift to online learning, markets for learning resources have shifted from local to global. Thus, a school in Australia may offer a course that attracts students from all over the world. A portal or Website may compete with a physical office of student services within a community college. These shifts in markets and audiences create new economies of scale, allowing larger investment and larger outreach, but they can also threaten locally-developed providers.

Globally Distributed Labor Pool

A company based in India may hire an experienced PhD at $7/hour to facilitate a graduate-level computer science course. This, in turn, may force a competitive response by a local school or learning-resource provider. By simple virtue of the Web, salary scales and hiring practices for online resource providers are starting to become more globalized.

Disaggregation of Products and Services

It can be hard to put a price tag on residential school experiences. What is a Harvard MBA worth, and where does the value lie? Many graduates would place great value on non-traditional outcomes, e.g., the network of friends and contacts; the exposure to a company's work practices via an internship; the rite-of-passage and developmental roles of schooling; the opportunity to take personal risks and test oneself. Online learning providers will need to somehow differentiate the valued outcomes of a schooling experience. Parsing out these valued outcomes will help to make sure the online experience can be specifically designed to include these outcomes. For example, if college graduates value the personal experimentation and growth accruing from going away to school, then online providers may want to design and encourage avenues for personal experimentation online; for example, through music or political involvement. Also, once valued outcomes are identified and understood, providers may be able to set up pricing schemes that differentiate among those outcomes. Credential costs, for example, may be priced separately from other learning costs.

Commoditization of Instruction

As suggested earlier, instruction can be seen either as a mass-produced product or as a unique experience. Because e-learning resources require more up-front development than typical classroom experiences, and because e-learning is still seen as an entrepreneurial enterprise, there is a tendency to see it as a commodity. Once investment has been made in the product, providers often want to distribute that product as far as the market will allow. This could also be called a shift from a craft to an industrial model of production and delivery. A view of instruction as commodity, of course, is compatible with viewing education in input-output terms.

As an industrial model of instruction is adopted, questions of owner-ship and control of distribution become more prominent, because a prod-uct is developed that, at least in principle, can be readily distributed (unlike the typical classroom experience). Publishers, concerned about losing their place in this changing environment, have introduced innova-tions such as the customizable textbook. To some extent, discussion of learning objects has been appropriated by publishers as part of an effort to maintain commercial control of content elements through proprietary standards.

Mixing of Commerce and Education

Many enthusiasts are disheartened at the commercialization of the Web, but it was a predictable effect coincident with increasing choice and individual control. A similar tendency is seen in schools as greater choices and perspectives are accommodated through charter and private schools. Commercial investment can provide the needed stimulus to innovation and development, but it can also reduce innovation and variation, espe-cially from small-niche perspectives at the fringes. Commercial appropri-ation of learning can result in some confusion through blurring of boundaries between consumption and education, between entertainment and learning. In an open market, where satisfaction of desire plays a criti-cal role, some low-demand learning outcomes may suffer from neglect.

The trends outlined above are largely conservative in nature, but only because I have grouped them in that manner. The following section rep-resents the progressive side of the same overall move toward global con-nectedness.

RADICAL FORCES INSPIRED BY GLOBAL CONNECTIVITY

The Web as Democratizing, Emancipating, Empowering Force

Early literature about the Internet was infused with optimism and ide-alism about universal sharing and access. The Web can indeed be an empowering force that gives information access to users who are physi-cally remote from resources (Ryder, 1995). At the same time, the Web, like so many other tools, reflects our own values and ideas. A divide still exists between the privileged and the disenfranchised, but the rules have changed somewhat. Principal barriers now include lack of access and lack of cultural or personal fit with the technology. Age can even be a barrier to empowerment, with younger people tending to have more time and familiarity with technology than do older generations.

Open Source

The commercial model of technology advancement, exemplified in the software industry by Microsoft, is being challenged right now by the open source movement. Linux, an operating system whose source code is open for the world to see and costs nothing to download and use, has become a major movement in the software development world. Open-source advocates are trying to create a world where software is freely available and a living is made through continuing relationships of service and support.

Open-source ideas may be applied to online learning and education: e.g., challenging commercial ownership of resources by making them freely available on the Web. If communities of practice can be organized around openly available tools and resources, then the system can become self-sustaining and reinforcing to participants (Schrage, 2000).

Self-Publishing and Knowledge Sharing

Self-publishing is to knowledge management as open source is to Microsoft: an alternative to a hierarchically-controlled system. Instead of fixed search categories and a computer-designed form, end-users themselves can publish solutions and locally valued resources. The Web epitomizes this growing trend, to the occasional chagrin of copyright owners and librarians (Ryder & Wilson, 1997).

Peer-to-Peer Networking

The Napster phenomenon taught us that downloading from central servers is not the only way to perpetuate an online enterprise. Peer-to-peer networking refers to individual users sharing resources by opening up their hard drives to each other. The core concept is even more radical than Napster's, because once out of the bag and in the hands of end-users, true peer-to-peer usage cannot be controlled. In this way, peer-to-peer networking constitutes a classic form of self-organizing system, using the technology to bypass every form of central control.

Self-Organized Learning- and Performance-Support Groups

Peer-to-peer connectivity is the extreme end of self-organizing on the Web, but there are other forms of organization that may occur. Interest groups, listservs, support groups of all kinds, each of these is a self-organizing system that draws on distributed energy and participation for its survival. An interesting example is slashdot.org, a news and discussion group for open-source and technical geeks. Run by a group of about a dozen editors, thousands of readers participate at multiple levels: by contributing stories, discussing the stories, rating the comments, and even rating the ratings. Together, these carefully crafted forms of participation result in a finely tuned environment for learning about news and technology. In short, it's a very successful informal learning environment exhibiting both designed and self-organizing qualities (Wiley & Edwards, 2002). And contrary to threaded discussions typical of online courses, the slashdot experience gets better with more students involved. It seems inevitable that educational institutions will see an advantage in exploiting these tools for more formal learning purposes. One can imagine, for example, a consortium of graduate programs sponsoring participation in a large-scale forum like slashlearn.org, only directed at academic discussions suitable for graduate learning (Wiley & Edwards, 2002). This is an important area for research because it combines the open-learning qualities of the Web with economies of scale associated with many technology advances.

Threats to Credentialing, Degree-Granting Institutions

For educational institutions to stay in business, graduates must hold some kind of advantage over the non-degreed person. The basis for accreditation and credentialing has historically been seat time: students live in residence and accumulate seat time until a requisite number of classes (with accompanying assessment and grades) is attained.

An alternative to seat time is the concept of demonstrated mastery of competencies. Professionally certified tests are an example of this approach. Competency-based alternatives have only been partly successful in their challenge of seat-time credentialing, partly because of technical and quality problems with competency measures. Also, it is argued, something unique happens in the experience of schooling. It's not just about the competency, advocates argue: it's about the learning experience itself. There is something in going to school that's irreducible down to a competency exam.

In recent years, however, competency-based approaches are enjoying a comeback, thanks largely to growth in online and self-directed learning.

For-profit outreach institutions like the University of Phoenix, once ridiculed for giving credit for "life experience," continue to gain market share against residential institutions. In spite of reliability problems, professional portfolios are increasingly used for competency demonstration and evaluation. Online learning, in which seat time loses much of its meaning, continues to improve its services and learning outcomes, along with market share. These "disruptive technologies" and accompanying competency-based tools are truly disrupting the status quo.

The challenge to seat-time credentialing is formidable. The fast-growing home schooling movement, for example, is increasingly dependent on online resources and interest groups, and has been fairly successful in demonstrating learning outcomes. Many working professionals are opting for narrower and shorter training certificates instead of full degrees, often with credit given for previously acquired competencies.

Global Education as an Alternative to a National Curriculum

Email exchanges and projects linking students from different parts of the world are not the only curricular impact of global connectivity. "Global education" refers to a new philosophy of learning that seeks to create responsible citizens of the world. Transcending national interests, the global education curriculum takes broadly-based positions on issues of nonviolence and conflict resolution, sustainable growth policies, treatment of rich and poor, and protection of the global environment (McEneaney, Kolker, & Ustinova, 1998).

REFLECTIONS

How do these various trends add up for the distance learning professional? I hope the reader engages in some reflection and conversation about this question. What follows is my best effort at generalizing upon the trends. Rather than paint a specific scenario, I highlight a few principles suggesting how the trends may combine.

The Trends Keep Marching On

Each of the trends listed above will continue to play a role in future developments of education and training, where distance technologies will play an expanding role. The trends may compete with one another, or sometimes cancel each other out, but they all represent significant aspects of the problem space within which distance education of the future will take shape.

Open Systems Trump Closed Ones

This is my way of saying that learners and communities will find a way to appropriate emerging tools and technologies, rather than the reverse. I have a bias that says that open systems (self-directed learners, self-organizing groups of learners and workers) constitute the most vital and thriving unit for understanding human actions and choices (*cf.* Hill, 1999). Process efficiencies and mass-produced tutorials can be appropriated and put into service by these learners and groups, and that is good. Where a group can appropriate a tool or technology and use it to learn from, let it do so. Where the technology breaks down, the group will adapt and make do.

This is not a utopian faith in the goodness of people; rather, it is an acknowledgement of the power and priority of groups that identify us and guide our behavior. Schools as collectivized learning institutions will not go away. Teachers or guides, responsible for the growth of novices, will not go away. Collective learning in real time will not go away. These practices are in place, not because we lack alternatives, but because we are social beings who invest considerable time and resources toward local interactions and support. I am confident that the same groups—schools, classrooms, families, workgroups, professional organizations—will find ways for distance education resources to work in their service.

Technologies are Still Reflections of Ourselves

Through technologies and new ideas, we are always in the process of re-inventing ourselves. Technologies serve as mirrors of our values and aspirations, as well as our weaknesses and intractable problems. This truth about technologies underscores the importance of subjecting our plans to continuing scrutiny. Whenever possible, we want our technologies to reflect our best selves and our highest ambitions.

Technology and Ideas Will Continue to Co-Evolve Together

Historians of technology tell us that a technology, often based on the best thinking available, in turn stimulates new thinking and new possibilities. This is certainly true of the Web and networked information systems.

A huge spike of promising ideas, models, and R & D efforts has accompanied the new technology. When these new efforts are seen as artifacts themselves, we see how one technology prompts the development of another, and how the cycle repeats itself through new iterations of technology, design, theorizing, and practice. Thus we can be sure that, as technology continues its onward march, new models and ideas will surely follow—and in some cases, precede the technology itself. As John Dewey said more than 70 years ago:

> Many are the conditions which must be fulfilled if the Great Society is to become a Great Community... The highest and most difficult kind of inquiry and a subtle, delicate, vivid and responsive art of communication must take possession of the physical machinery of transmission and circulation and breathe life into it. When the machine age has thus perfected its machinery, it will be a means of life and not its despotic master. (Dewey, 1954, p. 27)

REFERENCES

Archer, W., Garrison, D. R., & Anderson, T. (1999). Adopting disruptive technologies in traditional universities: Continuing education as an incubator for innovation. *DEOSNews*, 9(11). Retrieved July 23, 2004, from http://www.ed.psu.edu/acsde/deosarchives.html

Brown, J. S. (2000, February). Works in progress. Retrieved July 23, 2001, from http://www.parc.xerox.com/ops/members/brown/index.html

Brown, J. S., & Duguid, P. (1996, July/August). Universities in the Digital Age. *Change*, 10.

Carr, A. A. (1997). User-design in the creation of human learning systems. *Educational Technology Research & Development*, 45(3), 5-22.

Cave, D. (2001, July 10). Microsoft to schools: Give us your lunch money! Retrieved July 8, 2004, from http://www.salon.com/tech/feature/2001/07/10/microsoft_school/print.html

Collis, B., & Gommer, L. (2001). Stretching the mold or a new economy? Part I: Scenarios for the university in 2005. *Educational Technology*, 41(3), 5-18.

Collis, B., & Gommer, L. (2001). Stretching the mold or a new economy: Part 2: Realizing the scenarios for the university in 2005. *Educational Technology*, 41(4), 5-14.

Dewey, J. (1954/27). *The public and its problems*. Athens OH: Ohio University Press. Chapter 5: Search for the Great Community. Also found in J. A. Boydston (Ed.), *The collected works of John Dewey, 1882 - 1953, Later works*, 2, 325-350.

Hebb, D. O. (1949). *The organization of behavior: A neuropsychological theory*. New York: Wiley.

Hill, J. R. (1999). A conceptual framework for understanding information seeking in open-ended information systems. *Educational Technology Research and Development*, 47(1), 5-27.

Irving, J. (2001, July). SlashLearn: Discussion and debate for instructional technologists. Retrieved July 23, 2001, from http://www.beota.com/ilt/dwarticle.htm

Law, J., & Hetherington, K. (n. d.). *Materialities, spacialities, globalities*. Retrieved July 23, 2001, from http://www.comp.lancs.ac.uk/sociology/soc029jl.html

McEneaney, J. E., Kolker, J. M., & Ustinova, H. S. (1998, April). *Technology-based Global Education and its implications for school/university partnerships*. Paper presented at the meeting of the American Educational Research Association, San Diego. Retrieved July 23, 2001, from http://www.iusb.edu/~edud/global/pub2.htm

Naisbitt, J, (1982). *Megatrends: The new directions transforming our lives*. New York: Warner.

Norman, D. A. (1993). *Things that make us smart: Defending human attributes in the age of the machine*. Reading, MA: Addison-Wesley.

Parrish, P. E. (2004). The trouble with learning objects. *Educational Technology Research and Development, 52*(1), 49-67.

Ragan, T. J., & Smith. P. L. (2004). Conditions theory and models for designing instruction. In D. H. Jonassen (Ed.), *Handbook of research on educational communications and technology* (2nd ed.) (pp. 623-650). Mahwah NJ: Erlbaum.

Ryder, M. (2005, June). *Luddism and the neo-luddite reaction*. Retrieved June 29, 2005, from http://carbon.cudenver.edu/~mryder/itc_data/luddite.html

Ryder, M. (1995, November). *Production and consumption of meaning: The interplay between subject and object in open hypertext representation*. Paper presented at the meeting, Semiotics as a Bridge between the Humanities and the Sciences, Victoria College, University of Toronto. Retrieved July 8, 2004, from http://carbon.cudenver.edu/~mryder/semiotics_95.html

Ryder, M., & Wilson, B. (1997, March). *From center to periphery: Shifting agency in complex technical environments*. Paper presented at the meeting of the American Educational Research Association, Chicago. Retrieved July 8, 2004, from http://carbon.cudenver.edu/~mryder/coss.html

Schrage, M. (2000, August). The debriefing: John Seely Brown. Retrieved July 8, 2004, from http://www.wired.com/wired/archive/8.08/brown_pr.html

Spitzer, D. R. (2001). Don't forget the high-touch with the high-tech in distance learning. *Educational Technology, 41*(2), 51-55.

Tyack, D., & Cuban, L. (1995). *Tinkering toward Utopia: A century of public school reform*. Cambridge MA: Harvard University Press.

Wiley, D. A. (Ed.). (2002). *The instructional use of learning objects*. Bloomington IN: Agency for Instructional Technology and the Association for Educational Communications and Technology. Retrieved July 8, 2004, from http://reusability.org/read/

Wiley, D. A., & Edwards, E. K. (2002). Online self-organizing social systems: The decentralized future of online learning. *Quarterly Review of Distance Education, 3*(1). Retrieved July 8, 2004, from http://wiley.ed.usu.edu/docs/ososs.pdf

CHAPTER 2

QUALITY, ACCREDITATION, AND RECOGNITION

Issues in the Delivery of Transnational Education

Andrea Hope

INTRODUCTION

The rapid development of—and improved access to—information and communications technologies (ICTs) around the world in the past decade have fueled the development of a global knowledge economy. With the recognition that education and training hold the key to becoming beneficiaries of this development has come an unprecedented demand for educational products and services. Governments in developing countries who may hitherto have been the sole providers of educational opportunities to their citizens are seeking new ways to meet the urgent demand for new educational opportunities without bankrupting their economies. As agreements for the liberalization of trade in knowledge services are signed as part of the General Agreement on Trade in Services (GATS) arrangements by members of the World Trade Organization (WTO),

Trends and Issues in Distance Education: International Perspectives, 23–34
Copyright © 2005 by Information Age Publishing

international trade in educational services is being officially sanctioned, thus enabling public and private educational providers in the advanced economies to offer their programs across the world.

The trend towards internationalization in higher education that was characterized in the 1980s and 1990s by the international exchange of students and faculty has been superseded in the new millennium by the growth of transnational education. The Code of Good Practice in the Provision of Transnational Education defines transnational education as "those arrangements and partnerships between institutions and organizations in which students are located in a different country to the one where the institution providing the education is based" (UNESCO/CoE 2001).

For the past 30 years, open and distance learning has offered a cost-effective solution to national governments seeking to provide mass education at minimal cost. The current trend towards the transnational delivery of distance education raises significant issues of quality, equity, access, and recognition. These issues will be explored in this chapter.

THE NATURE OF TRANSNATIONAL EDUCATION

While transnational education is concerned with the mobility of, and trade in, educational goods and services, it specifically excludes the physical movement of students across international borders. Such study-related international travel of students represents a significant source of revenue for many developed nations. Figures from the United States indicate that U.S. universities and colleges recruited almost 500,000 international students in the 1998-1999 academic year. The United Kingdom was the second largest recipient of international students, with the recruitment of some 250,000 international students (Campbell & van der Wende, 2000).

International students represent a vital additional source of funding for universities and colleges in those developed countries where the proportion of state funding for higher education is being eroded. A recent report of the Productivity Commission in Australia noted that the country spent just 1.5% of its gross domestic product (GDP) on universities and academic research, down from 1.7% in 1995. A report of the study of 37 universities in ten developed countries also found that the 11 Australian universities included in the survey were much more reliant on overseas student fees than their international counterparts. Income from overseas student fees was expected to reach A$5 billion in 2002, a 35% increase over the 2000 figures, with China emerging as the fastest growing source of overseas students. Between 1999 and 2001, the number of Chinese students enrolled at Australian higher education institutions rose from 3400 to 8831 (Crabb, 2002).

A significant factor in this dramatic increase has been the rise of transnational education. One-fifth of overseas students undertaking an Australian university degree never go to Australia. Offshore campuses, online courses, and agreements with foreign universities mean that the education sector can earn fees from students who stay in their home countries. In Australia, offshore student numbers increased 45% between 1999 and 2001. For Australia, the United States, and the United Kingdom, Asia is the largest source of overseas students, with Singapore, Hong Kong, Malaysia, and Indonesia heading the list. The constant search for new markets has led to a significant increase of activity by Australian institutions of higher education in India, Pakistan, Bangladesh, and even in some African countries. The United States remains the leading exporter of educational services, with 58% of its exports going to the South East Asia region. Europe and Latin America are also significant destinations of U.S.-based educational services.

Typically, transnational educational arrangements cover the full range of distance education provision, including virtual universities. Examples include:

- Branch campuses, such as Nottingham University in Malaysia (http://www.unim.nottingham.ac.uk/) and De Montfort University in South Africa, (http://www.dmu.ac.uk/services/international/coll_south.jsp) where a foreign university establishes a presence in a host country;
- Franchises, such as the University of Bradford and the Management Development Institute of Singapore (http://www.mdis.edu.sg/) where institution A approves institution B to provide one or more of A's programs in B's country.
- Provision of education and training by international non-official higher education institutions, off-shore institutions, foreign public universities, various consortia, and corporate universities.

Transnational education is part of a wider global phenomenon, first defined as "borderless education" by a group of Australian researchers in 1998 (Cunningham et al., 1998). The term refers to those emerging forms of education that cut across a number of traditional boundaries including sectoral (education and industry), level (further and higher), public and private and, in the case of distance education, time and space. Fueled by technological developments and the spread of connectivity, new education providers and new forms of education are changing the traditional face of higher education in developed and developing nations alike. Such new providers include private for-profit universities such as the University of Phoenix (http://online.uophx.edu/); corporate universities such as Motorola University (mu.Motorola.com); media companies delivering educational programs, such as Thompson's Education Direct (http://www.educationdirect.com/index.html); and professional associations directly involved in the delivery of continuing professional development (http://www.accaglobal.com/). All are using the Internet as a delivery channel. In the longer term, it is likely that study program mobility will eclipse traditional student mobility, as more transnational programs are offered on-campus, in mixed-mode, and completely online.

ADVANTAGES OF TRANSNATIONAL EDUCATION

The proponents of transnational education extol its virtues as a force for modernization and progress. It widens learning opportunities by providing more choice, and it challenges traditional systems to reform by introducing more competition and innovative programs and delivery methods. Home institutions are able to improve their standing and reputation through links to prestigious foreign institutions. Transnational education enables countries like Malaysia—which have previously been a major source of foreign students on campuses in the United States, the United Kingdom, and Australia—to enhance their domestic capacity without concomitant infrastructure costs, while reducing the foreign exchange cost of traditional study abroad patterns and staunching the permanent loss of local talent characteristic of the "brain drain" from developing to developed economies.

The advantages to the exporting institutions in terms of access to new sources of income are clear. In December 2002, the Australian Commonwealth Minister for Education, Science and Technology announced a campaign to launch a new "offshore brand" to market Australian education and training overseas with the slogan "an education experience that makes a real difference" in an effort to distinguish Australian education and training from its competitors offshore (Nelson, 2002).

Transnational education is seen by the providers as a boost to the domestic economy and as a foundation for strong foreign and trade relations. It is not surprising therefore that Australia and the United States have made proposals under the General Agreement on Trade in Services (GATS) for the liberalization of trade in "knowledge services." The intention of GATS is to facilitate and promote ever more opportunities for trade. Forty-four of the 144 World Trade Organization (WTO) member states have made an unconditional commitment to such trade, and only 21 of those have included commitments to higher education (Knight 2002). They include the Congo, Lesotho, Jamaica, and Sierra Leone, countries hoping to encourage the entry of foreign providers to supplement their national systems which are failing to meet the demands of their citizens for greater access to educational opportunities.

DISADVANTAGES OF TRANSNATIONAL EDUCATION

The rise of transnational education provision raises issues of quality standards, equity, and access. Not all net recipient countries welcome the potential or the reality of transnational education as warmly as Malaysia or the signatories to GATS cited above. Where some see the benefits of increased access to educational opportunity for their citizens and greater foreign investment, others fear foreign domination or at least exploitation of their national system and culture. Greece, for example, deems franchising and other types of transnational provision to be illegal and seeks to outlaw it. Critics of transnational education point to:

- Problems associated with non-official, unregulated providers who remain outside of the official national quality assurance regimes and are not subject to internal or external auditing and monitoring processes;
- Consumer protection problems associated with a lack of adequate information available to potential students, employers, and competent recognition authorities;
- Marketization of education undermining the public good approach;
- Inequity of access resulting from use of information and communication technologies (the "digital divide");
- Difficulties with diploma mills and bogus institutions who exploit the public;
- Unfair competition to strictly regulated national institutions, particularly in lucrative popular subjects such as business, information technology, computer science, law, engineering, and other studies leading to professional accreditation; and
- Cultural imperialism as exemplified by the use of English rather than the national language; a standardized curriculum rather than a culturally embedded syllabus; and norms of degree architecture rather than a local model.

Despite concerns at the governmental level, consumer demand for transnational education remains buoyant. The main determinants of demand include the cost of the program; the brand name of the provider and product; the value-added of the program; the reputation, quality, and perceptions of the program; national and international recognition of the program; convenience and nature of the delivery; and level of dissatisfaction with local provision (Adam, 2001).

QUALITY, ACCREDITATION, AND RECOGNITION

Speaking at the 6th Biennial Conference of the International Network for Quality Assurance Agencies in Higher Education (INQAAHE) in 2001, the former Chief Executive of the U.K. Quality Assurance Agency for Higher Education (QAA) suggested that "individual decisions to participate in transnational higher education are driven by history, language, cost and recognition. Recognition of the qualifications gained, by governments, employers or professional bodies, is the single most important consideration for the individual" (Randall, 2001). Likewise, in her article on the General Agreement on Trade in Services (GATS), Knight (2002) states that"[q]uality and accreditation are at the heart of much of the debate. The importance of frameworks for licensing, accreditation, qualification recognition and quality assurance are important for all countries whether they are importing or exporting educational services. Developing countries have expressed their concerns about their capacity to have such frameworks in place in light of the push towards trade liberalization and increased transnational education." Some are turning to U.S.-based organizations offering a certification/accreditation service to meet this demand. The University of South Africa (UNISA) sought accreditation from the Distance Education and Training Council (DETC) (http://www.detc.org/) in 2002 "for a desire for national and international benchmarking of the quality of its teaching and services, an external source of stimulation to improve services, programmes and staff, benefits to its graduates of having a degree from a university accredited in the United States and the possibility of attracting US students because of the accreditation" (Gough, 2002).

Developing countries are increasingly becoming unregulated markets for higher education exporters because of insufficient government attention to regulation due to political and governance instability (Singh, 2002). Butcher and Welch (1996) describe the problem in Nigeria in graphic terms: "Adventurous entrepreneurs see a juicy field of operation because of the imbalance of demand and supply with a ready market for ever-increasing applicants who are desperate for educational qualifications through correspondence measures".

In an attempt to curb the worst excesses of the diploma mills and "web cowboys," some jurisdictions (such as Hong Kong), have established laws requiring all overseas providers that are not operating through accredited local institutions to register with the government and to meet the stringent quality criteria required for registration (www.hkcaa.edu.hk). In South Africa, the Higher Education Act (1997) requires private institutions operating in partnership with foreign universities to have their courses accredited or face being closed down (http://www.unesco.org/courier/2000_11/uk/doss23.htm). In the cases cited above, however, the laws cannot be applied to institutions that operate globally online and have no physical presence in the country. To address this problem, Australia has published its National Protocols for Higher Education Approval (http://www.detya.gov.au/highered/mceetya_cop.htm) that protect the use of the title "university" by making it illegal to use the term in Australia without formal accreditation by state government agencies and provide for virtual universities that breach national quality requirements to be prosecuted in the jurisdiction in which their operations have an adverse effect as well as in their home jurisdiction.

Transnational education presents challenges to existing national-level regulatory frameworks in terms of assuring the quality and standards of the study programs provided and the degrees awarded—as well as the recognition of the qualifications gained—through transnational study. Some of the leading provider countries have elaborated specific codes of practice; notably the Code of Practice for the assurance of academic quality and standards in higher education Section 2: Collaborative Provisions and flexible and distributed learning (including e-learning)—September 2004 (http://www.qaa.ac.uk/academicinfrastructure/codeOfPractice/section2/default.asp) from the U.K. Quality Assurance Agency; the Code of Ethical Practice in the offshore provision of Education and Educational services by Australian Higher Education Institutions from the Australian Vice-Chancellors' Committee (http://www.admin.uq.edu.au/HAI/00134.html); and the Principles of Good Practice for Educational Programs for non-U.S. nationals (http://www.neasc.org/cihe/overseas_programs.PDF), a code shared among the regional accrediting bodies in the U.S. The main concern of these codes of practice is to prevent any harmful effects on the reputation of their higher education systems caused by unscrupulous or unethical providers.

Conscious of the need to find commonly agreed solutions to practical recognition problems within Europe, and increasingly between European States and other nations, UNESCO/CEPES and the Council of Europe adopted a Code of Good Practice in the Provision of Transnational Education (http://www.cepes.ro/hed/recogn/groups/transnat/code.htm) in 2001. Qualifications issued through transnational education programs that comply with the provisions of the code will be assessed in accordance with the stipulations of the Lisbon Recognition Convention (1997), which provides a framework for the mutual recognition of qualifications among

European States. The Lisbon Convention is the most recent of six conventions on the mutual, transborder recognition of degrees in higher education that were brokered by UNESCO between ratifying countries worldwide. Their main objective is to promote international cooperation in higher education and to reduce obstacles to the mobility of teachers and students while preserving and strengthening cultural identity and diversity and promoting access to higher education as a human right. UNESCO serves as the secretariat to these conventions. (www.unesco.org/education/studyingabroad/index.shtml)

In 2002, UNESCO launched the Global Forum on International Quality Assurance, Accreditation and the Recognition of Qualifications. The forum's purpose is to provide a platform for dialogue by linking existing frameworks dealing with international issues of quality, accreditation, and the recognition of qualifications, and to develop an international policy framework on the impact of globalization and transborder higher education. Key players in the field of national and international quality assurance and accreditation are active in the forum.

To address the challenges raised by the development of transnational education, the quality assurance community has considered options ranging from improved communication between international accreditation agencies, to the development of a single international accrediting authority. The latter proposal was, not unsurprisingly, rejected by the majority of national quality assurance agencies as being too cumbersome and unachievable. In his argument for the establishment of such a supranational agency, Van Damme (2001) pointed to the immense diversity in national higher education systems and degree architecture mirrored by complicated (and protectionist) bureaucratic procedures that have been established to investigate whether a foreign or unknown degree matches the domestic ones. The Australian response to Van Damme's proposal is typical of the position of the national agencies: "the answer to the demand for improved quality assurance and qualifications recognition arrangements in international higher education lies in the maintenance of robust, flexible and transparent national arrangements with a strong commitment to international cooperation in terms of mutual recognition and sharing information about respective systems" (Pearce 2001). While one may be optimistic that this approach could be successful in regulating providers with a physical presence, the outcomes in the case of distance and virtual education are less clear. The Chief Executive Officer of the Center for Higher Education Accreditation (CHEA) does not underestimate the profound academic challenges presented to the accrediting community by distance education: "They speak to the fundamentals—classrooms, faculty roles, institutions, degrees. They have the potential to disrupt basic quality expectations within the academic community, throwing higher education and accreditation into disarray" (Eaton, 2001).

Significant attempts have been made by quality assurance agencies throughout the world to define quality in distance education. These attempts include the production of Code of Practice with specific reference to colloborative provision and flexible and distributed learning (including e-learning) by the U.K. Quality Assurance Agency referred to above; the publication of the New Zealand Academic Audit Unit's "External Quality Assurance for the Virtual Organisation" (Butterfield et al., 1999); the "Guide to Best Practice for electronically offered degree and certificate programs" (2001) from WCET (http://www.wcet.info/projects/balancing/principles.htm) and the Guidelines for Distance Education issued by the Higher Learning Commission (2000) (http://www.ncacihe.org/resources/guidelines/gdistance.html). All of these attempts take as their starting point that the well-established essentials of institutional quality found in existing accreditation standards are applicable to the emergent forms of learning and that too narrow a focus on a specific medium of teaching and learning is inappropriate, as the standards are independent of the method of delivery.

Pond (2002) proposes possible universal attributes of Quality Education and suggests that it provides continuity between advertising and reality; continuity between purpose and practice; preparation for external credentialing/further study; personal/professional academic growth for the learner; relevance; rich, multi-directional interaction; a functional, user-friendly interface; adequate resources for instructors, learners, curriculum; and appropriate assessment methods and opportunities.

While reputable providers of distance education courses and programs would not argue with these criteria, they do complain that current forms of accreditation are based on input rather than output measures: "not on what or how students learn but on how many feet of classroom space we have per student" (Gillis, in Anderson, 2002). The challenge to the accrediting community is summed up by Pond (2002): "Whether we are speaking of corporate training, continuing education, academic courses or even entire degree programs, the traditional mainstays of quality assurance such as physical attendance, contact hours, proctored testing, formal academic credentials for instructors and trainers, library holdings ... are often impractical or even irrational in today's educational reality." Nevertheless, both good and bad virtual universities remain vulnerable to the loss of consumer confidence that would be engendered by their inability to provide evidence that they can withstand scrutiny by the traditional measures of academic quality as evidenced by accreditation. One of the reasons suggested for the ultimate failure in 2002 of the U.K. Open University's attempt to establish itself in the U.S. (the United States Open

University) was not the quality of its provision, but the length of time taken to complete regional accreditation procedures, which, because of the link to federal student funds, in turn resulted in unsustainably low student numbers.

In a market-driven environment, the existing accredited providers of distance education are increasingly aware of the need to improve the transparency of their operations to increase consumer confidence. Technology-assisted delivery provides new opportunities for institutions to access data from the feedback-evaluation-quality improvement loop and make it available to existing and potential consumers wherever they are based.

The global marketplace for education is huge and growing fast. The Australian International Development Programme (IDP) estimates that in the year 2025 there will be 159 million learners in the world, and 87 million of them will be in Asia. The export of education and training services is one of the top five U.S. service exports, totaling more than US$14 billion in 2000 (Adam, 2001).

While both the accreditors and the institutions wrestle with the need to reform the system, and to put the learners' rather than the institution's needs first, ever–increasing numbers of learners worldwide are turning to technology-mediated learning offered from outside their national border to meet their professional and technical updating requirements. These learners are likely to be paying their own fees and, as consumers, will expect high cost-efficiency and effectiveness from their chosen providers (Hope, 2001). A number of means are available to them to evaluate their options. First, they could consult one of the entrepreneurial Web-based databases of student reviews of online courses (e.g., www.degreeInfo.com, which also offers an excellent guide to "Warning Signs of a 'Less-Than-Wonderful' School"). Alternatively, they could turn to Web sites offering self-assessment tests to enable potential consumers of e-learning to gauge their suitability for distance education and to get advice on how to choose a good course or program. Providers of this service include Degree.net (www.degree.net), AboutEducation (www.about.com/education), WorldwideLearn (http://www.worldwidelearn.com/), and QualitE-Learning Assurance.inc (www.Eqcheck.com). They could also follow the market's lead by perusing the annual rankings of universities and colleges published by magazines such as *U.S. News and World Report* (http://www.usnews.com/usnews/edu/eduhome.htm) and *AsiaWeek* (http://www.asiaweek.com/asiaweek/features/universities2000/index.html).

For learners, a quality education may ultimately be one that meets or exceeds their expectations for learning in the sense that—upon completion of the course or program—the learner has knowledge and/or skills that he/she did not possess before. In the face of the plethora of choice that characterizes online and distance education, Johnstone, Director of WCET (in Anderson, 2002) suggests: "Students should comb through their choices and make sure that the courses have good instructors, are taught through institutions that are accredited and that provide dependable services online and offer credits that are transferable." In the case of online courses, all of this information should be easily accessible on the institution's Web site.

The accreditation community recognizes that it is its responsibility to identify the distinctive features of distance learning, adjust accreditation scrutiny to reflect those distinctive features, and pay more attention to student learning outcomes (Eaton, 2001).

The accreditation community has much to learn from corporate distance learning providers such as Cisco (http://www.cisco.com/en/US/learning/le3/learning_career_certifications_and_learning_paths_home.html), Microsoft (http://www.microsoft.com/learning/), and Oracle (http://education.oracle.com/), all of which have developed effective competency-based models for information technology certification.

CONCLUSION

For the transnational learner, accreditation in the country of origin may not be an a priori foolproof indicator of quality, given that a number of bogus accrediting agencies have sprung up to service the needs of the web-cowboy providers. Nevertheless, accreditation offers at the very least a means of verifying the provider's formalized accountability as an institution of higher education. Accreditation therefore remains a useful indicator of probable quality. As important for the learner, however, is the issue of credibility. If the qualification or credential is not recognized for the purpose that the learner intends to use it for, the qualification has failed the first test of academic quality: fitness for purpose. National and international agencies have a key role to play in ensuring that best practice in this rapidly developing area is shared and subsequently codified into effective and relevant quality assurance, accreditation, and recognition arrangements.

REFERENCES

Adam, S. (2001). *Transnational education report.* Brussels: CEURC.

Anderson, B. C. (2002). Digital education: The Legitimacy of the higher education virtual campus. *DESIEN*, 7(6). Available online at (http://www.uwex.edu/disted/desien/2002/0207/full.htm)

Butcher, N., & Welch, T. (1996). *A distance education quality standards framework for South Africa*. Pretoria: Department of Education.

Butterfield, S. et al. (1999). *External quality assurance for the virtual university. AAU series on quality No.4*. Wellington: New Zealand Universities Academic Audit Unit.

Campbell, C., & van der Wende, M. (2000). *International trends in quality assurance for European higher education: Exploratory trend report*. Helsinki, Finland: ENQAHE.

Crabb, A. (2002, December 26). Overseas students worth $5 billion. Canberra, Australia: The Age. Retrieved 7/3/2003 from www.theage.com.au/articles/2002/12/26/1040511091084.html

Cunningham, S, Tapsall, S, Ryan, Y, Stedman, L, Bagdon, T, & Flew, T. (1998). New media and borderless education: A review of the convergence between global media networks and higher education provision. Retrieved from http://www.dest.gov.au/archive/highered/eippubs/eip97-22/eip9722.pdf

Eaton, J. (2001). Distance learning: Academic and political challenges for higher education accreditation, CHEA Monograph Series 2001, Number 1. Retrieved from http://www.chea.org/pdf/mono_1_dist_learning_2001.pdf

Gough, D. (2002, February). quoted in http://allafrica.com/stories/200202120002.html

Hope, A. (2001). Quality assurance. In G. Farrell (Ed.), *The changing faces of virtual education*. Vancouver: The Commonwealth of Learning. Retrieved from (http://www.col.org/virtualed/index2.htm)

Knight, J. (2002). Trade in higher education services: The implications of GATS. London: The Observatory on Borderless Higher Education.

Nelson, B. (2002, December 9). New offshore brand for Australia's $5 billion international education industry. Retrieved 7/3/2003 from (http://www.dest.gov.au/ministers/nelson/dec02/n258_091202.htm).

Pearce, M. (2001). Report to the UNESCO Expert meeting on the impact of globalisation on quality assurance, accreditation and the recognition of qualifications in higher education. Retrieved from http://www.unesco.org/education/studyingabroad/highlights/presentations/pearce1.doc

Pond, W. K. (2002). Distributed education in the 21st century: Implications for quality assurance. *Online Journal of Distance Learning Administration, 5*(2). Retrieved from http://www.westga.edu/~distance/ojdla/summer52/pond52.html

Randall, J. (2001). Defining standards: Developing a global currency for higher education qualifications. Paper delivered at the 6th biennial conference of INQAAHE, Bangalore, India, March 2001.

Singh, M. (2002). International quality assurance, ethics and the market: A view from developing countries. UNESCO-IAU.

Uvalic-Trumbic, S. (2002). UNESCO conventions on the recognition of qualifications and GATS: Conflict or common ground? Paris: GATE.

Van Damme, D. (2001). *Higher education in the age of globalisation: The need for a new regulatory framework for recognition, quality assurance and accreditation*. Introductory paper for the UNESCO Expert meeting, Paris, September 2001.

CHAPTER 3

THE LONG AND SHORT OF DISTANCE EDUCATION

Trends and Issues from a Planetary Human Development Perspective

Jan Visser

THE AUTHOR'S VANTAGE POINT

Trends and issues exist in the mind of the beholder. To look at trends and issues requires having an overall vision that serves as a conceptual frame in which issues are embedded and against which trends become distinguishable. It is therefore proper that I start off explaining what my specific vantage point is.

In this chapter I look at trends and issues in the evolution of distance education from the perspective of someone who has worked around the globe while trying to make his modest contribution to improving the human condition. I consider consciousness to be among the most human of human characteristics. Consciousness is key to the idea that the human condition can be improved. Humans are able to look at their world and at themselves as agents in that world, asking themselves questions about it

Trends and Issues in Distance Education: International Perspectives, 35–50
Copyright © 2005 by Information Age Publishing
All rights of reproduction in any form reserved.

and thinking about alternative ways of intervening in their world. Learning—not to be confounded with memorization of facts—is a particularly important road towards continually developing the capacity to consciously intervene in one's environment so as to make life better for the largest number of people possible, including oneself. In that context, distance education should be seen as one among multiple alternatives through which human learning can be deliberately stimulated, structured, and facilitated.

I thus define distance education as any set of purposely-devised procedures and resources to support people's learning in ways that focus on the learners' ability to choose when and where to engage in a particular act of learning. This definition is wider than definitions employed by most other authors (see e.g., Delling, 1987; Keegan, 1986; Moore & Kearsley, 1996; and Perraton, 1988). It makes no reference, explicitly or implicitly, to the presence of a teacher, in whatever guise. I adopt the term distance education not because I find it particularly appropriate—which it is not, at least not from my perspective—but rather because it has become a well-established term that vaguely binds together a community of practice that reads books like this. A notion like "environmental design for the provision of distributed learning resources" comes closer to my interpretation of the term, but it is, of course, a clumsy phrase. An advantage of using the well-established term distance education is also that one places oneself within an important historical perspective. That perspective is cognizant of early efforts to offer learning opportunities using postal services, i.e. correspondence education; the later expansion of these practices to include other communication media such as radio or TV, leading to the replacement of the term correspondence education by the more encompassing notion of distance education; and current visions of building distributed learning environments using facilities created through computer networking, often referred to as e-learning.

In terms of the above definition I consider myself both a distance learner and a distance educator. For instance, after a secondary school history of being bad at—and thus disliking—the learning of foreign languages, I joyfully learned in my late twenties a new foreign language, Spanish, using self-instructional books and records, developing my linguistic abilities to speaking the language well (so I'm told). Another instance in which I was allowed to use my ability to choose when and where to engage in a particular act of learning was the following one. After completing at a regular age my academic training as a theoretical physicist in a traditional manner and in a traditional university context, I went back, more than two decades later, to another university to pursue advanced degrees in Instructional Systems Design. It was at a time when I was working full time and didn't want to give up my job. So, I set up my own scheduled sequence of learning events over the course of four years through negotiation with an established face-to-face institution of higher education where no one had yet heard about distance education. Doing so involved organizing a variety of communication processes and alternative uses of media as well as convincing faculty and administrators that rules can—and in certain cases should—be bent. It allowed combining study in one continent, North America, with full-time working in another continent, Africa. Over my entire life's history I cannot recall a time when learning and working were more perfectly each other's complement, both modalities of existence benefiting greatly from each other through their constant interaction.

The above two personal experiences would not normally be recognized as examples of distance education. However, I defend that they should, for the following two reasons. First of all, my case is far from unique. Secondly, to the extent that cases like the above are more the exception than the rule, I believe that the cause of human learning will benefit from the greater flexibility implied by my definition of distance education, allowing the rules to be bent more frequently and in a greater variety of ways. Many people go through learning experiences similar to the ones described in the above examples, wholly or in part, negotiating their deliberate interaction with resources and opportunities that come their way or that they actively seek (usually it's a combination of the two). A continuing issue in the development of distance education is thus to remain true to its original impulse; namely, to find ways to escape from the straightjacket of the traditional schooling practice, which largely assumes that there is but one way of doing things. This is thus the first issue I wish to discuss.

MEETING LEARNING NEEDS BY BEING INNOVATIVE: THE UNFULFILLED PROMISES OF DISTANCE EDUCATION, PARTICULARLY FOR THE DEVELOPING WORLD

My motivation to work on matters of distance education largely originates from my having lived and worked for an extensive proportion of my life in parts of the world where going to school is a privilege rather than the exercise of the fundamental right defined in the Universal Declaration of Human Rights (1948; cited in UNESCO, 2000). Beyond the question that human rights should not be violated, I add to this the consideration that a majority proportion of human potential to contribute to positive change is wasted as long as 121 million children around the world do not go to school (UNICEF, 2004) and hundreds of millions who do go to school do so in conditions that make it less likely that their learning will profoundly touch their lives. Consequently, so long as this situation perpetuates, any significant advance in our understanding of the workings of nature and the intricacies of human individual and social behavior is unlikely to come from those parts of the world where opportunities to engage in serious systematic learning are absent or deficient. This means that the chances that a major response will be found to urgent challenges the world is facing—think, for instance, of a cure for AIDS or the development of a truly workable mechanism for sustainable and equitable development at the level of our small planet—remain limited to only a minor, privileged proportion of the available brain mass present around the world. Consider in this context that, as the history of science shows, nothing whatsoever indicates that major advances in human understanding are predicated on a particular segment, be it race or any other subdivision, of the human species, and it will be immediately clear that humanity is seriously and stupendously foolishly shortchanging itself in opportunities to develop its so much needed shared wisdom.

Thus, for the sake of human rights, and for the sake of good common sense, there is increasingly a need to dramatically develop the learning capacity of our species in its entirety. I believe that distance education has the potential to make its contribution to this goal. The assumed promise of distance education to make a major impact on the developing world has long been touted. For instance, it motivated UNESCO to undertake a major study in the mid-1960s concerning the potential of media to improve education (UNESCO: International Institute for Educational Planning, 1967a, 1967b); it was the premise of an influential book, *Distance Teaching for the Third World*, published a decade and a half later (Young, Perraton, Jenkins, & Dodds, 1980); it inspired the discourse that emerged from the World Conference on Education for All held in Jomtien, Thailand, in March 1990 (Inter-Agency Commission World Conference on Education for All, 1990); and it prompted a major UN initiative for the cooperative development of distance education in the nine so-called high-population countries, home to more than half the world's population and the large majority of its illiterates (J. Visser, 1995). However, while gradual improvements can be gleaned from a comparison of data collected over time, no major breakthrough can, unfortunately, be reported. What went wrong? I propose considering the following possible reasons.

The desire to innovate, which drove the work of early distance education developers, led to a tendency to think in terms of "found solutions" that could be plugged into identified problems elsewhere without much further thinking. The fact that contexts could be greatly different was often ignored. In fact, the need to take context into account, particularly as regards the huge differences that distinguish developing nations among themselves and that differentiate them from industrialized nations, while occasionally noted in the literature of the past, has only recently received serious attention in the instructional design field, thanks to a much-quoted article by Tessmer and Richey (1995). Arias and Clark (2004) pay attention to this matter with a view to the particular circumstances in developing countries.

A related issue is the gradual development in the distance education field of a sharp focus on cost-effectiveness and economies of scale. The fact that learning needs can be attended to through distance education at a reduced cost as long as high development costs can be spread over a large number of users has gradually become a major argument in defense of distance education over traditional modalities of educational provision. The argument is obviously valid, but its importance has sometimes been overemphasized to the extent that distance education has become attractive to politicians who want to claim that they have at least done something to reduce deficits in schooling. A trend has thus emerged to document best practices and make information about such practices available to potential users in different parts of the world to adopt or adapt them. While there are obvious advantages to following this trend, the disadvantage is that it stifles creativity and innovation. A better balance between the desire to apply quick fixes and the long-term need to develop real solutions must be found.

In the above context it is essential to go beyond superficial interpretations of what it means to learn. In fact, the opportunity offered by the advent of distance education—now often in the form of online learning—has, surprisingly perhaps, not led to asking any substantially deeper questions than the one asked by Simonson (2000), How can we best provide learning experiences that are equivalent for all learners, whether they learn in the traditional context of some kind of classroom environment or through any particular form of media-facilitated distance education? It is obviously perfectly reasonable to ask such a question in a world in which the classroom is still the dominant educational model but in which increasingly also other media are available to extend and enhance the classroom experience as well as to create learning environments beyond the classroom of a varied nature. Nonetheless, further questioning is necessary.

What if the classroom weren't the best of all possible alternatives and it would thus not be appropriate to consider the classroom as the standard of ultimate quality? What about the critique of the schooling culture (e.g., Shikshantar, n.d.) and the banking concept of education (Freire, 1972)? Can the possibilities offered by distance education help overcome, at least to an extent, the shortcomings of existing practice and the flaws of the schooling culture? Would it be possible to create something entirely better than what we have by taking a few steps back and first ask ourselves what we actually want when we create the conditions of human learning for the generations of the third millennium and only then start creating anew and from scratch the environments that are most propitious for achieving what we want? Doing so would avoid what now often is the trend, namely that we adopt, without further ado, the same assumptions that underlie educational practice of the past and build around those assumptions distance education systems that surprisingly closely resemble the existing face-to-face practice? Considering that the brain, the seat of consciousness and the processing of information, plays a crucial role in how we learn, what is it that we now know about brain functioning and the growth of neural networks in ways that reflect our life's experience (Greenfield, 2000) that could relevantly inform the creative design of media-facilitated learning environments? And as we rebuild the environments in which people learn, can they be built so as to allow those who participate in their processes to attain a truly deep and critical understanding and appreciation of their world? (e.g., Perkins, 1993; Perkins, 1998; Bereiter, 2002; Bereiter & Scardamalia, 2003). These are but a few of the questions that ought to be asked if distance education is to remain true to its original inspiration to advance the state of learning through innovation rather than to merely replicate its current occurrences using alternative means.

COMMODITIZED EDUCATION OR DIGNIFIED LEARNING?

In the wake of privatization and globalization, and in the context of a dominant development philosophy that has a strong focus on economic development as a prime force and on consumer behavior as the driving mechanism within it, a trend has emerged to equate the creation of learning opportunities with the provision of commodities to consumers whose particular preferences and tastes for them and whose styles of consumption can be made to match the items available on a limited menu. An obviously important backdrop to this trend is the aforementioned focus on increased cost-effectiveness through economies of scale. A particularly poignant expression of this philosophy can be found in an editorial note by the then Assistant Director-General for Education of UNESCO, John Daniel (2003), in *Education Today*, the newsletter of UNESCO's Education Sector. "Is the commoditization of learning material a way to bring education to all?" (p. 1), asks Daniel rhetorically. And his answer: "Yes it is, and open universities in a number of countries have shown the way. By developing courseware for large numbers of students they can justify the investment required to produce high quality learning materials at low unit cost" (p. 1).

In addition to the economic argument, the trend towards commoditization is, of course, also rooted in a rather limited, superficial and noncomplex vision of what actually happens when someone interacts with a given learning environment. Certainly, part of what learning is—and that is the part covered by most conventional definitions of learning—can be taken care of by that vision. That part is not unimportant, I believe, and for some researchers or developers of learning environments it is the only part that should count. From my vantage point, however, as explained at the beginning of this chapter, I see good reasons why one should go beyond such a vision. I particularly wish to argue that a more comprehensive and encompassing perspective on learning will allow the complexity of the world's problems to be properly reflected in the complexity of learning processes and of the learning ecology in which such processes evolve (see also J. Visser, 2001; J. Visser & Y. L. Visser, 2002; J. Visser, 2003). The implication of my above argument is that, yes, to an extent certain dimensions of the rich and complex reality of human learning can benefit from Daniel's (2003) vision. However, great care should be taken not to overemphasize this aspect and to be well aware of the great inherent risks of too strong a focus on learning as consumption of commodities.

The question of commoditization is also linked to the emerging trend to think of instruction as something that can be designed based on the use of reusable and scalable so-called learning objects. Learning objects are building blocks whose potential use to facilitate learning can be described in the form of metadata. They can be plugged in and out of a particular instructional context in any instructionally relevant manner. This allows instruction to be adaptable as well as generative. The assumed scalability of object-oriented instructional design makes this procedure attractive, at least at first sight, from an economic point of view in much the same way as discussed above for the economies of scale concept that has pushed the development of distance education along. However, actual practice is often at odds with otherwise rational expectations. Why? Probably in the first place because we find it difficult—if not outright impossible—to entertain different mindsets simultaneously. Having put our focus on a particular technology, a particular way of addressing problems, be it through the procedures of distance education in general or, more specifically, by means of object-oriented instructional design, or indeed any other problem-solving modality, we are at great risk of closing our eyes to other technologies or to aspects that are not in the first place technological but, rather, human. Parrish (2004) observes in this connection that "the problems of education are always more complex than technology alone can solve" (p. 51). Along with other authors, such as Jonassen and Land (2000), he also draws attention to how a particular focus, in conjunction with the terminology in which it is expressed, sets one up in terms of attitudes and perspective to look at learning in only one way, ignoring alternative views.

By extension of the above argument, it is equally likely that the use of the commoditization metaphor is not innocent. Thinking of learning in terms of the provision of commodities engenders a view of a planet populated by consuming human organisms. I assume that most people who read this chapter would agree that consumption is but one aspect of what humans do. While some may decide to limit their existence to mere consumption, many other people create meaning and dignity in their lives by actually transcending such basic patterns of behavior. Consequently, learning can also be greatly more dignified than the commoditization metaphor suggests, and I thus conclude that the identified trend should be resisted. In fact, one of the major challenges for the new modalities of learning that technology allows us to create is exactly to restore the dignity of learning.

LEARNING AUTONOMOUSLY IN AN ENVIRONMENT OF DISTRIBUTED RESOURCES

The conditions under which people can learn have greatly diversified, thanks to the development of distance education and, in general, the rapid and pervasive spread of technologies for interpersonal and mass communication, as well as for storage, retrieval, and processing of information. Despite these developments, little has changed in the way human beings are being prepared to reap the full benefit of available opportunities and resources for learning. In countries with well-established education systems, people come face-to-face with more-or-less conscious learning efforts when they first go to school or kindergarten at a young age, usually when they are somewhere between four and six years old. This is when they not only start learning in a systematic way; it is also their first opportunity to start reflecting on how they learn and what learning means to them. In countries with a less perfect school system, young people's initiation in such a reflection on learning will be more haphazard and therefore also more varied. However, for those who enter the world of learning via the school system, their initiation into thinking about learning will naturally be oriented towards what happens in school.

Sfard (1998) identifies two major metaphors that guide learners, teachers, and researchers in their thinking about what happens in the context of deliberately-planned learning events. She calls them the "acquisition metaphor" (p. 5) and the "participation metaphor" (p. 6), respectively, and warns against choosing just one of those metaphors. Looking at learning from the perspective of the acquisition metaphor leads, according to Sfard, to a vision that:

- emphasizes the individual learner and that person's individual enrichment as the prime goal of the learning event;
- interprets learning as an act of acquiring something;
- sees the student as recipient or (re-)constructor of a commodity that becomes the student's property and views the teacher as a provider, facilitator and/or mediator in helping the students to acquire that property; and
- perceives knowing as having or possessing something.

By contrast, the perspective provided by the participation metaphor leads to a view of learning that:

- emphasizes community building as the prime goal of the learning event;
- interprets learning in terms of becoming a participant in a social learning event and the environment that affords the event;
- sees students and teachers as co-participants with roles as apprentices and experts, respectively; and
- perceives knowing as "belonging, participating, [and] communicating" (p. 7).

In her essay, Sfard (1998) draws particular attention to how the vocabulary associated with the acquisition metaphor pervades the language in which we express ourselves and think about learning. It should thus be no surprise that those who enter into the world of learning through the gates of the school—which is, in and of itself, an expression of that metaphor—end up being prepared for further learning in terms of that same metaphor. It should also be of little surprise that many of the distance education experiences, including the modern day e-learning variety of them, simply replicate the school model by different means. After all, those experiences were devised mainly by people who are themselves the (at least, partial) product of the acquisition metaphor. Somewhere this cycle of the self-asserting acquisition metaphor will have to be broken and replaced by a richer level of thinking that recognizes that various metaphors may be used to enhance our understanding of this most complex phenomenon we call learning. I believe that the information and communication technologies currently available and the experience gathered over the decades to build new learning experiences provide an excellent opportunity to do so. But where should we start?

The current trend is to prepare learners for their entry and participation in an unfamiliar learning experience such as online learning by providing them with just-in-time advice, often in the form of checklists of what to do and what not to do. A worthy example of this approach is the *E-Learning Companion* by Watkins and Corry (2005). Many online learning providers also offer their students advice via their various Web sites. Two examples out of very many that can be found on the Web are the pages provided by the University of Guelph (n.d.) and the Illinois Online Network (n.d.). I have no doubt that such advice is called for in the present circumstances. However, I should like to argue that much more is needed and that proper preparation to reap the benefits of new opportunities to learn should start in kindergarten, or even earlier at home, and that the skills to explore distributed learning resources, autonomously and in collaboration with others, should continue to be perfected as learning individuals progress through their course of life. To make this really work it will be necessary as well to initiate new generations in their thinking about learning by turning the tables on current mainstream practice and provide deliberate learning experiences that are varied in meaning and that can be described using vocabulary associated with multiple metaphors. And where better to begin than right at the start?

Research, rather than mere intuition, will be necessary in this context to identify and validate the competencies today's learners must possess. Focused efforts are underway to undertake such research. A good example is the project recently initiated by the International Board of Standards for Training, Performance and Instruction (ibstpi, 2003) to identify and validate learner competencies in an international context with a particular focus on online learning. The effort recognizes that online learning environments currently provide the broadest range of challenges to learners. Thus, the complete set of competencies and related specific performance statements to be developed must be expected to also be relevant for other settings and circumstances in which people learn. It is important, though, that such research efforts be guided by visions of human learning that go beyond the traditional views. Work to establish such enhanced visions was initiated in the late 1990s by UNESCO in the framework of its trans-sectoral Learning Without Frontiers (1999) initiative and is currently being carried forward by the Learning Development Institute (2004) and its partners.

STARTING ANEW OR BUILDING ON FOUNDATIONS ALREADY LAID?

There is a tendency throughout the history of the development of distance education to replace technologies whenever new ones become available rather than continuing to perfect the use of existing technologies and enhance them through the inclusion of new ones while at the same time exploring the additional benefits such new technologies may offer. The tendency is understandable if one considers that most of those involved in developing educational alternatives such as distance education are, by nature of their trade, innovators in the sense defined by Rogers (2003). They are only too eager to try out anything new. It is one of the psychological traits present among a significant minority of humans that is necessary to lead others to eventually follow them. Without it innovation would not diffuse the way it does. However, there is a costly downside to being innovative in too uncontrolled a fashion or, rather, in a manner of being too much focused on the tools instead of the issues.

A typical example of the above phenomenon could be observed when the computer science community realized that its tools—which so perfectly allow everyone to communicate with everyone, and stored information to be accessible throughout a network—had great potential for building virtual learning environments. They quickly coined the term e-learning for electronic variants they constructed of learning procedures that usually closely resembled the well-known practice of how people are made to learn in schools, with the exception that the teacher was not in the same location as the student. It took them some time to discover that something called distance education had preceded the invention of e-learning for decades and, though it had employed older technologies, wasn't conceptually too different from e-learning. One can see advantages and disadvantages in such a development. The clear advantage of ignoring the past is that one will not be bogged down by it. The disadvantage, though, is that one cannot learn from past mistakes or build on past achievements. Rather than choosing between ignorance or slavishly persisting in patterns of the past, the greater wisdom is, of course, to be critically aware of the past. Such awareness can then be the basis for approaches that are innovative in a much more profound way as they go deeper than merely changing a superficial detail. What is required here is a back-to-basics approach, asking ourselves questions about what kind of learning is required for citizens of today's world and what facilitating factors will best provide opportunities for such learning. Among those factors are technological ones. Answers to the question of what technologies to use and how to use them will then naturally follow from these prior considerations.

By way of example, I should like to refer in the above context to an international discussion that took place under the auspices of UNESCO regarding the kind of education that would be required for the 21st century. The discussion culminated in a report that was published in 1996. Among four pillars of the desired education, the commission that responded to the challenge formulated by UNESCO defined "learning to live together, learning to live with others" as "probably one of the major issues in education today" (Delors et al., 1996, p. 91). It so happens that only years before the above report was published technologies had become pervasively available that are particularly well suited to creating learning environments in which participants from around the world can creatively and collaboratively engage in exchanging and generating knowledge. However, with the fine exception of such cases as reported by Patarakin and Y. L. Visser (2003), little of the established practice of using the World Wide Web for educational purposes is a result of the conscious decision to explore the technology for the kind of purposes highlighted in the Delors report. Why? Because for most people who design virtual learning environments, the major challenge is to replicate as well as possible—and, if possible, improve—the practice of school learning as we know it by different means and not to design something entirely new for a fully new conception of what human learning in this day and age should be about.

LEARNING BEYOND SKILLS DEVELOPMENT

As promised in the title, this chapter discusses trends and issues in distance education from a planetary human development perspective. The United Nations Development Programme (UNDP) annually publishes the Human Development Report (HDR/UNDP, 2004). In addition to statistical data regarding different aspects of human development such as literacy, school attendance, life expectancy, access to water, poverty, and health-related indicators, these reports also focus, on a year-by-year basis, on issues of overall planetary import. The specific focus of the 2004 report, for instance, has to do with cultural liberty in a diverse world. Among the areas covered in previous years we find issues like poverty eradication; deepening of democracy; and the impact on human development of technological development, human rights, aspects of economic development, and gender. Particularly during the 1990s, the United Nations system as a whole, together with bilateral partners, non-governmental organizations, and other representations of civil society organized debate around such planetary issues in the context of so-called world conferences, starting in 1990 with the earlier mentioned World Conference on Education for All.

I believe the above shift of attention to global issues to have been timely. We live in an increasingly planetary world; that is, in a world in which key issues can no longer be dealt with appropriately solely at a level lower than that of the planet as a whole. French sociologist Edgar Morin's work, particularly his more recent writings, has had a strong focus on this idea. Regarding implications of his thinking for education, I refer specifically to his *Seven Complex Lessons in Education for the Future* (Morin, 2001). The need to take planetary issues seriously is a new turn in the development of humanity that has critical implications for what and how we learn (see also J. Visser, 2003), a consideration that should have equally vital implications for how we design the conditions under which people learn. There is, in my view, a definite need to work concurrently on two fronts. One of those fronts is the one that has existed all along the history of deliberate intervention in human learning, namely the concern to develop useful skills. The successive Human Development Reports mentioned above show great discrepancy in the various indicators that make up the Human Development Index across nations and geographical areas. Many of those discrepancies can be resolved by creating more equitable conditions for the development of specific skills among members of the human species in different parts of the world, provided such development goes hand-in-hand with developing facilitating contextual factors— for instance, in such areas as the development of economic conditions, environmental management, transparent governance, and the creation of legal and policy frameworks—that allow people to explore using their skills and, by doing so, enhance existence for themselves and their fellow human beings.

The trend so far in educational development, including in the development of distance education, has been to concentrate on skills development, something that is clearly demonstrated in how we decompose the purpose of educational efforts into specific learning goals, each of them specifying something the successful student will be able to do upon completion of the learning task. This is an obviously useful trend. It has allowed the instructional design discipline to develop into a mature science and learning conditions to be deliberately created for specific learning needs, often in response to important social needs. However, the development of the aforementioned contextual factors, particularly in a planetary perspective, depends on more than merely having skills, more than having the ability to do certain things. This "more than skills" area of concern is what I consider to be the second front on which we must focus our attention in conjunction with the first front mentioned above. That area has to do with the formation of the entire person, with a process of contributing to the continual building of someone's mind in the sense defined by brain researcher Greenfield (2000): "Mind," says Greenfield, "is the seething morass of cell circuitry that has been configured by personal experiences and is constantly being updated as we live out each moment" (p. 13). She refers to this process as "the personalization of the physical brain" (p. 14).

I am not implying with the above reference that the brain is the only organ involved in human learning, or that human learning is a mere individual act. No doubt, the brain is an essential organ, and much is still to be discovered about its role in helping us all to learn. However, we learn with everything we have and are, individually as well as socially. Our entire bodies are involved. Our entire life's experience counts in who we are and how each of us participates in this huge interplay, throughout the history of humankind, of members of our species interacting with each other and with their environment, producing continual change while aiming at making existence progressively better for all of us and for the planet as a whole. At that level, the level of what I called the second front, the immense diversity among us is not "an issue to be dealt with," which is typically what one does when designing skills oriented instruction for a diverse population; rather, it is an issue to be embraced and exploited for the benefit of the species and the planet. To do so requires a vision of the essential issues regarding the development of human learning for the planetary era, focusing not so much on specific skills, but rather on how to live with the skills we have and those we are able to develop; that is, emphasizing meta-competencies. The seven complex issues identified by Morin (2001) form a good starting point. This is, I believe, an area in which the field of distance education, with its powerful potential to use media that connect people across the planet, has a prime responsibility to start a trend that is still absent.

REFERENCES

Arias, S., & Clark, K. A. (2004). Instructional technologies in developing countries: A contextual analysis approach. *TechTrends, 48*(4), 52-55, 70.

Bereiter, C. (2002). Education and mind in the knowledge age. Mahwah, NJ: Erlbaum.

Bereiter, C., & Scardamalia, M. (2003). Learning to Work Creatively With Knowledge. In E. De Corte, N. Verschaffel, N. Entwistle & J. van Merrienboer (Eds.), *Powerful learning environments : unravelling basic components and dimensions* (pp. 55-70). Amsterdam: Pergamon.

Daniel, J. (2002, October-December). Higher education for sale. *Education Today*, No. 3, 1.

Delling, R. M. (1987). Towards a theory of distance education. *ICDE Bulletin, 13*, 21–25.

Delors, J., Al Mufti, I., Amagi, I., Carneiro, R., Chung, F., Geremek, B., Gorham, W., Kornhauser, A., Manley, M., Padrón Quero, M., Savané, M-A., Singh, K., Stavenhagen, R., Suhr, M.W., & Zhou N. (1996). *Learning: The treasure within.* Report to UNESCO of the International Commission on Education for the Twenty- first Century. Paris: UNESCO.

Freire, P. (1972). *Pedagogy of the oppressed*. Harmondsworth, UK: Penguin Books.

Greenfield, S. (2000). *The private life of the brain: Emotions, consciousness and the secret of the self.* New York: Wiley.

HDR/UNDP (2004). Website of the *Human Development Reports* of the United Nations Development Programme (UNDP) [Online]. Retrieved August 8, 2004 from http://hdr.undp.org/

Ibstpi (2003). Web site of the *International Board of Standards for Training, Performance and Instruction* [Online]. Retrieved August 6, 2004 from http://www.ibstpi.org

Illinois Online Network (n.d.). Web site of the Illinois Online Network on *What makes a successful online student?* [Online]. Retrieved August 4, 2004 from http://www.ion.illinois.edu/IONresources/onlineLearning/StudentProfile.asp

Inter-Agency Commission World Conference on Education for All. (1990). *World declaration on education for all and framework for action to meet basic learning needs.* Paris: UNESCO.

Jonassen, D. H., & Land, S. M. (2000). Preface. In D. H. Jonassen & S. M. Land (Eds.), *Theoretical foundations of learning environments* (pp. iii-ix). Mahwah, NJ: Erlbaum.

Keegan, D. (1986). *The foundations of distance education*. London: Croom Helm.

Learning Development Institute (2004). Web site of the *Learning Development Institute* [Online]. Retrieved August 6, 2004 from http://www.learndev.org

Learning Without Frontiers. (1999). Website of the *Learning Without Frontiers* trans-sectoral initiative of the United Nations Educational, Scientific and Cultural Organization (UNESCO) [Online]. Retrieved August 6, 2004 from http://www.unesco.org/education/lwf/

Moore, M. G., & Kearsley, G. (1996). *Distance education: A systems view.* Belmont, CA: Wadsworth.

Morin, E. (2001). *Seven complex lessons in education for the future.* Paris: UNESCO.

Parrish, P. P. (2004). The trouble with learning objects. *Educational Technology Research and Development, 52*(1), 49-67.

Patarakin, E., & Visser, Y. L. (2003). *Creativity and creative learning in the context of electronic communication networks: A framework for analysis of practice and research.* LDI Working Paper # 4 [Online]. Retrieved August 7, 2004 from http://www.learndev.org/dl/Creativity&CreativeLearning.pdf

Perkins, D. (1993). Teaching for understanding. *American Educator, 17*(3), 8, 28-35 [Also Online]. Retrieved August 2, 2004 from http://www.exploratorium.edu/IFI/resources/workshops/teachingforunderstanding.html

Perkins, D. N. (1998). What is understanding. In M. S. Wiske (Ed.), *Teaching for understanding: Linking research to practice* (pp. 39-57). San Francisco: Jossey-Bass.

Perraton, H. (1988). A theory for distance education. In D. Sewart, D. Keegan, & B. Holmberg (Eds.), *Distance education: International perspectives* (pp. 34–45). New York: Routledge.

Rogers, E. M. (2003). *Diffusion of innovations* (5th ed.). New York: Free Press.

Sfard, A. (1998). On two metaphors for learning and on the dangers of choosing just one. *Educational Researcher, 27*(2), 4-13.

Simonson, M. (2000). Making decisions: The use of electronic technology in online classrooms. *New Directions for Teaching and Learning, 84*, 29-34.

Shikshantar (n.d.). Website of Shikshantar: The Peoples' Institute for Rethinking Education and Development [Online]. Retrieved July 23, 2004 from http://www.swaraj.org/shikshantar

Tessmer, M., & Richey, R. C. (1997). The Role of Context in Learning and Instructional Design. *Educational Technology Research & Development, (45)*2, 1042-1629.

UNESCO. (2000). *World education report 2000—The right to education: Towards education for all throughout life*. Paris: UNESCO Publishing.

UNESCO: International Institute for Educational Planning. (1967a). New educational media in action: Case studies for planners – I, II & III. Paris: United Nations Educational, Scientific and Cultural Organization.

UNESCO: International Institute for Educational Planning. (1967b). The new media: Memo to educational planners. Paris: United Nations Educational, Scientific and Cultural Organization.

UNICEF. (2004). *The state of the world's children 2004*. New York: UNICEF. Retrieved July 9, 2004 from http://www.unicef.org/sowc04/

University of Guelph (n.d.). Web site of the University of Guelph on *Learner resources: Learner skills development: Hints for learning online* [Online]. Retrieved August 4, 2004 from http://www.open.uoguelph.ca/resources/skills/hints.html

Visser, J. (1995). International cooperation in distance education: The DE9 initiative, a case in point. In D. Sewart (Ed.), *One World Many Voices: Quality in Open and Distance Learning. Selected papers from the 17th World Conference of the International Council for Distance Education, Birmingham, United Kingdom, June 1995* (pp. 38-42). Milton Keynes, UK: the International Council for Distance Education and The Open University. Retrieved July 6, 2004 from http://www1.worldbank.org/disted/Policy/Global/int-02.html

Visser, J. (2001). Integrity, completeness and comprehensiveness of the learning environment: Meeting the basic learning needs of all throughout life. In D. N. Aspin, J. D. Chapman, M. J. Hatton, and Y. Sawano (Eds), *International handbook of lifelong learning* (pp. 447-472). Dordrecht, The Netherlands: Kluwer.

Visser, J. (2003). Distance education in the perspective of global issues and concerns. In M. G. Moore & W. G. Anderson (Eds.), *Handbook of distance education* (pp. 793-810). Mahwah, NJ: Erlbaum.

Visser, J., & Visser, Y. L. (2002). Undefining learning: Implications for instructional designers and educational technologists. *Educational Technology Magazine, 42*(2), 15-20.

Watkins, R., & Corry, M. (2005). *E-learning companion: A student's guide to online success*. Boston: Houghton Mifflin.

Young, M., Perraton, H., Jenkins, J., & Dodds, T. (1980). *Distance teaching for the third world: The lion and the clockwork mouse*. London, UK: Routledge & Kegan Paul.

CHAPTER 4

DISTANCE EDUCATION REAPPRAISED

Emerging Trends and Patterns in Traditional Face-to-Face Universities and Corporate Training Institutions

François Marchessou

The reflections and comments that follow do not claim to be an exhaustive analysis of the state of distance education in the first years of the twenty-first century. The purpose of this chapter is to clarify some of the underlying tendencies which affect those lighter forms of open and distance learning (ODL) that came into being with the advent of the Internet and its related technologies, within formal educational systems as well as within the corporate world.

When I talk about lighter forms of distance education I mean those distance education courses or programs that have recently been established in universities and training centres which are otherwise primarily devoted to face-to-face instruction. Another characteristic of the lighter forms of ODL is that the programs can easily be adapted if they fail to match

Trends and Issues in Distance Education: International Perspectives, 51–66
Copyright © 2005 by Information Age Publishing
All rights of reproduction in any form reserved.

expectations, as they do not involve extensive or massive human and technological resources.

It was not easy to identify some of the emerging trends in what is almost uncharted territory, a novel field consisting of highly diversified experiments where dissemination of feedback and evaluation is often restricted to the project administrators and where techno-political, economic and commercial factors have often concealed the critical evaluation of a media-based learning process. The views that follow are based on experiences acquired in, among others, consultancy work involving overseas projects, mostly in Africa and Latin America. These projects include a strong educational technology component. To avoid that a critical appraisal in this chapter could jeopardize the possibly hitherto shining image and/or the successful relationships within the business world or the academic community, some names are withheld. The sheer multiplicity and diversity of ongoing distance education ventures means that it is impossible to include them all. It is hoped that the reader will be reminded of other cases that contradict or confirm those discussed below. In the sections that follow I will successively attempt to analyse some of the cultural factors that affect positively or negatively the distance learning process, then I will try to shed light on some of the major obstacles that impede such a process in this first decade of the twenty-first century before describing a few of the light and diversified formats that are emerging with a respectable measure of success and may constitute lasting trends for the future.

THREE CULTURAL FACTORS

In the emerging diversified formats of post-2000 ODL, the social vision of the 'sixties and 'seventies on which the large open and distance universities were built, namely the mission to provide higher learning to those who were denied it earlier for reasons of cost, age, gender, etc., seems to have lost some of its strength, perhaps because those noble goals have partly been attained through democratization campaigns that include, among other things, the availability of Open and Distance Learning in some form or other. In the new emerging patterns, the cultural factors are all important, and the word "cultural" is used in a broad sense that goes beyond the obvious differences that can be noted in any cross-border activity. Culture here is seen as shared habits, values, memories and beliefs that unite a group of people and make communication between and among them easier. The expressions "multi-cultural society," "corporate culture," etc., will sound familiar to many readers.

To keep it simple, it could be said that there are at least three cultures, three sets of mental images and implicit beliefs that inform and guide teachers and students involved in open and distance learning. On the one hand there is the traditional top-down view of the master, the competent, knowledgeable provider of instruction, sometimes helped by tutors or instructors, who designs the programs and courses and assigns tasks. This has created a context where functions are clearly identified and where almost everyone feels at ease. In large distance education systems, the teacher/instructor, the tutor, the printed learning materials, the written assignments generally reproduce the traditional school pattern. It has been noted that many of those adults who enroll in a distance education program, find it comfortable to rediscover the benign authority and clearly defined guidance they were accustomed to in their school days. They may resent being forced to become actively involved in more open systems where they have to map out some of their learning itineraries. In a filmed interview, one of the facilitators in charge of an open learning centre for adults known throughout France as "Ateliers Pédagogiques Personnalisés" (Personalized Pedagogical Workshops) would insist on the difficulties many of the new trainees had in adjusting to a flexible system where they would have to take the initiative, choose the subject of the day, formulate specific questions , ask for advice, without being told what to do (for the film and the APP movement evaluations, etc., see below).

The second culture is media-based. It is not usually associated with schools and education, but it is strong and pervasive. For the past 40 years, the impact of radio, television, and advertising has been so strong that any educational programme has to follow the pattern of commercial broadcasting if the students' attention is to be attracted and retained. This is reflected in the short impacting sequences as well as in the breaks that come up regularly just like the commercials in a run-of-the-mill soap opera. One of the earliest successful attempts to emulate the rhythm of commercial TV is to be found in the first episodes of *Sesame Street* (Greenfield, 1984), whose influence soon proved so significant that it inspired a highly diversified collection of academic interpretations across the globe, as can be seen in any Internet search. In Brazil, with its deeply rooted *telenovela* (soap opera) culture, the locally produced distance education programmes that are being disseminated by the general as well as by the specialized channels, notably *TV Escola* (2002), try to follow the same dynamic pace and friendly tone as the main prime-time shows. This is the positive impact of media culture. On the negative side, many educators note that the speed and spectacular effects of TV and video games have certainly contributed to what could be called "student impatience," a reduction of the attention span, which is felt very strongly at the primary school level and is also noticeable among adults.

From another point of view, distance education programs are generally produced on a fairly tight budget. They cannot in any way compete with the spectacular shots, sound effects, actors, and stages of the main networks, and students may subconsciously resent those programs. This has been apparent in perfectly acceptable, well-designed multimedia programs for the training of prospective physical education teachers, where people expect World Cup standards from the people who perform on screen as well as from the camera work (Nascimento, 2002).

The third culture that strongly affects distance education students more than teachers, as a result of a generation and culture gap that will probably vanish in the coming years, is best described by Manuel Castells (2001) in his recent and comprehensive analysis of the diversified Internet paradigms, *The Internet Galaxy*. He reveals the post-1968 belief in communication and non-commercial exchange that underlies the development of the earliest networks, as well as the design of what eventually became the World Wide Web, all the way through to the open-source software culture as exemplified by Linux. At this stage of his momentous in-depth survey of the "networked society," Castells does not wish to analyze all the implications of the Internet for education, but his study does reveal some of the underlying causes of the tensions that presently affect many online distance education and training ventures, both in institutions and in the corporate world. Students, especially those who came of age with the Web, resent the commercial overtones and all-too-often behavioristic top-down nature of the on-line courses they are taking and the discrepancy between the instruction offered and the medium itself. To them, the Internet is *the* emblem of mutual enrichment, of creativity shared among equals, not a channel for school-type learning tasks prescribed by some unquestioned educational authority. Perhaps, subconsciously, they expect to find in distance learning something akin to the successful e-enterprise, online as well as offline, as described by Castells as

> based on a horizontal hierarchy, team-work and an easy, open interaction, between workers and managers, between the various departments as well as between the various levels of the enterprise. (Castells, 2001, p. 109)

This ideal view of things may exist in small circles of research scientists who share strong cultural or corporate bonds, but we should not forget that, for many traditional universities, offering online programs has primarily been an attempt to increase student enrollments and raise badly-needed extra income. In many cases, the authoritarian tendency has, at least temporarily, been reinforced by the adoption of a new technological mode of communication, the Internet, in contradiction with the very nature of that medium, which is fundamentally participative.

Conversely, in all the instances that we know of, where distance education/training is being offered to members of tightly knit groups sharing the same culture, the major indicators point to success. The most outstanding examples are to be found among Europe's smaller countries and ethnic minorities. I will name just a few: Wales, The Basque Country, and Catalonia. Ireland, where educational creativity and the widespread use of IT have led to outstanding economic achievements, could also be added to the list.

The word *country* has a strong cultural connotation in contemporary Europe: it refers to the habitat, values, and language of a given group of people. It is much more than a province, which is an administrative term. The notion does, however, not necessarily extend to that of the nation-state as such, although there are many political movements that strive towards full political independence.

In the beginning of the 1980s in Wales, as well as in the Basque country, people were faced with a harsh physical environment where a long industrial tradition based in both cases on mining, steelworks, and shipyards was coming to grief with the prospect of massive unemployment and few opportunities for the younger generations. In both cases, this would have resulted in a massive emigration of the young towards the major cities of England or Spain, with an ensuing loss of identity, language, and culture. The urgency to look for a solution was felt by the local politicians, who quickly realized that a strong emphasis had to be put on new, easily accessible training facilities for tomorrow's jobs, alongside the traditional academic infrastructure of schools, vocational colleges, and universities. The result has been an impressive series of innovative plans, all of them related to open and distance learning. In Wales, the focus has been on providing remote schools and communities with programs that first used audioconferencing, then satellite and, today, Internet. The array of subjects ranges from efficient rugby coaching to science or to a mixture of face-to-face and distance education courses for, among others, middle-aged women who wish to reach the required level in electronics before applying for a job in one of the new Japanese-owned factories that have replaced the old steel mills. In the Basque country, open and distance learning is closely built into the fabric of the Basque cooperative movement, originally based in the town of Mondragón. This includes the world's largest industrial cooperative (manufacturers of robots as well as buses and household appliances), a large network of cooperative savings banks, and a powerful cultural drive based on a local form of social catholicism and on the revival of the Basque language and culture. In both regions, migration has now slowed down to a manageable trickle, the once-endangered languages, Welsh and Euskera (the Basque language), are used spontaneously in everyday life, and spanking new buildings like the Cardiff Rugby stadium or the Bilbao Guggenheim museum testify to the rebirth of civic pride in cities that seemed forever associated with the decline of Victorian industries.

The creative approach to open and distance learning is not the one and only cause of this revival, but it has certainly played an important part. Furthermore, the success of those new flexible forms of open and distance learning has attracted a great deal of attention in academic as well as in socio-economic circles wishing to import the proven technological platforms and pedagogical models. To give a few examples: The Welsh have provided training programs to Norway for people working on oil rigs in the North Sea (Roberts, 2004) while Mondragón exports its turn-key on/off line technological degrees to several countries in Latin America, such as Mexico.

Distance education expertise is not only a powerful identity-building agent, it also proves to be a valuable source of exports. It is only fair to say that, outside their respective borders, Welsh programs are being disseminated in English, and Basque courses in Castilian. The same holds true for Catalonia, where the Open University was the first to be exclusively Web-based (Universitat Oberta de Catalunya, 2003) and is now offering its Masters' programs in Spanish in, among other countries, Mexico.

These examples show how the presence/absence of shared values, whether cultural in the broader sense, or linguistic, can affect, positively or negatively, the successful design and implementation of open and distance learning. In a more anecdotal way, we could add the recent testimony of one of the Poitiers exchange postgraduates, who attended one of the online courses offered to teachers by Utah State University. One of the most striking elements the student noted was how the geographic and religious (in this case the Church of Jesus Christ of Latter-day Saints) factors would act as powerful incentives for middle-aged students, mostly from Utah and Idaho, and helped them engage actively in chatroom dialogues and general discussions, often enriched with a wealth of personal details (Brossard, 2002).

NON-CULTURAL OBSTACLES

Beyond those obstacles related to religion, linguistics, and ethnics, we can also identify other, less visible obstacles. Some obstacles obviously stem from the misunderstandings that tend to separate information science specialists from educators, in the same way as they, in the past, frequently separated broadcasting people from teachers of the British Open University (Bates, 1984). Strange as it may seem, in a cold, rational world of bytes and algorithms, computer science and network administration seem to elicit passionate responses and rejections.

Once the inter-campus optical fiber cables were in place, I have found it extremely difficult when trying to lay the foundations of the "Digital Campuses" project for French universities (EducNet, 2004), to convince network specialists that if distance education is to reach new target groups, especially those adults who wish to work from their homes, one has to be fully aware that Internet access has to be reconsidered: ADSL connections are getting cheaper and are spreading quite fast in Europe and the Americas, but one should keep in mind in rural areas and in most developing countries the need for alternative channels that offer high capacity Internet access at sustainable "family" prices. Cable TV networks and/or satellite dishes could provide part of the answer, but this is not considered a technologically noble solution by many engineers. On the other hand, teachers make little effort to discover and understand the actual possibilities of technological media, while imported software is all-too-often ignored as part of the "not invented here "syndrome. Hence, the time and energy wasted in trying to design another Web-based plat-form (CNED, 2004) every time a distance education programme comes into being. Educators do not seem to realize that what matters is not the newness, but the flexibility and ergonomics of a given educational soft-ware, and the way feedback from distance education students has been taken into account over the years and reincorporated into the original platform.

It is difficult to move beyond the strict borders of one's scientific or educational field and, after supervising generations of graduate students in educational technology, I have noticed some progress in mutual respect and understanding between media specialists and teachers. There often remains, however, a barrier that can be called "the macro-educational obstacle." I have often found, even among those colleagues who have suc-cessfully adopted IT within their own face-to-face courses, the inability to replace and refocus their own teaching within a broader context that will then include the provision of some form of open and distance learning. The new emerging needs and their social importance are often not per-ceived, even by professors who claim to be (and are) genuinely committed to promoting equity and democracy through education. This is especially true in Europe within the established school and university systems where, possibly with the exception of the schools of business administration, the decisions to promote ODL and the necessary financial incentives have always come from above, especially from the national ministries or the various Directorates General (DG) of the European Union. The integra-tion of information technologies, the building of inter-European partner-ships for the cooperative design and testing of flexible learning systems that involve distance courses, have been helped by the various *framework programmes* (Union, 2004) which are now being extended to, among others, Eastern Europe and Latin America (Union, 2004).

Looking back at the past decade, experts in distance education will discover the networking that has slowly been established, to a large extent, through the incentives provided by the DELTA, COMENIUS, LEONARDO, and other European Community-sponsored projects. Their objective was the cooperative creation and provision of multimedia for open and flexible learning in order to maximize Europe's competitiveness in a knowledge-based economy, and distance education was always present in the planners' minds as a desirable option.

The end-products, such as the multimedia that were co-designed and produced, have not always been put to their full use, but European educators who did not really know each other and who had little or no experience of working together, have now built cross-border operational alliances that will make it easier to test and implement new forms of distance learning. One of those alliances is the *Coimbra Group*, an informal alliance of some of Europe's oldest universities, including Salamanca, Leuven, Edinburgh, Abo, Poitiers, and Leiden. Their educational technology departments are often involved in projects sponsored by the European Union and range from surveys of actual IT uses among students and teachers to parallel experiments in online teacher training in The Netherlands, Belgium, France, Italy, and Finland (Coimbra Group, 2002). Historical fault lines and the prevailing lack of communication have now been overcome, and the basic social prerequisites for the launching of voluntary bottom-up experiments in distance education have now been established.

The historical and cultural obstacles have largely been erased through working together, through the joint fight against the same bureaucracy, through the discovery of the values actually shared by all the participating institutions, whatever their tradition and culture may be. When the values that were previously taken for granted are not (or no longer) there, then the best distance education endeavours will be seriously impaired.

The case that follows has been documented by an OAVUP (Poitiers, 1993) postgraduate student in educational technology, during her internship within a reputable 200-year old French institution of higher learning (Goutner, 2002). This institution, which includes a national center and several regional branches, was built on the idea of offering evening classes to working adults, in this way enabling them to gain a valid university degree in areas like accounting, economics, and engineering. The tradition remains first-rate and the institution has incorporated the latest technologies into its curricula.

In the mid 1980s, one of the regional centers, assisted by local authorities, decided to go "online," using an existing network that connected the computer classes in several *lycées* and offering adults the possibility to work in small groups in the evenings. The proprietary software they used was somewhat comparable to the one used by the University of Maryland (USA) for its extension courses. In both the United States and France, the shift to the Internet actually took place in the late 'nineties. In the French case, the platform has been designed and tested in-house, and is constantly being upgraded and modified in response to students' and teachers' suggestions. It is generally considered to be both flexible and "user-friendly." At the same time, the institution spends a good deal of time and effort informing and training the tutors/instructors who have a long experience of using online education with adult students.

Things had been running smoothly until the academic year 2001-2002, when the institution was asked to address the training needs of a new social group made up of adults who wished to gain academic accreditation for their past professional experience (Poitiers, 2003), and thus were required to take some on-line courses. When the tutors/instructors actually met in the Spring of 2002 and compared their impressions about the course, they realized that there had been, and was, a breakdown in communication between the students and the instructors, and among the students themselves. It had not been easy for the tutors to establish contacts with the students, chats remained inactive and "friendly" personal phone calls were considered intrusive. Overall it had been very difficult to establish, on a mutually accepted basis, a participative dialogue. This was something the online tutors had never encountered during their many years of practice with adult distance education students working towards a degree. The causes of this specific, unexpected breakdown have not been fully analyzed yet, and the following explanations are just tentative:

- In some cases, the move from the autonomous small-group work in the lycées to individual study using Internet at home may have affected the human contacts and the peer-learning bonds that existed and were felt to be important metacognitive factors. With the problem group, however, one may suppose that the learners actually resented having to go through a complex process in order to put an academic label on the skills and expertise they had acquired through their years of professional practice and for which they were recognized in the workplace.

- The uneasiness of the students possibly increased because Web-based distance courses include peer-to-peer activities, chats, forums, and other activities, often different from the traditional single teacher-student relationship they had been exposed to in their own school-days. The fear to appear less competent when communicating their impressions and responses to the group was also voiced by some students participating in the Utah State University class (Brossard, 2002) mentioned above, and may have been the actual reason for their refusal to communicate.

The case discussed is a specific one within a limited French context and, knowing the care, professionalism, and flexibility of the team in charge, it has probably been sorted out by now.

On a broader scale, the flexibility dimension—or rather the lack thereof—remains one of the major obstacles to the integrated, non-conflictual development of open and distance learning. In most countries, but even more so in Europe where tradition is revered, many mainstream university lecturers think of distance education as something distinct, a field in which they take no part because they believe it is somehow substandard. This is still true in many areas although, in my own recent experience, some departments are more open than others, especially in modern languages and medicine.

This is reinforced by the barely-concealed fear that distance teaching and its attendant technology are in fact an undercover attempt to cut costs by reducing the number of teachers. I have personally heard that fear voiced by teachers' union representatives in several countries.

LIGHT, LEAN, AND FLEXIBLE:
THE KEYS TO SURVIVAL AND EXPANSION

Although traditional distance universities based on the British Open University model may not be planned and implemented in the near future, at least not in the richer countries of the northern hemisphere, ODL remains, nevertheless, a highly creative field where hundreds of small-scale experiments are taking root worldwide, especially since the advent of the Internet. This means that, although it remains expensive for many individuals in developing countries, the cost of the indispensable interface--that is, a connected work station, is now accessible to most schools and training centers. In some cases, downloading of HTML pages can effectively be carried out through a portable digital radio with a tiny dish aimed at one of the Worldspace satellites (International, 2004) whose footprints now cover all of Africa and Asia. Those radio sets cost about US $100 and provide high-quality digital sound. They can be connected to a computer, thereby offering fast, cheap, sustainable access to Web-based course pages, Powerpoint slides, etc. Prospects for transmission and delivery of educational material are infinite, but so far, beyond the test transmissions of data, the technology has only been used mostly as an efficient channel for radio. Several projects, generally funded by international aid agencies, are under way with a view to implementing *ad-hoc* mini-networks that would combine community radio animation with the regular delivery of instructional written material (International, 2004). This is a slow process, and one more example of the difficulties encountered when trying to make full use of a light, sustainable technology which appeals to educators and trainers in the field, but does not sound exciting enough to some of the decision-makers because it does not call for massive funds and spectacular equipment.

The Kothmale Community Radio in Sri Lanka represents an efficient way of bridging the North/South digital divide through a combination of digital technology, the Internet, radio, and local human interaction. The experiment has been thoroughly documented, and the following description comes from the United Nations Human Development Report (2001):

> The Kothmale Community Radio in Sri Lanka uses radio as a gateway to the Internet for the listeners in remote rural communities. Children or their teachers send requests for information about school topics for which no local resources exist; other listeners may also submit requests. The broadcasters search for the information on the Internet, download it and make it available by constructing a broadcast around the information, mailing it to the school or placing it in the radio station's open-access resource centre...This mediated access brings the Internet's resources to rural and underserved communities and community rebroadcasting can relay the information in local languages rather than English, the dominant language of the Internet. (United Nations Development Report, 2001, p. 87)

Development economists and educators will note here the use of the cheapest medium available—radio—for the dissemination of off-Internet information to rural communities with obvious education and training needs. Although there is no denying the elegance and efficiency of the solution adopted, we insist on mentioning another factor that is all too often underestimated in the planning of local distance education networks. This factor is the appeal of the human voice—verbal communication—that can be enhanced and multiplied by electronic and digital means, as we can see in the Kothmale experiment. This explains the enduring power of radio, which is constantly reincarnating itself into new formats across the world: on FM airwaves, on the Internet, and on digital satellite transmitters (Visser, 2002) A distance education project in a southern country that would ignore the importance of oral communication in the local context and its power as a learning tool, would certainly limit its potential audience and impact. This is very different from the north, where I have often made the subjective observation that people sometimes prefer to communicate through the screen of the written page for fear of meeting their peers' critical comments.

In the ongoing graduate course at Utah State University, one of the students, a middle-aged schoolteacher, says that he finds it easier to communicate through WebCT than face-to-face.

> I also like the fact that online courses require more writing than speaking. I can usually express myself more competently in writing than in speaking— as many of you may know given my less-than-stellar presentations over the past two semesters. (Brossard, 2002, p. 48)

In other cultures, however, where school infrastructures are the norm, oral verbalization serves two functions: from the meta-cognitive viewpoint, it integrates the learning process within the familiar, socially accepted communication patterns, thereby facilitating learning; from the cognitive angle, it is well-known that the echo of something that was actually heard several times, helps students initiate that inner dialogue, the personal storytelling that activates the new knowledge and is an essential part of the learning process.

One could add to this the economic factors that industrialized-world specialists tend to overlook: most distance education programs worldwide rely to a large extent on print: books, photocopies, the hundreds of pages students download for Web-based courses, and so on. The function of books is, and will remain, essential, but the cost of paper as we use it in Europe and/or North America, and printer cartridges often is not within reach of most distance education students in developing countries. Public funding and international assistance will almost always help secure funds for the acquisition of equipment and some of the other costs, but the repetitive purchase of paper and toner may be too costly to individuals and organizations. Using oral communication could help keep spending within sustainable limits.

The last two cases we will analyze have been selected because they represent, in two very different contexts, examples of what future light and diversified trends in distance education could actually be.

The first project, called PIE (Pedagogia para Profesores em Exercício no Início da Escolarizaçào) or Pedagogical Training for Teachers at the Start of their Careers, has been operating in Brasilia's Federal District for a little over two years and is closely linked to the formal education system, namely a public university, The University of Brasilia (UNB) The aim of the project, as Prof. Magalhaes (2004) will explain, is to increase the numbers and improve the quality of primary school teachers. Until recently, they would study at the Faculty of Education of the UNB, with teaching practice in the schools. The introduction of an open and distance learning project here was not meant as a short cut, an industrial approach aimed at producing more teachers at lower cost, but rather as a qualitative change, a complete rethinking of the training to make it more observation-based, more inductive, and more rewarding for trainees and children alike.

Those students who wish to become primary school teachers have to be admitted by the Faculty of Education through the very selective Brazilian university admission test known as the *vestibular*. Once they have been admitted, they are appointed to one of the Federal District schools. Their first obligation is to study the written material and the online course that has been provided by the Faculty with their peers. In addition to the mutual support students can offer each other, they can turn to the human assistance provided by *monitores* who are, in fact, experienced teachers currently working towards a master's degree in education and who are appointed to perform this contact-tutoring job based on the Web course. When there are doubts, e-mails can be sent to the designers of the course, professors of the Faculty of Education. The list of resources available includes also the TV Escola programs (2002) that are being broadcast several hours a day across Brazil. In the afternoons, student teachers go to their assigned primary schools in the vicinity of the education office and they try to apply in their classes what they have learned online in the morning. To my knowledge, this is one of the most thorough attempts to renew the concept and practice of teacher training, which is often quite rightly considered overly theoretical and cut off from the realities of the classrooms in fast-changing multicultural societies. The choice of open and distance learning/training here has not been motivated by geography: student teachers could probably have managed to attend regular classes at the Faculty of Education and visit schools in Brasilia itself, but they could certainly not have had the opportunity to split their working days between theoretical classes in the mornings and the opportunity to test that theory the same day in remote schools that receive children whose families have come from all over Brazil, attracted by the opportunities of a booming region. The provision of online material and the physical assistance of the *monitores* mean that student teachers live from their first year onwards in the professional environment they have chosen, and that the delays and gaps between the discovery of theory and methodology, tentative applications, and children's feedback have been dramatically reduced. Backed up by study-groups, this leads, as I noted in meetings with the trainees, to permanent, constructive, focused dialogues conducive to new classroom experiments, readjustments of previously selected strategies, and so on. Those students who have been or are enrolled at the same time in other, traditional university courses have mentioned the creative stimulation brought about by the ODL format to the field of teacher training. The PIE project is constantly being assessed and modified, but so far the experiment has proved positive and it is currently being expanded (Coutinho, 2004).

The second case shows things that are quite different. The in-house distance training system developed over the years by a banking group known as *Banque Fédérale des Banques Populaires* is now discussed. This is the coordinating unit for the twenty-some banks operating along cooperative lines on a regional basis. Banques Populaires constitute France's fourth-largest banking group, with assets in the hundreds of billions of euros and, according to international standards, a Triple-A credit rating. The cooperative culture remains strong and there is a close working relationship with small and medium enterprises. Banque Fédérale offers its partners assistance in such fields as international relations and staff training, since many employees wish to advance in their careers and obtain the accredited professional diplomas of an inter-bank training institute (CFPB, 2004). E-learning facilities have been available for over six years. The original offer was built around *Cybernef* (Cybership), an inter-bank intranet whose function was to provide the banks with information about available training sessions and facilities. The Cybernef training intranet (Hauswirth, 2003) is now about eight years old and several functions have been added, notably online resources that can be used by trainers at the local/regional level.

Along with Cybernef, at a later stage, Banque Fédérale launched its own complementary educational platform of structured instruction, *Campus BP*, which was meant to be a full, online system of courses. The venture did not prove successful and less than 10% of the potential users did actually register, in spite of the established reputation and success of Cybernef. Although the Intranet culture is well established across the Banques, the proposed shift probably came too early. High-ranking executives were not fully convinced, and this certainly had an impact on the average staff members. Though institutional inertia is certainly a factor, another cause could also be a new shift in paradigm, closer to the evolution described by Manuel Castells (2001) in *The Internet Galaxy*. Alongside Campus BP, Banque Fédérale has created a database of pedagogical resources *Médiabanque*, which offers, free of charge, over 300 archives on HTML/PDF. These are widely used by trainers and trainees across the Banques Populaires network. They have also been made available to the French interbank training institute in open source format. Trainers like the design of those archives and their ease of access. They spontaneously use them when they design their own small, ad-hoc, open and distance training courses.

Educators may wonder whether they are not confronted here with one of the emerging trends in open and distance learning: a strong cooperative culture and a well established tradition of lifelong learning across the banks, together with a longstanding familiarity with Web tools. At this stage, formal courses from outside are no longer necessary, since it is easy to assemble quality online material "just in time" for specific synchronous or asynchronous training programs.

The Brazilian teacher training venture may point into the direction some university courses could take in a broad attempt to weave together from the start theoretical studies, professional practice, and inductive thinking. The Cybernef/Médiabanque story shows a mature system in which the formats and contents of ODL are easily put together for a mature, experienced learning public by mature, experienced trainers, on a cooperative basis.

In both cases, however, the emphasis is on ease of access as well as on the supply of constantly upgraded, quality learning material.

The need for quality assurance in ODL is now being emphasized in response to the development of the field. In a country like France, where adult education is embedded in the laws and where every employee has a legal right to choose his or her own course of studies, one example would be CCIP, the Paris Chamber of Commerce and Industry, which has large, official responsibilities in the training field. To help clarify the situation, it has set up its own independent watchdog unit called Le Préau (2004) in cooperation with several universities. The aim is to provide assistance to potential learners who are informed of the legal requirements for e-learning programs to be accredited, and of the skills they should develop in order to know "how to learn." Several other independent institutes are also offering their services in the quality assessment of e-learning (Barker, 2004). There is also a strong emphasis on the confidentiality criteria, since it has been noted that many employees drop out of online distance education programs because they are afraid of being spied upon by their bosses.

The over-inflated technology bubble collapsed at the turn of this new century, along with the Nasdaq. For the first time in generations, we notice that some telecommunications developments—cheap worldwide satellite-based cellphone access (Iridium), among others—have slowed down or halted for lack of suitable educational developments they could transmit, and yet, modest, sustainable, flexible distance training is alive and well. The emphasis is no longer on technology but on the complex human factors involved, as it should have been from the start. It is to be hoped that the years to come will surprise us with a wealth of inventive projects that may help bridge those digital divides—north/south and north/north—that still alienate so many by denying them access to the benefits of knowledge both theoretical and practical.

REFERENCES

Barker, K. C. (2004). *Introducing the open eQuality learning standards*. Retrieved July 4 2004 from http://www.eQcheck.com

Bates, A. W. (1984). *Broadcasting in education*. London: Constable.

Brossard, R. (2002). *Intégration du forum dans un dispositif d'enseignement à distance*. Unpublished Master's thesis, Université de Poitiers.

Castells, M. (2001). *La galaxia Internet*. Barcelona: Plaza & Janes.

Catalunya, U. O. d. (2003). *Universitat Oberta de Catalunya*. Retrieved July 4, 2004 from http://www.uoc.es

CFPB. (2004). *Centre de formation de la profession bancaire*. Retrieved November 2004 from http://www.cfpb.fr

CNED. (2004). *Cned*. Retrieved October 2004 from http://www.cned.fr

Coutinho, L. M. (2004). Personal communication. Brasilia.

Diallo, S., & Brissonnet, P. (1993). Ateliers pédagogiques personnalisés [Video]. Poitiers: Université de Poitiers.

EducNet. (2004). *Les campus numériques français*. Retrieved July 4 2004 from http://www.educnet.education.fr/superieur/campus.htm

Escola, T. (2002). *TV Escola O Canal da Educaçào*. Retrieved July 4, 2004 from http://www.mec.gov.br/seed/tvescola

Goutner, A. (2002). *Mémoire de Stage de D.E.S.S. Ingéniérie des Médias pour l'Education*. Unpublished Master's thesis, Université de Poitiers.

Greenfield, P. M. (1984). *Mind and media*. Cambridge, MA: Harvard University Press.

Group, C. (2002). *Coimbra Group universities*. Retrieved July 4, 2004 from http://coimbra-group.be

Hauswirth, E. (2003). Personal communication. Paris.

International, F. V. (2004). *Worldspace survey report on distance education for southern Sudan*. Washington, DC: Worldspace Corporation.

Magalhaes, M. R. A. d. M. (2004). Personal communication. Brasilia.

Nascimento, R. J. (2002). *Uso das tecnologias da informaçâo e comunicaçâo na formaçâo de professores de educaçâo física e desporto*. Unpublished doctoral dissertation, Universidade Tecnologica de Lisboa.

Poitiers, U. d. (2003). *Support juridique*. Retrieved July, 2004 from http://www.univ-poitiers.fr/formation/vap_support_jur.htm

Préau, L. (2004). *Le préau veille et accompangnement en e-formation*. Retrieved July 4, 2004 from http://www.preau.ccip.fr

Program, U. N. D. (2001). *Human development report-UNDP*. Oxford: United Nations.

Roberts, G. W. (2004). Personal communication. Anglesey.

Union, E. (2004). *Europa gateway to the European Union*. Retrieved June 2004 from http://www.europa.eu.int

Visser, J. (2002). Technology, learning, and corruption: Opportunities and hurdles in the search for the development of mind in an international development context. *Educational Technology Research and Development, 50*(2).

CHAPTER 5

DISTANCE EDUCATION INTERNATIONAL RESEARCH

What the World Needs Now

Deborah K. LaPointe

INTRODUCTION

In the majority of our world, education is the means by which the building of human capital occurs. Today, both developing and industrialized countries recognize global productivity and competitiveness are increasingly based on enhancing the caliber and resilience of the workforce, and that the only real long-term society is the perpetually learning society (Shive & Jegede, 2001). Today's call for a knowledge economy means every society must shift from "one-time" education to "lifelong" education (Ding, 2001). The once useful elite-sorting model of who receives an education is no longer practical and efficient in today's knowledge-based economy, and a nation will likely not advance if the thinking is left to just a few (Florida, 2002). While a village or neighborhood can support a primary school, or perhaps a basic clinic staffed by a local general teacher and doctor, more sophisticated education and health care requires greater, specialized skills (World Development Report, 2003). Today,

Trends and Issues in Distance Education: International Perspectives, 67–79
Copyright © 2005 by Information Age Publishing
All rights of reproduction in any form reserved.

everyone in the workforce must contribute more than just manual labor (Florida, 2002) by working on the generation, distribution, and application of knowledge.

Education symbolizes more than economic development. Education is the conduit that facilitates the knowledge construction of the individuals who will solve the world's global problems and promote human rights. With education, people create ways to promote higher standards of health and nutrition, reduce poverty, promote cleaner environments, increase the access to—and quality of—opportunity, increase individual freedom, facilitate a richer cultural life, and generally add meaning and value to human lives. This makes education a key component to protecting the full spectrum of human rights (Aderinoye & Ojokheta, 2004). The right to an education is nothing less than the individual's right to participate in the life of the modern world (UNESCO, 2004). Education represents the key to society's sustainable and humane development and the path to international peace and security, founded on mutual respect. Clearly, the importance of education is crucial for the society as a whole, as well as for individuals.

It is interesting to note that no country has been able to meet these critical educational goals and development needs solely through face-to-face classroom instruction (Jegede, 2001). Today, as in the past, distance education plays a critical role in a variety of settings in achieving these goals. Universities use distance education to increase the number of students who have access to higher education. Learners use distance education to meet their educational goals, some as a convenience, and others as the sole means to an education. Companies use distance education to upgrade employee skills and bring HIV/AIDS training and education to their workforce. Workers use distance education for professional development to enhance career opportunities. Governments use distance education to deliver literacy instruction, to create community learning centers that disseminate information and entrepreneurial skills to remote rural areas, to provide on-the-job training to teachers and other workers, and to enhance the quality of traditional primary, secondary, and home schooling. UNESCO, the educational arm of the United Nations, uses distance education to foster literacy and basic education, sustainable development, gender equality, and non-violence education for all.

For many countries, distance education offers the sole opportunity for many populations to gain access to education. Distance education has presented a way of providing education to the Fulbe nomadic women who herd cattle and market perishable milk, butter, and yogurt in Nigeria. Distance education is also used for teachers educating youngsters in isolated areas in western China. In the "industrialized west," distance learning is used by working adults with family and community responsibilities living in rural areas of the United States, Canada, and Australia, and other countries.

Such openness of distance education is perhaps its most remarkable character, widening opportunity for access to higher education for employed adults, school leavers, and the less-advantaged (Ding, 2001). To continue to provide such open access, distance education has always been responsive to new technologies and media, striving to provide access and autonomous learning to more learners, and sometimes offering new teaching and learning methods for schools and the workplace. These attributes of distance education explain why education at a distance of one type or another has been practiced in many countries regardless of cultural situation and stage of development since Sir Isaac Pitman began teaching shorthand by mail in England in the 1840s (Maeroff, 2003).

While education can be justified as a human right, and has increasingly over the years provided more access for more people, evidence suggests quality has taken a back seat to quantity. The relation between investment in education and economic growth is distressing, according to Hülsmann (2004), who quoting Pritchett (1999), writes that the correlation between growth of educational capital and conventional measures of total factor productivity is "large, strongly statistically significant, and negative." Hülsmann's work suggests that a conflict exists among the demand for education, the available budgets for funding that demand, and calls for cost-effective resource allocation. Educational investment has been of low quality and in amounts inadequate to affect productivity. While more people have access, what they learn is not always useful, and drop-out rates are high.

Unfortunately, examples supporting Hülsmann's warning prevail. The Improving Access and Quality of Teacher Education in Africa Program (2004) faces critical challenges, including an increase in the number of students seeking access to education, while simultaneously facing a lack of adequately qualified personnel. Further, appropriate mechanisms to keep well-trained and experienced staff, and lack of adequate funding and up-to-date educational resources continue to be present. The failure of on-time creation, production, and delivery of course materials at Bangladesh Open University (due to lack of funding and personnel added to an unstable supply of electricity and frequent TV and radio transmission disruptions) seriously hampers the sustainability of its programs (Faruque, 2004). In Lesotho, the number of people seeking formal certification exceeds the available personnel and facilities providing such certification, and "fly-by-night" continuing education centers exploit the situation by charging high tuition without delivering quality (Braimoh, 2001).

Developing countries are not alone in their struggle to educate while facing inadequately funded technology-enhanced programs. The United

States, for example, also suffers from a lack of access to computing technology. Specific classrooms have computing technologies and innovative teaching and learning methods while operating under a grant written by a committed faculty member, but precious few lasting "footprints" have been left by technology (Norris, Sullivan, Poirot, & Soloway, 2003). Often, when the faculty member who initiates the grant leaves, or the grant funding ends, a lack of recurrent funding to acquire or develop updated software and maintain or replace technology often prevails. Innovative courses developed under the grant are, therefore, frequently abandoned for more manageable—and more traditional—modes of instruction (Herrington, Reeves, Oliver, & Woo, 2004). This reversion to more traditional modes of learning—and with technology used in non-innovative ways— often results in a more passive learning environment with inferior learning experiences.

Additional problems substantiate Hülsmann's (2004) warning. Evaluations of online learning environments frequently reveal that, after the necessary expenditures are made on Web technologies and infrastructure, courses offered still tend to be electronic versions of the conventional print-based versions. Some of the responsibility for this situation lies, inter alia, with the predominant focus of obtaining the technology over using the technology. Technology often has been used as a "solution looking for a problem," as illustrated by universities' use of the Web's hyperlinked environment and streaming video to post and deliver hour-long lectures. Often distance education courses are designed in such a way that the technology is used to help the learner memorize and store information for subsequent recall, when technology could be better utilized by assisting learners to construct knowledge by searching for information to solve a problem; create a project; evaluate the credibility, relevance, and quality of content; or preparing and presenting a solution to discuss with others (Jonassen, 1994). Institutions without a tradition of using technology effectively in this manner attempt to earn a profit from pursuing an online learning business model, and design, sell, and export courses as face-to-face replications (Shive & Jegede, 2001). Regardless of the reason, distance education frequently has unreflectively borrowed traditional teacher-centered course designs, replicating face-to-face lectures and using technology as delivery media for content delivery and transmission. Why is that so?

BELIEFS ABOUT LEARNING AT A DISTANCE

Quality in design and learning outcomes has long been a characteristic of distance education from the early days of Peters' (1993) industrialized model of distance education with distribution of quality print materials.

Quality was foremost in Moore's theory of the structure and dialog of transactional distance (Moore & Kearsley, 1996). Structure is the measure of an educational program's responsiveness to learners' individual needs, and dialog is the interaction required between learner and instructor as the distance learner becomes an autonomous learner and accomplishes the goals of the educational program. Taking the learners where they are (i.e., at their learning level, in their own environment, and with the specific technology at their disposal) and interacting with them in ways that help them meet learning outcomes, is the basis of Moore's theory.

Effective learning environments, including those in the distance paradigm, acknowledge individual differences and contexts, motivate the student by mindfully engaging learners through complex, authentic tasks, avoid information overload through chunking, provide hands-on activities, and encourage student reflection. In a quality learning environment, students complete tasks with relevant cognitive tools in interaction with other students, instructors, tutors, or expert members of the learning community. Learners construct their own knowledge in the domain and assign meaning to that knowledge, relating new knowledge to prior knowledge. In so doing, they become autonomous learners, applying self-regulated learning strategies to regulate their own learning process. Learners search for information, publish results, and create products to solve problems with teachers providing structure, monitoring progress, and assessing accomplishments; all the while, the technology is a constant—yet transparent—component of the course design.

We have always had isolated examples of effective distance education environments. The Speak2Me online synchronous English as a Second Language program offered by Ladder Publishing, Ltd., in Taiwan is an example of a distance education program that effectively harnesses technology to achieve learning outcomes. The Speak2Me program offers Taiwanese students a multimedia approach to learn conversational English. Learners purchase a monthly magazine that contains articles in English about American and Taiwanese culture, as well as an audio CD-ROM to which they can listen as they read the written text. With a high-speed Internet connection and inexpensive headsets and microphone, learners can log onto a Web site and converse about the magazine articles in English with instructors from the United States as well as teaching assistants from Taiwan. A textbox on the Web site allows learners, instructors, and teaching assistants to type out more difficult questions and answers as needed. Learners report that having the opportunity to regularly speak English with English speakers improves their English-speaking ability and increases their confidence to communicate when they travel overseas to English-speaking countries and take English proficiency examinations (LaPointe, Greysen, & Barrett, 2004). The Speak2Me program is, therefore, a case in which technology facilitates the development of the desired learning outcomes of a distance-based educational program.

Another case in point will illustrate these concepts. The National Commission for Nomadic Education, established in December 1989 to implement the government's Nomadic Educational Policy Blueprint, delivers radio broadcasts to the Fulbe women in Nigeria (Usman, 2001). The women herd cattle, are entrepreneurs in the processing and marketing of perishable milk products, and travel as a group to the market to sell their dairy products. The women have radios that previously were purchased at a subsidized rate by their husbands through the men's cattle breeders' association. The Commission sends four repeated radio broadcasts a week on topics related to nomadic work roles, such as prevention of certain animal diseases. The courses are designed to be self-instructional and to stimulate discussion when the women gather to market their products. The women, along with their families, complete self-assessments at the end of each broadcast.

The Fulbe educational program may illustrate, after some modifications, an effective example of distance education based on the community of practice model. The pedagogical system in use is supportive of women's circumstances, the demands of their life roles, and the technology to which they have access, all in the context of their nomadic lifestyle. The program provides information needed by their community of practice, and that community decides how the information will solve problems faced by the community. Although Usman (2001) reports that the timing of the broadcasts should be modified to more carefully meet the women's availability (and the women themselves have requested more information on animal and child care and improved ways of milking, topics not yet covered in the broadcasts), evaluation of the program could be evidenced in better health of cattle, increased productivity of the women's cheese, milk, and butter businesses, and improvement in the women's and their families' health. This project, therefore, represents a exemplar of how distance learning can be implemented in a truly enriching and meaningful manner.

CASES CONFLICTING WITH BELIEFS

The case of the Fulbe women in Nigeria, however, is perhaps more the exception than the rule. Why are such cases isolated examples? Frequently, the distance education literature subdivides course design into "high touch" or "high tech." The interactive model, or "high touch," is considered better quality, yet too expensive in terms of monitoring and facilitating learner interaction with faculty. Faculty members have to be recruited, and class size has to be kept small. The literature reports that the "high touch" model is unsustainable, and even impossible in developing countries needing to educate millions of individuals. Anadolu University, a dual-mode university in Turkey, enrolled 800,000 distance learners in 2004 (C. H. Aydin, Fulbright lecture, February 2004), and China Central broadcasts radio and TV lectures to students at 2,600 branch campuses, 29,000 study centers, and workplaces (Bollag, 2001). The "high touch" model of faculty interacting with students will not scale to large classes, and learners have to forego a satisfying, quality learning environment. Class size, however—at least in the online learning environment—is not a major predictor of learner satisfaction (Ouellette, Gayol, & Ali, 2004) or learning outcomes.

In fact, course designs that have incorporated faculty/tutor interaction have failed. Mhehe (2001) reports on a pedagogical model designed by the Open University of Tanzania that failed to meet the content and context needs of women learners. The program was based on print materials, two written assignments, an orientation, two face-to-face tutoring sessions, two timed tests, and an annual and supplementary examination given at 25 regional centers. While common in many open universities, this model failed for women learners in Tanzania. The women did not receive study materials before the courses started; did not have the money required to pay for accommodations, food, and transportation to the regional centers for attendance in the required interactive activities; and had to find time to complete all requirements after working a full-time job, looking after the children, running the household, and caring for small farming projects. Their husbands did not support their learning efforts, and without their husbands' permission, women could neither study nor use family money for educational expenses, travel, or interaction with tutors. Their employers required special favors in order to grant time away from work. The attempts to incorporate teacher or tutor interaction (often with males) outside of the context (both in terms of relevancy and location) conflicted with the women's lives. The course design and required interaction placed women at risk and certainly could have endangered women's lives and positions in the Tanzania situation. In this case, student-teacher interaction was not successful.

Distance education's ability to create unrestricted access comes at the expense of encouraging local initiatives, which value local culture and promote national beliefs, skills, and knowledge (Braimoh, 2001). The technology and course design of the designing cultures have embodied within them elements of the designing culture (Piecowye, 2003), as illustrated by the Tanzania study. The literature suggests that, in such situations, detriment to the local culture will result. Piecowye (2003), however, suggests that, when international students enroll in courses designed or taught by people from different cultures, the students consciously choose what elements, if any, of the offering cultures they want to appropriate. In fact, Piecowye (2003) found that courses designed with computer-mediated communication technology under a socio-constructivist paradigm reinforced United Arab Emirate culture by simulating the majlis, a traditional meeting environment where people meet to talk and seek guidance.

More conflicting information stems from retention studies. Although the numerous definitions and measurements of retention are problematic, research frequently shows that studying at a distance often conflicts with the learning process of constructing meaning through dialogue and reflection with others. Research reports that distance education's isolating experience is frequently the cause of high drop-out rates, ranging from 21 percent (Simpson, 2002) upward. Richardson (2000), however, found that drop-out rates are frequently due to the characteristics of distance learners. These individuals are typically more mature learners with family, work, and community responsibilities. Learners who fail to complete a course are "stop-outs" rather than "drop-outs," frequently due to other reasons than lack of interaction.

The cost of drop-outs and stop-outs is a hidden cost. These hidden costs once exposed represent an opportunity to re-examine current mental models about education. Reducing the costs associated with drop-outs and stop-outs then presents a possible source for funding increased quality in courses, if quality requires increased funding. Twigg (2003) reports that, of 37,000 students enrolled in an introductory math class at one community college, only 800 successfully complete their math requirement. Alleviating the cost of course repetitions and courses that fail to meet expectations by rethinking course design could provide the source of adequate funding for high quality, high-touch investment in education.

That distance education processes are lagging in comparison to demand, as well as failing to meet specified learning goals, presents a huge problem on a global scale to the educational community. This failure of learning means that human preparedness remains globally underdeveloped, and the world's people are, therefore, limited in their capacity to deal with the issues they face (Maeroff, 2003). When people cannot gain access to or drop out of distance education, the loss to the world is significant. The lack of graduates curtails the supply of teachers, doctors, engineers, and other professionals, and global problems such as gender equality, the HIV/AIDS pandemic, and poverty go unaddressed. The presence of such failings when distance education has such important, global issues to address is an important issue to solve.

AN INTERNATIONAL RESEARCH AGENDA

Finding a way to meet global learning needs and enhance the learning experience by fitting the learners' context and available technology remains a challenge that distance education must meet (Yoon, 2003). Now that distance education is viewed as a reputable educational alternative for global development and human rights, and a respected partner to traditional face-to-face education, it is time to take a critical look at distance education (Visser, 2003) and determine which lessons we should learn from and share with others.

Research is distance education's next important development (Shive & Jegede, 2001) and will contribute to global economic development.

Good research is grounded in theory. Theory makes it possible to generate hypotheses about good practice, to frame experiments that will test these hypotheses and, as a result, develop more soundly based guides to practice (Perraton, 2000). However, despite the fact distance education has been on the educational scene since the 1800s, the field has not made research a central focus of its practice. The field of distance education has been too busy meeting the teaching and learning needs of hundreds of thousands of off-campus students to make room for research activities, and the result has been detrimental. Distance education has been left as a practice-driven rather than a research-driven effort, drawing upon theories and practices of many disciplines with little if any modification. Like course design, research into distance education can be criticized for being less than systematic (Zirkle, 2003), unreflectively borrowing concepts and methods from research on campus-based students (Richardson, 2000). Distance education is a field of many speculations, but few systematic observations and analysis (Astleitner, 2003). There is little specific distance education theory and no commonly-held, theory-based agenda regarding its use and implementation.

When theory is absent, good research begins with a problem (Perraton, 2000). Perhaps the fundamental problem facing distance education is the question of how we can expand coverage, reduce inequalities of access and outcomes, and improve educational quality and relevance in financially sustainable ways (Daniel & Mackintosh, 2003). This problem is likely a good start for generating a distance education research agenda that will eventually result in some form of theory base that can be used to improve practice.

In the United States, researchers working under a Pew Grant (Twigg, 2003) are asking questions such as, "When do students need to be in class and when do they need to be in a tutorial?" "When do students need to read a lecture, and when do they need to hear a lecture?" "When do students learn by being actively engaged in solving relevant problems?"

"What questions must be answered by an instructor?" "When should students take advantage of computer-based quizzes or self-assessment activities?" "When do students need examples from real-life settings?" "What instructional activities can be handled by technology in order to free teachers for interaction with students?"

Do we need to continue the distinction between teaching and learning as they have been understood as specific, separate activities (Raschke, 2003)? We believe learning is the construction of meaning when the learner is deeply engaged in an interesting, relevant, authentic learning activity. Can teaching and learning take place simultaneously, as in the Fulbe radio broadcasts? Most learners have easy access to people, including other students, employers, and experts, major libraries and museums, and other information sources throughout the nation and the world (Jalobeanu, 2003). Can we use those contexts and settings to provide a quality learning environment? Many people have been touched and motivated by a "distance teacher," a mentor, the author of a book that spoke to them, or a person encountered only once but who left an impression in that single interaction (John-Steiner, 1997). Could we follow this pattern of interaction? Who will want to and who will be successful learning in these settings? Will a community of practice model work in all settings? What kinds of learning are needed? What instructional approaches will best meet those needs? What are the best technologies for supporting simultaneous teaching and learning? Should we focus on low-cost solutions instead of "high touch," "high tech" solutions? Who knows how to teach and assess learning this way (Shive & Jegede, 2001)?

Distance education needs a systemic research theory agenda that captures the intellectual spirit, identifies the issues currently receiving major attention of scholars and the wider social context, heeded by expert practitioners, influencing the selection of articles for publications in journals and presentations at conferences, shapes university curricula (Roblyer & Knezek, 2003), and addresses the issues of human rights and economic development. Concentrating on getting the "soft" technologies of people, institutions, structures, and pedagogical processes right will be important, as the "hard" technology will change before the "soft" technologies are perfected (Daniel & Mackintosh, 2003). Research should focus on the relationship between the use of a technology and different levels or types of learning (Bates, 2000).

Necessity is the mother of invention. The critical need has now surfaced for distance education to develop an international research agenda that features systematic, longitudinal, in-depth component analyses; theoretical comparisons of strategies for fostering transformative learning of individuals and societies; and use of alternative methodological designs. Distance education research needs microscopic orientations on particular components that are known to be essential to distance education—possibly course design, pedagogy, interaction, class size, and active learning. Large-scale, summative and formative evaluations are also needed, so that learning gains are empirically documented (Bork & Gunnarsdottir, 2001). What is needed is a set of reliable, consistent research results that can be used as the basis for a theory of distance education.

CONCLUSION

Distance education should not be charged with solving all educational problems. Distance education has become a recognized, valued partner in meeting global learning needs, but is only a part of the larger educational system that can creatively offer lifelong learning. Distance learning can promote economic development that assists people in solving critical global problems, as well as meeting the challenge of higher standards of health and nutrition, poverty reduction, cleaner and sustainable environments, mutual respect, and international peace and security. The development and implementation of a rigorous, systematic distance education international research agenda is critical, for without such, educational efforts may be met with continuing failure. When education is unsuccessful in developing teachers, doctors, engineers, researchers, and members of the workforce, these people will no longer by able to meaningfully contribute to the human condition, and our world will continue to suffer.

REFERENCES

Aderinoye, R., & Ojokheta, K. (2004). Open-distance education as a mechanism for sustainable development: Reflections on the Nigerian experience. *The International Review of Research in Open and Distance Learning, 5*(1). Available at http://www.irrodl.org/content/v5.1/aderinoye_ojokheta.html

African Virtual University (2004). The AVU teacher training program. Retrieved June 10, 2004, http://www.avu.org/ap_new_programs.asp.

Astleitner, A. (2003). Web-based instruction and learning: What do we know from experimental research? In N. Nistor, S. English, S. Wheeler, & M. Jalobeanu (Eds.), *Toward the virtual university: International online perspectives* (pp. 37-63). Greenwich, CT: Information Age.

Bates, A. W. (2000). *Managing Technological Change*. San Francisco: Jossey-Bass.

Bollag, B. (2001, June 15). Developing countries turn to distance education. *The Chronicle of Higher Education*. Retrieved from http://chronicle.com/free/v47/i40/40a02901.htm

Bork, A., Gunnarsdottir, S. (2001). *Tutorial distance learning: Rebuilding our educational system*. New York: Kluwer Academic.

Braimoh, D. (2001). *The effectiveness of distance education delivery methods in continuing education programs in Lesotho.* Retrieved June 2, 2004 from http://www.deakin.edu.au/education/RIPVET/conferences/2000/RIDE/Ch_9_Braimoh.pdf

Daniel, J., & Mackintosh, W. (2003). Leading ODL Futures in the Eternal Triangle: The Mega-University Response to the Greatest Moral Challenge of Our Age. (pp. 811-827). In M. Moore and W. Anderson (Eds.) *Handbook of Distance Education.* Mahwah, NJ: Erlbaum.

Ding, X. (2001). Information technology revolution and development of distance education in china. *Global E-Journal of Open, Flexible & Distance Education, 1* (1). Retrieved from http://www.ignou.ac.in/e-journal/ejournal.htm

Faruque, A. M. (2004). *Agricultural education in distant mode in Bangladesh Open University: A new approach to transfer of technology.* Retrieved June 10, 2004 from http://www.col.org/pcf2/papers%5Cfaruque.pdf

Florida, R. (2003). *The rise of the creative class.* New York, NY: Basic Books.

Herrington, J., Reeves, R. C., Oliver, R., & Woo, Y. (2004). Designing authentic activities in web-based courses. *Journal of Computing in Higher Education, 16*(1).

Hülsmann, T. (2004). Guest editorial: Low cost distance education strategies: the use of appropriate information and communication technologies. *International Review of Research in Open and Distance Learning, 5*(1). Retrieved from http://www.irrodl.org/content/v5.1/editorial.html

Jalobeanu, M. (2003). The Internet in education. In N. Nistor, S. English, S. Wheeler, & M. Jalobeanu (Eds.) *Toward the virtual university: International online perspectives* (pp. 23-36). Greenwich, CT: Information Age.

Jegede, O. (2001). Hong Kong. In O. Jegede and G. Shive (Eds.) *Open and distance education in the Asia Pacific region* (pp. 44-79). Hong Kong: Open University of Hong Kong Press.

John-Steiner, V. (1997). *Notebooks of the mind: Explorations of thinking.* Albuquerque, NM: University of New Mexico Press.

Jonassen, D. (1994). Technology as cognitive tools: Learners as designers. *ITForum Paper 1.* Retrieved June 1, 2004 from http://it.coe.uga.edu/itforum/paper1/paper1.html

LaPointe, D. K., Greysen, K. R. B., & Barrett, K. A. (2004, February). *Bridging the cultural divide—Social construction of meaning and community: The "Speak2Me" English as a second language synchronous distance education program.* Paper presented at the meeting of the International Council on Distance Education, Hong Kong.

Maeroff, G. (2003). *A classroom of one.* New York: Palgrave Macmillan.

Mhehe, E. (2003). Confronting barriers to distance study in Tanzania. In E. J. Burge and M. Haughey (Eds.) *Using learning technologies: International perspectives on practice* (pp. 102-114). New York: RoutledgeFalmer.

Moore, M. G., & Kearsley, G. (1996). *Distance education: A systems view.* San Francisco: Wadsworth.

Norris, C., Sullivan, T., Poirot, J., & Soloway, E. (2003). No access, no use, no impact: Snapshot surveys of educational technology in k-12. *Journal of Research on Technology in Education, 36*(1), 15-27.

Ouellette, R., Gayol, Y., & Ali, A. (2004, February). *Class size and satisfaction in on-line learning environments*. Paper presented at the meeting of the International Council on Distance Education, Hong Kong.

Perraton, H. (2000). Rethinking the research agenda. *International Review of Research in Open and Distance Learning, 1*(1). Retrieved from http://www.irrodl.org/

Peters, O. (1993). Distance education in a postindustrial society. (pp. 39-58). In D. Keegan (Ed.), *Theoretical Principles of Distance Education*. New York: Routledge.

Piecowye, J. (2003). Habitus in transition? CMC use and impacts among young women in the United Arab Emirates. *Journal of Computer Mediated Communication, 8*(2). Retrieved from http://www.ascusc.org/jcmc/vol8/issue2/

Pritchett, L. (1999, December). *Where has all the education gone?* World Bank. Retrieved November 5, 2003, from http://www.worldbank.org/research/growth/pdfiles/Where_r4.pdf

Raschke, C. A. (2003). *The digital revolution and the coming of the postmodern university*. New York: RoutledgeFalmer.

Richardson, J. T. E. (2000). Researching student learning: Approaches to studying in campus-based and distance education (pp. 123-136). Philadelphia, PA: Open University Press.

Roblyer, M. D., & Knezek, G. A. (2003). New millennium research for educational technology: A call for a national research agenda. *Journal of Research on Technology in Education, 36*(1), 60-71.

Shive, G. & Jegede, O. (2001). Introduction: Trends and issues in open and distance education in Asia and the Pacific. In O. Jegede and G. Shive (Eds.) *Open and Distance Education in the Asia Pacific Region* (pp. 1-24). Hong Kong: Open University of Hong Kong Press.

Simpson, O. (2002). *Supporting students in online, open and distance learning*. Sterling, VA: Stylus.

Twigg, C. A. (2003). Quality, cost, and access: The case for redesign. In M. S. Pittinsky (Ed.), *The wired tower* (pp. 111-143). San Francisco: Pearson Education.

UNESCO (2004). *World Forum On Human Rights 2004 - Follow-Up*. Retrieved June 2, 2004 from http://portal.unesco.org/shs/en/ev.php-url_id=4658&url_do=do_topic&url_section=201.html

Usman, L. (2003). "No one will listen to us": Rural Fulbe women learning by radio in Nigeria. In E. J. Burge and M. Haughey (Eds.), *Using learning technologies: International perspectives on practice*, (pp. 92-101). New York: RoutledgeFalmer.

Visser, J. (2003). Distance education in the perspective of global issues and concerns. (pp. 793-810). In M. G. Moore and W. G. Anderson (Eds.) *Handbook of distance education*. Mahwah, NJ: Erlbaum.

World Development Report (2003). Retrieved June 1, 2004 from http://www.dynamicsustainabledevelopment.org/

Yoon, S. W. (2003). In search of meaningful online learning experiences. (pp. 19-30). In S. R. Aragon (Ed.) *Facilitating learning in online environments: New directions for adult and continuing education, No. 100*. San Francisco: Jossey-Bass.

Zirkle, C. (2003). Distance education and career and technical education: A review of the research literature. *Journal of Vocational Education Research, 28*(2), 161-181.

PART II

CHAPTER 6

DEFINING "TRENDS" AND "ISSUES" IN DISTANCE EDUCATION

An Interview with Don Ely

Lya Visser and Kristen Gagnon

INTRODUCTION[1]

In attempting to truly "understand" a subject, one must develop a solid knowledge of the facts and information inherent to that subject. But acquisition of a subject's factual information base is insufficient to develop a comprehensive understanding of that subject. Although facts and information form the core of almost any discipline, the patterns at work within the discipline, as well as the unresolved disputes surrounding that discipline, make up a critical portion of what it means to "understand" that field.

Distance education is a good case in point. Being a relatively young discipline (existing in its current form for only slightly over 100 years), the field consists of many varied and unresolved viewpoints and attitudes. If one were to memorize the mere factual aspects of distance education—

Trends and Issues in Distance Education: International Perspectives, 83–89
Copyright © 2005 by Information Age Publishing
All rights of reproduction in any form reserved.

say, for example, the number of students taking distance courses, the name of institutions offering such courses, and the specific number of teachers teaching these courses—one would have an undeveloped, incomplete mental image of the world of distance education. Critical to gaining a comprehensive knowledge of distance education is an understanding of the movements and developments within the field, as well as the unresolved questions that are currently debated within the distance education community.

We often use the phrase "trends and issues" to capture the more abstract features of a discipline. But what specifically do the terms "trends" and "issues" mean? In this chapter, we take a careful look at these terms, and develop a common understanding of how these terms should be used in the distance context.

TRENDS

The term *trend* is often misused within the educational community. When preparing for our interview with Don Ely, the authors consulted the literature to locate specific information concerning "trends" in education, and found that many articles, chapters of books, and conference papers discuss what they call "trends" without actually defining the term. In reality, many so-called "trends" cannot in actuality be considered *trends*, the term being misappropriated and misused to name other types of occurrences.

Ely defines a trend as "A line of general direction of movement and a prevailing tendency or inclination. The general movement over a course of time of a statistically detectable change."

The key factor in this definition is that a trend is a general direction and prevailing tendency. We cannot simply decide that a certain development is a trend. Trends are developed over time. If we see, for example, that in the last four days the number of applicants for a particular course has increased, we cannot define this fact as a "trend." If, however, we have data that show that in the last four days of every month there are more student applications than in any other period during the month, and that this has repeatedly been the case over a period of time, we may then correctly identify this phenomenon as a "trend," even though we may still be unable to fully explain why the phenomenon is occurring.

In addition, we can look at *current* trends, which are just like a photo of what has been happening up until today, but we can also be looking forward to *emerging* trends. Emerging trends are those that are likely to be realized in the near future. In either case, however, the definition for "trend" remains the same, regardless of whether that trend has started earlier in time, or is just now beginning to emerge.

Trends are rarely specific reports on "the truth." Trends are indicators of direction. Trends help us to see where we are heading, and may point the way in making decisions. Trends usually develop over a period of years. A trend is related to movement, to a shift in direction that takes place and which is clearly supported by recorded information. Trends do not predict the future; rather, they show a current report of what is happening during a specific period of time.

There are many ways in which trends can be identified, including content analysis, expert opinion, panels of specialists, surveys, or informal observation (Creswell, 2002). In a content analysis, a procedure that analyses general themes in, say, the annual literature of distance education journals, conference papers and other publications, a literature review is undertaken to uncover the data that may support the presence of a trend. The literature review in a content analysis should not be the work of one person, but rather should be conducted across many individuals for purposes of increasing reliability. Translation from quantitative summaries to qualitative trend statements is mostly subjective (Ely, 1996), and so therefore any ambiguities arising from such investigations should be thoroughly reviewed and answered before determining a particular phenomenon a "trend."

Researchers often make use of trends studies, which are longitudinal surveys of an identified population conducted over time. A good example that has yielded important findings is the administration of achievement tests. Focusing on national samples of students at different grade levels in order to decide whether the effectiveness of the nation's educational system is improving (Gall, Borg, & Gall, 1996), a downward or upward trend can become clear when many years of achievement data are collated and compared. Trends identified as a result of such a process can become valuable pieces of information to other researchers who are examining or attempting to explain associated phenomena within the educational domain.

Trends are generally associated with only one or two topics or items, not on whole sets of issues, and therefore stand out from other random occurrences. For example, in discussing distance education, Ely provides the example of educational technology. It is not very useful to say that a trend is that "the use of educational technology in distance education will increase." Educational technology is not a simple concept; it consists of many different areas, involves a multitude of coordinate concepts, and spans a range of technology types. Thus, the identified trend is likely to occur in a few of the many subsections contained within educational technology, for example, an increase in the use of computers in inner-city schools, or the decrease in the use of instructional radio in rural areas. Some trends may be contradictory or complementary, depending on the situation. For example, the trend of increased use of radio for distance education programs in a country may also be complimented by the increased student enrollment for such programs, or perhaps the contradictory case of a decrease in student enrollment for these courses. In the specific case of educational technology, we find that Seels and Richey (1994) defined five "domains" of educational technology: development, utilization, design, evaluation and management. This framework is useful in helping us categorize trends in educational technology within these five specific areas.

Determining when a trend starts is also an important issue. Ely notes the specific case of the trend of increased use of computers in a particular context. Do we assign the official start of this trend as the first day the computers began to be used, the first instance the computers were used in research, or the point at which general acceptance of computer use occurred? Part of trend's description should include this important marker of when we have assigned a starting point for the trend. A clear and defensible starting point for a trend is valuable in defining the trend, describing the trend's impact, and comparing that trend with other associated pieces of information.

According to Ely, the identification of a trend almost always requires hard data. Trends are thus data-driven, not ad hoc or informal guesses about a situation. Take, for example, the trend of an increase in the salaries of teachers. What data support this claim? Where, specifically, did the trend begin? What do the most recent data say concerning this trend; i.e., does it appear to be continuing? A trend is not identified by guessing or hypothesizing, but rather is determined through objective information that can be examined by anyone.

Ely warns that trends should come from international, and not just national, sources. National trends are too limited, and may only be representative for a national context, not an international one. In this book, we take an international approach toward the identification of trends. It is sometimes fascinating to learn from and about the different trends in different countries. We may see in distance education that while there may be a trend in the United States to use learning networks, a developing country may have a trend to use radio. We may identify a trend in Europe to increase student support groups, while we see a trend in South Africa to use SMS to support the learner. Knowing and understanding the trends in an international context may contribute to international understanding, to improve educational exchanges, and to learning from each other.

An important problem when we look at trends is that the available data may not be accurate. For example, in one country in southern Africa, the number of people dying from tuberculosis has increased dramatically; in fact, the number has increased ten-fold during the last five years, while the number of people dying from AIDS in this same region appears to be rather constant. However, this description is not an accurate portrayal of the situation in this country. A closer examination of the situation will find that the government of this country does not want to recognize the pandemic of AIDS, and thus states as cause of death with people dying of AIDS some type of related disease, such as tuberculosis. This inaccurate reporting on the part of the government makes it appear, therefore, that more and more people are dying of tuberculosis when, in fact, more and more people are dying of AIDS. Thus can be seen the situation in which an apparent trend (an increase in tuberculosis) is actually no trend at all; in point of fact, the true trend is an increase in death by AIDS. Identification of trends, therefore, can be no better than the accuracy of the data by which the trend was identified.

ISSUES

We are all likely aware of the many pressing "issues" that education currently faces, including access, quality of programs and courses, equity, rising costs and decreasing funds. Identifying these issues and working on solutions to each of them is important in both national as well as in international contexts.

Ely defines an issue as "a fact or matter that is in dispute between two or more parties. It's a debatable question that experts in the field try to resolve in some way."

An issue is a vital, burning question that people are trying to resolve in some way. In order to find a solution to an issue, individuals typically look for pertinent data surrounding the issue, and often attempt to draw on past experiences for additional insight, clarity, or guidance in developing such a solution.

There are many issues surrounding distance education, and we mention only two of them here as examples. The issue of course management, for example, is a clear example of an issue faced within the distance education community. There are often strong feelings on how courses should be organized, how student monitoring should be set up, or how evaluation should be administered. These differences of opinion and viewpoint constitute an issue for the distance education community. Another example of an issue is in the use of World Wide Web resources: is it proper to use such resources without express permission from the author? Such a question might intuitively be answered "no" with little thought, until one considers the fact the Web was designed from its inception as a free and open repository of information. The intent of the Web was to make universally accessible anything made available on that system. So, the question remains, is permission required for reuse of Web-based materials? That's an issue, a debated, vital question of great importance to anyone in the distance education community.

We can identify a number of key areas in the distance education community in which issues are prevalent but, although we should be familiar with these issues within our own context, it is also important to be aware of issues that reside outside our own milieu, including our national context. Awareness of issues gives us time and opportunity to think about them in a rationale manner without having to be unexpectedly faced with them in an inopportune moment and be forced to come up with quick, often unexamined and unsupportable answers. Awareness of issues is an essential part of our education, regardless of the field in which we operate.

In this book, a number of issues are discussed in relationship to distance education. These issues can be categorized into four areas: academic, financial, management and technology, and student support. Table 6.1 lists some of the specific issues mentioned in this text, grouped within these four categories.

In closing, it should be noted that identification of issues is a powerful tool for assisting individuals in understanding several points of view on one topic, even when those issues reside outside of our direct area of concern. Ely has stated, "I think it is important to be aware of the trends and

Table 6.1.   Key Issues in the Area of Distance Education

Issue Category	Specific Issues
Academic	Admission Transfer of credits Accreditation Evaluation
Financial	Course fees Technology fees Free use of facilities Remuneration for instructors and staff
Management and Technology	Acquiring materials Tasks and compensation Accountability Delivery of courses/programs Ethics and integrity
Student Support	Student-centered learning Library services Tutorial support Call-back services

issues outside of our milieu. There are signposts of things to come, to prepare for, and to assess value, current ideas and directions that are why it is
important so that we can be on top of things that happen so that they
don't all of a sudden come and surprise us." A knowledge of pertinent
issues both within and outside of our own context can be used as a key to
understanding the larger picture, explore potential solutions, and come
to agreement over pressing concerns. The field of distance education is
replete with issues needing sound solutions. Identification of and discussion about these issues are the first steps in creating those solutions.

NOTES

1. Although this chapter is largely based on two interviews with Don Ely, the
    authors have also incorporated their own ideas, opinions, and experiences.

REFERENCES

Creswell, J. W. (2002). *Educational research*. Upper Saddle River, NJ: Merrill Pren-
    tice Hall.
Ely D. P. (1996). *Trends in educational technology 1995*. Syracuse, NY: ERIC Clear-
    inghouse on Information and Technology
Gall, M. D., Borg, W. R., & Gall, J. P. (1996). *Educational research: An introduction*.
    New York: Longman
Seels, B. B., & Richey, R. C. (1994). *Instructional technology: The definition and
    domains of the field*. Washington, DC: Association for Educational Communica-
    tions and Technology.

CHAPTER 7

A CAREER IN INTERNATIONAL DISTANCE EDUCATION

An Interview with Barbara Spronk

Michael Simonson and Margaret Crawford

A distance learning leader is a visionary capable of action, an individual who guides an organization's distance learning future. This guidance often includes developing and setting the tone of the organization's vision, mission, goals, and objectives. The distance learning leader guides the organization and its people, and develops faith in those individuals who will follow the leader's vision. The end result is an organization with individuals who possess a clear understanding and acceptance of the leader's worthwhile and shared vision and goals.

Barbara Spronk is such a visionary leader. The following interview allows access to some of the thinking and ideas that are of great benefit to anyone working in this distance environment. The text has been edited for readability in a written format.

QUESTION: How did you get your start in distance education?
I first became involved in distance learning in 1974, when distance education was a very new thing. At the time, the Open University in the

Trends and Issues in Distance Education: International Perspectives, 91–96
Copyright © 2005 by Information Age Publishing
All rights of reproduction in any form reserved.

U.K. had been running for just a few years, and I was working at Athabasca University in Canada, where distance learning was, to some extent, a new thing. I was interested in distance education and got involved because I was really becoming intrigued by the idea of opening up educational opportunities to as many people as possible. I eventually earned my Ph.D. in anthropology, and continued to teach anthropology at a distance, but also managed to widen my scope of interest to include distance education for native people in Canada. Later, I widened my scope even further to include international education.

QUESTION: *What is your involvement in distance learning today?*

As of April, 2002, I left my position at the International Extension College in the U.K. Since then, I've been dong tutoring for Athabasca University's Master's Program in Distance Education. I have also been doing some course revision work for Athabasca University. I've been writing and reviewing courses for the online version of the University of London's Master's in Distance Education, which is delivered via the Internet to an international audience. I've also been doing a bit of advising for people who are involved in proposals for distance education-related international development, and I also do some international consulting.

QUESTION: *What have been the most significant trends in distance education? What are the characteristics of these trends, particularly over the last decades?*

First, there has been an incredible expansion of distance education. In international terms, this is in terms of its geographic spread and geographic reach. It also includes the development of major universities throughout the world that deliver single-mode distance education, as well as the incredible expansion of institutions that are now involved in doing a significantly greater amount of distance education, although perhaps not in terms of completely dual-mode provision. This is even the case when these providers remain pretty firmly campus-based. That's one enormous change. Secondly, there is the advent of the Internet and the World Wide Web. The latter two have really changed distance education in significant ways in the affluent nations. Most of the countries I have worked in are so poverty-stricken that the use of the Internet for making education available is simply not a possibility, and won't be for a significant time to come. I can't even predict a point when countries like Bangladesh, Sudan, or Mozambique will have an infrastructure that makes access to the Internet possible in rural areas. But in the affluent countries—in North America, and Europe and parts of Latin America and Asia—the Internet has changed both how we present education and learning and the way we think about education.

QUESTION: You indicate that the Internet has changed the way we "think" about education. What do you mean by this?

It refers to the way we conceptualize the whole nature of teaching and learning. With the advent of the Internet, there has been a convergence of a learner-centric orientation in distance education. In distance education, we have long prided ourselves on recognizing the significance of the learner. Increasingly, I see a shift from teaching to learning which I saw while I worked in the U.K. This shift was a very significant development there, and it will be an increasingly significant development in other countries as well.

The shift from teaching to learning encourages university teachers to think about learning, and how best to use the remarkable new technological developments we have experienced. There is a considerable shift taking place in terms of how learning opportunities and education are provided, at both the course level and the programmatic level. These changes are driven by the learners' needs for flexibility in terms of scheduling and pacing, and the types of learning modalities that are available to the students. It has opened up enormous possibilities for making both teaching and learning more flexible.

I believe that this convergence has taken distance educators unawares. Up to the late 1980s, the focus in distance education was very much on a single-mode provider. The Open University in the UK, the "five-star hotel" of distance education providers, had all the resources they could throw at facilitating learning by using television or radio in an effective way. It is remarkable that a lot of the innovations in terms of electronic teaching and learning have come from campus-based institutions that are discovering electronic teaching and learning as an important way for providing expanding opportunities for the student body.

QUESTION: What other trends have you witnessed over the last several decades?

My focus over the past six years has been the Internet. And frankly, the trends I see there is that increasing poverty is widening the digital divide. In developing countries, the elite are becoming very proficient and effective users of the Internet. Degrees like the Master's Degree in Distance Education are reaching more affluent people through the use of the Internet. The elite are thus very much benefiting from this explosion in the availability of electronic resources. The fact that that universities and agencies now offer online courses has made virtually no impact on the masses, because it is not within their financial reach. I find that trend alarming. So much of our energy in our affluent world is focused on electronics that we forget that we are leaving 95% of the world behind.

There are agencies like the Commonwealth of Learning that are working very hard to ensure that distance educators remain aware that an affordable worldwide infrastructure to support mass education by electronics does not yet exist. There are still very effective programs that are operating on a mass basis, using print and sometimes face-to-face tutorials. Since these programs are still working, we have to focus on these kinds of approaches to distance education in addition to the more advanced Internet-based distance education program. It also worries me that we depend so much on the Internet, because this dependence affects donor agencies very much. For example, the World Bank will increase funding for education delivered electronically, but this will not solve the larger problem that needs to be solved: universal availability of education.

QUESTION: What is your hypothesis concerning how distance education may progress in the next five to ten years and what issues do you think distance education will face in both national and international contexts?

In the affluent world—North America, Europe and Australia—the focus will be on flexible learning. Universities will focus more on learning and making learning available in a variety of modes. This means a move beyond face-to-face instruction and toward learning modes that will involve the use of the Internet and other technology.

There are other potential developments that I cannot project because I am not a technician or planner; I am a user of technology and don't consider myself on the cutting edge of technological advances. There are technologies that are being developed right now that I know little about. These developments will continue to amaze us. It is a welcome development, because there is a wide diversity of learners and learner needs. When used appropriately, technology can go a long way to help meet those needs. I think this realization is filtering into potentially new areas for distance education opportunities, such as secondary and even primary education. In fact, this is an area to which we should dedicate more attention than we have done in the past.

There is exciting potential for the use of electronic teaching and learning, particularly at the secondary levels. For example, students in rural areas could take Web-based physics and high school math courses when a local math and physics teacher is not present. Federal governments and state-level governments are very alert to these possibilities, and are working hard to find avenues—perhaps through collaboration with private providers—to make this infrastructure work and make it available on a universal basis. I find that really exciting. On the other hand, as I said before, I think the digital divide between the affluent world and the developing world is continuing to widen. I don't see anything that would affect that trend for the foreseeable future.

QUESTION: What other issues do you see impacting the field of distance education?

In all of our excitement about electronic education, we forget that there are people right under our noses, right next door to us, in our own neighborhoods, who don't have access to distance education because they can't afford it. Affordability and access remain the big issues surrounding distance education, but we don't talk enough about them. Amongst women, for example, the use of the Internet is growing by leaps and bounds. But what I would like to see is more programs to make the Internet useful and available and appropriate for single mothers. There are wonderful programs available for single mothers. But these individuals cannot access them because they do not have the equipment and are not hooked up to the Internet. Some of these individuals struggle to feed their families, and so they certainly can't afford another $20 to $50 monthly to connect to the Internet.

QUESTION: What do you think are examples of best practices in distance education?

Best practices are always contingent upon finding and creating what works for a particular context. For example, at the International Extension College we worked with the Sudanese Open Learning Organization (SOLO), providing distance education for people in refugee and displaced persons camps. These people want to continue their education, further their opportunities, and further their life chances. SOLO makes useful programs available to people using paper-based courses with face-to-face tutorials, an approach that is very modest in cost, yet incredibly effective.

When I think of modest cost, I think of the incredibly effective teacher training taking place all over the world using distance education, using well-designed paper-based instructional materials. These materials are treated like gold by the teachers who are getting their teacher training while they are teaching in the classroom. The evaluations that have been done of these programs show that they are making a difference in serving the teachers in the primary and secondary school classrooms. They are the type of examples that give me the most inspiration because of my first-hand experience with them.

QUESTION: What is the impact of cultural differences on distance learning?

After 30 years of involvement in distance education, I have become very aware of the impact of cultural issues. Cultural differences play a large role in how distance learners from different parts of the world interact with teaching and learning. As practitioners, we get so hung up with the notions of the economies of scale and the incredible reach of these materials that we easily forget the reality of cultural differences. Distance educators need to be alert to diversity of all kinds, whether it is in terms of gender, culture, or religion. It is important that we make our teaching and learning approaches truly flexible so as to ensure that we are getting across the concepts that are central to a discipline or to a subject in a way that makes sense within a given learner's cultural framework.

QUESTION: Who would you identify as key individuals with whom all distance learning workers should be familiar?

My personal hero is Michael Young, the founder of the National Extension College in the U.K., and one of the unsung heroes of the Open University. Michael died last year at the age of 87, and up to his last breath he was still brimming with ideas for furthering the cause of social justice.

Next, I would mention the former Director of the National Extension College (IEC's mother institution), Ros Morpet. Ros is a shining example of a person who can maintain her personal integrity as an educational leader. At the same time, she stays alert to the opportunities for marketing education without becoming enslaved to commercial values.

In the international context, I would mention Tony Dodds, first director of the International Extension College. Tony was almost single-handedly responsible for the founding of extension units and distance education programs in almost every country in Africa. He is another unsung hero of distance education.

CHAPTER 8

IMPLEMENTING A DISTANCE EDUCATION PROGRAM: LESSONS FROM FLORIDA STATE UNIVERSITY

An Interview with Robert M. Morgan

Ray J. Amirault and Jeffery Sievert

It is often said that we *learn by doing*. In any area of learning, the knowledge surrounding that subject, the philosophical basis of the subject, and the various opinions of theoreticians about the subject—admittedly all essential components—could conceivably be considered "inert" knowledge until the added voice of real experience becomes part of the discourse. We say "theory *and* practice" because both worlds have important things to contribute to our understanding and practice in the field of education.

The implementation of a full-scale distance education system is perhaps the archetypical case in point. Many distance education projects, like other large organizational undertakings, are filled with unknowns and uncertainties, particularly if the undertaking is an institution's first foray into the distance modality. A distance education project entails all the

Trends and Issues in Distance Education: International Perspectives, 97–106
Copyright © 2005 by Information Age Publishing
All rights of reproduction in any form reserved.

aspects of any large educational project: costing and financial issues, acquisition of staff, training of existing staff and faculty, student recruitment, development of instructional materials, and evaluation, to name a few. However, distance education programs also bring a whole new range of issues to the table. What type of technical infrastructure will be needed to house, disseminate, and make instructional materials available to students 24X7 anytime and anywhere? Who should have the responsibility for setting up and maintaining such an infrastructure? How should subject matter currently existing in traditional format be converted to the distance modality for optimal learning outcomes? How will students be assessed, and how can the institution validate that the assessment is being properly administered? What student support structures should be developed, and how should they be staffed? These are but a few of the questions that speak to the value in listening to those individuals who have had actual experience in the development and implementation of a large-scale distance education initiative. Indeed, it is often experience—a precious and sometimes rare contribution to any project—that is most frequently desired by those charged with the responsibility of implementing new distance programs.

In this enlightening interview, Robert M. Morgan, Professor Emeritus of Florida State University (FSU), and past Director of FSU's Learning Systems Institute, presents his insights and experiences as one of the lead architects of Florida State University's implementation of its centralized distance education initiative. Focusing on issues surrounding the early phases of this initiative, Morgan provides valuable details on how FSU began its design and implementation of a distance education program, how the program was viewed by members working in the traditional face-to-face education setting, and how the transition to the distance modality occurred over time. In describing his first-hand experience with FSU's distance education initiative, Morgan also covers issues such as enrollment sizes, the population characteristics of distance learners, and the work investment required to make such systems successful. While describing these experiences, Morgan offers his unique insights on a broader range of surrounding issues, including a valuable comparison of the American and British distance education models, the potential impact of distance education programs on the traditional university, and the cost of education. The interview was conducted in spring 2004, in Tallahassee, Florida. The text has been edited for readability in a written format.

QUESTION: *How and why did Florida State University initiate its distance education program, and what was your role in this undertaking?*

FSU's president (Dale Lick) investigated the whether or not there was a need for distance education in the southeastern part of the United States, and whether Florida State had any particular capacities or credibility for moving in that direction. Dr. Lick created a University -wide task force to address these questions. The task force conducted a statewide study on the subject as well as an audit of the resources here at FSU that were relevant to distance education. Dr. Kaufman, who was chairing the task force, worked with me at the Learning Systems Institute (LSI), and through my interactions with him I became aware of the ongoing effort. The task force generated a report which, in summary, stated that there was a strong need for higher education distance learning in Florida and the southeast United States in general, and that Florida State University had some unusual qualifications and resources to equip the institution for getting into that line of work.

I became quite interested in the investigation as I read the report. The report contained much documentation concerning the number of people who, for a large variety of reasons, couldn't access higher education. That seemed remarkable to me, because for many years the State of Florida had been at the forefront of easy access to higher education through its community college systems. For example, there is a community college within driving distance of every citizen in the State. But, there are also many other reasons why people can't access higher education: some people cannot afford higher education, some do not have the time for taking coursework due to employment or familial responsibilities, and so on. So, the report concluded that there were many people who could take advantage of a higher education program through distance education if such opportunities were available. Even though FSU, like other state universities, has had some form of *off-campus* instruction for many years, these efforts were not truly *distance* learning; it was lecture and home study combined with attending off-campus lectures. So the documentation of need as reported by the task force was valid.

On the other hand, it was clear that FSU already possessed a very strong media program. We had a good media center, and we had the Instructional Systems Program which was experienced in developing instruction using systematic approaches. FSU also had a very strong computer capacity on campus. We also had television production resources on campus. And even though these resources were scattered around under different organizational authorities, they were all present and in operation at FSU. It became clear that these strong institutions could be brought together to build a distance education program.

Next, FSU got a new University President (Sandy D'Alemberte). Those of us who were now "caught up" in the distance education fervor met with the new University president, and we summarized the findings on both sides of the equation, describing what the State of Florida needed and what we already had in place at FSU. The President decided we would move ahead with the distance learning initiative, that we would seek additional budgetary resources, and that we would dedicate some of our own internal resources, as well. The President also cast the Learning Systems Institute to be the startup organization to get the initiative underway until there would be a transition to a permanent distance education authority within the University. The President also asked the Dean of the College of Communication (John Mayo) to organize a trip to visit the British Open University and see what kinds of things they were doing. So, that's how things got going.

QUESTION: *What were the next steps after the initial groundwork had been laid?*

The first task we undertook was to create a University-wide Distance Education Council. These types of counsels are traditionally very important here at the FSU. These groups are comprised of members representing different aspects of the University. The councils either create or recommend policy and support programs within their area or domain. The Distance Education Council was appointed by the President, and I became its first chair.

Our next task was to develop initial policies, as well as a plan of action regarding types of classes and target populations. We also set up a search committee to look for a permanent director of the distance education center who would be assigned to the *Learning Systems Institute*. LSI had four active centers at that time, and the distance education program was added as an additional center. Finally, we hired a Director for the center.

Following a visit to the British Open University (BOU) in England, we established an ongoing relationship with BOU so that we could draw on their expertise in distance learning. We also arranged with the BOU for Dr. David Hawkridge to come to FSU to consult with us for various time lengths. Dr. Hawkridge was one of the pioneers at British Open University, and was extremely helpful in teaching us about the "ins and outs" of distance education, how distance programs are typically built, how these programs disseminate information, how the programs are managed and staffed, and so on. The input from Dr. Hawkridge was very critical to us in these formative stages of our own program.

At the same time, the President was securing a request from MCI communications. MCI offered to provide FSU one million dollars for the distance effort, and the State of Florida matched that with about three-quarters of a million dollars, which provided us a small initial endowment to begin our work. One of the things we did was to create an *MCI Fellowship*, which was assumed by Dr. Hawkridge to continue to provide us with assistance as we continued in the development process.

Over time, we began to realize more clearly that the Learning Systems Institute was not an academic unit, but a development, support and research group, and since any distance education courses that were going to be developed and offered at a distance for credit had to be done through academic units within existing University departments and colleges, we were going to eventually need to make some decisions concerning the specific programs that would eventually be offered at a distance at FSU. Looking at the vast menu of programs offered at Florida State, the question became which ones were most appropriate for distance education and represented the fewest logistical problems for conversion into the distance format. Answering this question involved some searching and talking to administrators and faculty members at the various levels throughout the University.

QUESTION: Did you encounter any misperceptions regarding FSU's ability to achieve the desired learning outcomes of traditional programs converted to the distance modality?

Yes, many. There were many different views, although the common view was "no view at all." Many individuals didn't really know much about distance learning. And most people didn't have a very high opinion of that modality. It was similar to the past situation where correspondence schools were regarded as a third-rate alternative to higher education. But there were also people who understood that with the changes in technology distance education could be a great deal more powerful than perhaps it had been in the past. There were folks who were interested, and we began to initiate a dialogue with them.

By this point in time, we had put together a budget and began to authorize development of pilot programs. We started with the School of Information Studies. The Dean of that school and her faculty were very responsive to developing distance education courses. They agreed as a faculty that they would all be involved in the building of courses, with the intent of eventually offering an undergraduate degree program in Information Studies by way of distance education. The effort was very successful, and it is still underway.

At the same time, we were looking very closely at the British Open University as a model to guide our efforts. Some of the BOU courses were offered by way of national television, but the real fundamental basis of the approach was programs of instruction that were developed for use exclusively by students at a distance, working with a tutor and a faculty member. In the BOU model, lessons were sent out for completion, students would send the completed lessons back, receive feedback, repeat these steps as required, and finally go through a controlled examination. At the end, if the student was successful with completing all the lessons and passing the exams, he or she got credit for that particular course of study. The accumulation of these courses would eventually lead to a college degree.

FSU was initially looking at a combination of television and print for our distance courses, but there was a technological development that quickly made that obsolete, and that was, of course, the rise of the Internet and the World Wide Web. I must confess that I was very skeptical about the use of the Web, at least initially, for any large scale distance program; I was pretty certain that the system would become saturated, with students not being able to get online, perform the necessary course functions, and so on. If the Web had not been expanded as rapidly as it had, then that would have been true, but this type of distance education did, of course, catch on due to the capacity growth of the Internet. It soon became apparent that the traditional method of sending lessons through the mail was obsolete, as were televised lessons. And so our initial offerings were all Internet-based, providing for interaction between faculty and students on a continuing and instantaneous basis. We had to learn how to do that, as did the British. I think one of BOU's motives for working with FSU was that we were ahead of them with respect to the use of the Internet, whereas we learned a great deal of other lessons about distance education from them.

Different people had different motives for getting into distance education. Some thought these courses could be profitable; I was one of them, and I still feel the same way. Of course, if you set a distance program up and operate it on the traditional faculty load basis, and you measure faculty load by the number of hours that a professor teaches, the teaching load taught via distance education won't be classified as any different a load than a face to face course taught on campus. So, there is no fiscal benefit for doing it—no profit. On the other hand, if you follow the British model, where you have one professor per course and a group of paid tutors who are paid considerably less than the instructor but share in the instructional work, then what you get is some leveraging of your instructional cost. From a cost point of view, this situation can be very beneficial. But as the British regularly pointed out, you can't do this approach with only 20 students—you have to have a lot of students. It is not unusual for BOU, based on this model, to have a thousand students, where a single professor would have oversight of both the development and the offering of the program, and where a number of tutors are assigned specific students for whom they are responsible.

As many institutions found out, to design a distance course, you didn't just grab a textbook off the shelf and throw something together; there was a front-end development investment that was substantial in nature. The British told us about this front-end investment, so we knew about it, and were not surprised. But I think a great many universities working in this new modality were surprised. When a university decides to offer a face-to-face course, it hires a professor, gives them a classroom, announces the course, enrolls students, gives the professor a piece of chalk, and off they go: there is little front-end investment as an institution. But in distance education, from beginning to end, you have to build a program that is tailored for students who are not going to be meeting with you in person. It is technically difficult. It takes time and it is costly, so a lot of institutions, I think, got into it, faced strong difficulties, and decided to exit the effort.

QUESTION: What do you think that distance education will do to the traditional "brick and mortar" university?

When the distance learning option first began to become popular, it created an enormous explosion on the American education and training scene. Everyone was talking about distance learning in the journals and the popular press. The University of Phoenix came into being, and all the universities got to talking about this modality and became interested in determining if they could also pursue it. There was an enormous amount of excitement. This was around 1995, and FSU was right at the front end of it. In fact, I think we might have been in it before the excitement kicked off, but within a year or so, it had captured everyone's imagination. And it looked for a while like everyone would be moving to this type of education. A lot of traditionalists on campus felt this was a threat to the conventional university, because students who could easily and economically get the higher education they wanted through online distance education, might choose this route instead of coming to campus. This turned out not to happen. The people who take distance education are generally people who *cannot* go to a campus. Almost anyone you talk to who takes distance education courses or degrees state they would much prefer a conventional campus face-to-face education if it were feasible.

One might wonder whether distance education will reduce enrollment in traditional education as technology evolves even further, but I do not think this will happen. I think high school graduates who want to go to college go for a lot of things other than college credit. Such students will continue to come to the traditional university, and they will, in FSU's case, continue to overload our campus into the foreseeable future. Adults who for one reason or another miss that opportunity will, I think, continue to expand the enrollments through distance education. For adults it is often not possible to attend classes on a regular basis. So, distance education represents a very attractive alternative for adults. I think distance education will continue to grow, but it will not grow at the expense of residential enrollments in America, either at the graduate or undergraduate level.

QUESTION: Many working professionals are using distance education as a means to advance their careers without having to quit their jobs or relocate their families. As a result, they are looking for shorter programs of study than are offered by traditional institutions. How is the American distance education system addressing the needs of these corporate and professional learners?

There are quite a number of developments that respond to that particular need. Duke University created an executive master's program. It has been very successful, and also very expensive. I don't think it's shorter; I think it still takes about 18 months to get the degree. It is not totally lockstep, but it does offer a learning schedule. You enroll, and there are certain benchmarks or milestones that you are responsible for meeting. People finish up at the same amount of time. Between those milestones, however, there is a lot of variation. The advantage it has is that you can schedule your own time. You don't have to leave your job working for Sony in Tokyo to enroll in this degree program. I think two-thirds of Duke's enrollments are foreign executives. I say executives, because the people enrolling are already managers and the cost is so high that you normally wouldn't enroll in it unless you have corporate backing.

I did look at the program at Duke, and it is an excellent program. The enrollees are provided laptops loaded with the necessary software, and students meet periodically, some two or three times during the course of studies. Students work at a distance except for those meetings. So a midlevel manager at Samsung or Mercedes-Benz, for example, if they speak English, can enroll in the program and get through it in 18 months. The cost is high, but on the other hand, you don't have to move, relocate your family, or leave your job. So it is very beneficial to the corporation in terms of not losing management time. And it is very beneficial to the individual. It is, indeed, an immense amount of work. Most of these students put in regular work hours, and then study during weekends, holidays, and evenings.

I think that over time we will see an increase in the number of "shortened" programs. Many of the programs, such as at the University of Phoenix, are flexible with the timing. If a student wanted to study intensively, he or she could get through the program in less time. You can, of course, do that at a conventional school, as well. I went through my baccalaureate program in two years, and my whole baccalaureate, masters, and doctoral program in four and a half years, so it can be done.

QUESTION: Will the American universities be able to tap into the global distance education market?

I suppose we can. Since World War II, American universities have been the most popular places in the world for foreign students to come for graduate education, as well as some undergraduate programs. I suspect that when we have high quality and widespread distance education programs, foreign students will find those attractive as well. I suspect we will have, as the British have, a lot of appeal to an international student body.

QUESTION: Will accessibility devalue online degrees?

I don't think so. The population of the world is growing faster than we are educating people now, so I don't think it will devalue the degree. If you effectively develop marketable knowledge and skills, a degree will continue to hold its value. If you don't do that, whether it's traditional education or distance instruction, it will loose its value.

QUESTION: You mentioned earlier that there was a subset of Florida's population that does not have adequate access to certain higher educational opportunities, and that this was one of FSU's reasons for offering distance education courses. With that in mind, do you think Florida State's distance efforts responded adequately to that need?

I would say that the programs that FSU is offering are directly responsive to that need. People can enroll, they don't have to come to campus, and they can complete an entire bachelor's or master's degree and never set foot on campus. I was at commencement recently, and there were some the distance education graduates getting their diplomas. That was the first time they had been on campus. So yes, it is affordable, it is flexible, and it is accessible. But it is *not* easy. The students who follow a degree program through distance education have to work hard. I taught two or three of the first distance courses in the Department of Educational Research, so I could see what the students were doing—and they were working extremely hard. It was not a shortcut. I think the education they got was pretty nearly equivalent to what they would get on campus. As a matter of fact, we gave these online learners access to people that they wouldn't be able to access normally, people like Dr. David Hawkridge.

While I do think that we have been responsive, I also feel we are not offering as many degree programs as I had hoped we would by now. I think this is because distance learning requires a substantial investment of time and energy on the part of faculty and departments. I think we will continue to grow. We now have a permanent organization, apart from the Learning Systems Institute, whose job it is to build and support the distance education program.

QUESTION: Where do you think we will be in 10 years?

I think that education is getting enormously expensive. Even relatively low-cost, state-wide campus educational costs have gone up significantly over the years. The cost of private schools is almost prohibitive, unless you are wealthy. I think the American higher education system is one of the best things we have going in our society. Distance education will get a lot more sophisticated, and technology will continue to improve. We are already able to have televised motion pictures over the Web, and it's inexpensive to do so. As the population of users grows, universities and private groups will see the prudence of making investments in those types of educational technologies.

I do not know whether a university like Florida State University should strive to get that big in terms of distance education. What we do on the campus, we do well. Should we try to do more? Well, we obviously have attempted to do more, but how big should we get? Should we try to be an "open" university with a hundred thousand students? I suppose that if I was the President of the University, I would say, "No. Let's respond to the most urgent needs in our region, and be satisfied." I think that private schools and other non-traditional types of schools like the University of Phoenix, will respond to the demand.

It is interesting to see the trend of education and information becoming a commodity. We are in the information era, so there is going to be a growing value in having and controlling information. So for that reason, if no other, I think distance education will continue to expand.

CHAPTER 9

EXPLORING TRENDS AND ISSUES IN DISTANCE EDUCATION

An Interview with Dr. Otto Peters

Lya Visser and Meira van der Spa

The last few years have offered the authors of this chapter a number of opportunities to exchange ideas with Otto Peters and to learn from him. For over four decades, Peters has emphasized the unique potential of distance education in providing access to large numbers of students in both industrialized and developing countries. During the last decade, Peters has assessed the potential and impact of digital information and communication technologies on education. The results of some of this work appear in his recently published *Distance Education in Transition: New Trends and Challenges* (2003).

This chapter addresses six distance education trends that we discussed with Peters in a series of interviews and discussions.[1] In the course of the interaction, Peters not only commented on the trends, but also shared his vision on related issues.

Trends and Issues in Distance Education: International Perspectives, 107–113
Copyright © 2005 by Information Age Publishing
All rights of reproduction in any form reserved.

In laying the foundation for the interview, it was agreed to adhere to the definition of a *trend* given by Ely in Chapter 1 of this book: "A line of general direction of movement and a prevailing tendency or inclination. The general movement over a course of time of a statistically detectable change."

The following trends were discussed with Peters:

1. The economic recession of the past few years has, in many countries, considerably decreased funds for (higher) education, and has increased the interest of traditional universities in offering distance education as a cost-cutting initiative.

2. Some faculty in traditional teaching institutions show a somewhat adverse attitude towards online course delivery, or may even show strong resistance to this mode.

3. In many countries there is a significant rise in the number of for-profit distance education institutions. However, these institutions generally offer only easy-to-deliver courses such as management, computer-science, and so on.

4. Traditional universities are becoming more like distance education universities, not vice versa.

5. Academic accountability is growing, but the training of instructors and faculty is not keeping pace and is often not in place.

6. Developments in digitized learning will make it likely that "the very nature of scientific knowledge will not remain the same. It will change to a degree that is similar to the transformation caused by the use of books."

One of the trends that we observe is that with the economic recession, funds for education, and specifically for higher education, are decreasing, and the unique possibilities of distance education are commanding more attention. This can be seen at conferences about education and has resulted in an increased number of traditional colleges and universities exploring the possibility of offering distance education as a solution to control costs (Jones, 2003). Such increased interest in distance learning may, in turn, lead to an increase in the number of institutions offering distance learning courses and programs.

One of the first questions we asked Peters was whether this trend would threaten the existing open universities. The answer was a very decisive "no." According to Peters, open universities are a type of university *sui generis* with a philosophy and mission that is different from traditional universities. As he sees it, open universities focus on helping those who are not served well, not only in the industrialized world, but also in the developing countries. Peters emphasized that an important characteristic of open universities is that their faculty have an undivided loyalty toward their learners, while this may be different in traditional institutions where faculty may have a divided loyalty between the students who are physically present (and can thus easily contact the instructor), and the students who are at a distance (and therefore have less contact with their instructor).

A trend has been observed that some faculty members are resisting technological (digital) course delivery (Dunn, 2000). We therefore asked Peters whether he believed that faculty in traditional education have an adverse attitude toward distance education and may, as a result, favor their traditional (and physically present) students. In response, Peters brought up the related issue of the media as a medium for teaching rather than for simply transmitting information. He distinguished between teaching media and teaching through media. Open universities, with their extensive experience, may be better equipped and better prepared to make optimal use of the available media, especially where large groups are involved.

As a possible competitor to open universities, Peters mentioned the possibility that a number of traditional universities could unite and design an organizational structure that is prepared to optimally serve those (adult) students who are employed on a full-time basis. As he noted, "This has already happened quite often, but these organizations cannot become real competitors (to the open universities), as they are based on different approaches and experiences. I do not believe that open universities are threatened by them. Competition will stimulate and strengthen our efforts."

Peters went on to state that he believes that open universities are better prepared for new forms of online learning than are traditional universities, which offer only part of their programs at a distance. The latter often use the distance mode as an add-on to their traditional teaching practice and, in Peters' opinion, this is the wrong approach. In addition, he remarked that many traditional universities dedicate comparatively few faculty to the distance education programs and that courses are often written by just one faculty member, while open universities typically work with course teams.

To quote from Peters' *Distance Education in Transition: New Trends and Challenges* (2003): "Distance learning is not just campus-based learning with the help of particular technical media. It is an entirely different approach, with different students, objectives, methods, media, strategies and above all different goals in educational policy."

Peters added some additional thoughts, mentioning that digital information technology is becoming increasingly important, both in the world at large and in universities. Experts predict a constant growth in digitized communication and in digitized teaching and learning. In the universities, networked computers have become important and are already indispensable in research. While many professors are still hesitant users, students use computers for real-time communication and for surfing the Web, in this way changing the teaching-learning process. By and by, the learning process will become a distinct process of knowledge management. This trend is as strong as it is irreversible.

According to Rubin (2003), there is a trend that traditional universities are becoming more like distance education universities, rather than vice-versa. Given the history of distance education in a country like England, and its positive and innovative approaches towards open and distance learning which have resulted in the establishment of the British Open University, we asked Peters his opinion on the situation in the United States, where there is no tradition of an open university to build on. We further asked Dr. Peters whether he thought that countries such as the U.S., that lack the experience of an open university, might perform more poorly than countries with a rich history in distance education. Peters believes that this is not necessarily the case, and that it is difficult to compare the two. He argues that many open universities offer courses and programs developed and facilitated by experts, in order to generate a high-quality education. In many U.S. continuing education programs, only one professor designs the course. In Peters' opinion, this does not contribute to improving the quality of cooperation and team teaching. The most important issue, according to Peters, is that student support is not organized in the same way as in open universities, where there are study centers and many tutors and mentors. Thus, it is impossible to say that one is poor and the other excellent, because traditional universities cannot offer the same conditions as open universities. Peters notes that traditional universities were not designed for the purpose of offering distance education. Distance education is only an additional function in traditional universities, while in open universities it is the main function.

A recent trend has been an increased emphasis on academic accountability. In his book *Distance Education in Transition: New Trends and Challenges* (2003), Peters states that it is completely inadequate to judge distance education by applying the criteria used to assess face-to-face education. This hints at differences in approach and differences in implementation. We discussed with Peters the notion that many of the professionals working and teaching in distance education environments have never been exposed to distance learning themselves: some have just made the switch from traditional "teaching" to distance "teaching." We asked Peters if he believes there is an increasing demand for academic accountability, and whether the time is ripe for a better training of distance education instructors. Asked whether he feels that there should be agreement on the need for a minor academic degree or diploma—a specialization in distance education, so that faculty and instructors are better prepared for their task, Dr. Peters exclaimed: "Yes, I can only say yes," adding "It seems to me that this specialization would introduce participants to the theory of constructivist learning, which is very important as preparation for a change in thinking, in outlook. Students in this specialization course should also know the theory and practice of independent, autonomous learning."

In Peters' opinion, good instructors have always recognized the importance of moving away from a pedagogy of expository teaching toward engaging, self-directed and meaningful learning. In distance education, we identified a trend of motion away from the transmission model toward a constructivist and meta-cognitive model. Peters states that digitized learning environments open up new possibilities and chances for autonomous learning, as there is already a wealth of desirable pre-conditions for such learning. The student will enter into an interactive relationship with all types of information from the onset. Instead of a passive and receptive learning situation, we encounter independent, self-determined, and self-regulated acquisition of knowledge based on students' own learning strategies, their capacity and willingness to engage in searching for and finding information, and their capacity and desire to select and apply the acquired information. The beauty of such an approach is that it has the ability to modify the traditional methods of presentational teaching and learning, while also providing a completely different challenge for learning.

When asked to dwell a little more on autonomous learning, learning processes, and critical thinking, Peters stated that "learning is basically a process in which the individual person reacts to his or her environment, its objects, human beings and cultural patterns. Autonomous learners should be aware of this interactive process. This means that all interactions with classmates, tutors, counselors, teachers, professors, and experts are extremely significant. This interaction can be critical if the learner has developed a critical attitude which induces him or her to put forward critical questions. In open universities—single-mode, distance-teaching universities—the 'external critical input' is provided by several services in study centers. Digital information technology also provides a wealth of additional critical communication possibilities which can be used in order to obtain critical input as well."

One of the last questions we asked Peters refers to scientific knowledge. Our question read "Educators and policymakers should ask fundamental questions that will influence the future viability not only of their institution but of distance education in general. In our rapidly changing world we should be able to identify the important issues that keep us busy and the trends that will help us to make informed decisions. In *Distance Education in Transition: New Trends and Challenges*, one of the important trends that you identified is that the very nature of scientific knowledge will not remain the same. It will change to a degree that is similar to the transformation caused by the use of books. Could you discuss this further?" In his answer, Dr. Peters started by identifying the problem. According to him, digitalization and computerization are changing teaching and learning in various ways. Reflecting on the progress of online learning in schools, institutes of higher education, and continuing education, we might be tempted to think that changes are taking place with regard to new pedagogical scenarios, organizational forms, and strategies and methods of teaching and learning. In reality, however, content is *also* affected, in terms of the knowledge that is to be imparted or acquired. The change is much more fundamental here, and it affects the core of the pedagogical process. The knowledge that is developed with the use of a computer and with the help of an unimaginable abundance of easily accessible information differs structurally from classical knowledge. By concentrating on this fact we hit a nerve that radiates out to other areas of learning and changes them. But there is more to it: even our thinking, the way in which we gather knowledge and apply it, in fact our whole intellectual life, is affected by this change and process.

An external sign of the changes mentioned here is the almost inflationary use of the terms "information" and "knowledge." We will examine this phenomenon and discuss the impact this change has on teaching and learning in continuing education and turn to Norbert Bolz, philosopher and media theorist. Exact conceptions of what knowledge will look like in the age of digitalisation are offered by Bolz, because he characterises the thought processes in the virtual world which brings forth this knowledge.

> Today, instead of the linear rationality of the Gutenberg galaxy, we are thinking in configurations. The *adequatio* theory of truth is being replaced by the constructivist theory of the "fitting" of a theory; recurrence replaces causality, pattern recognition replaces classification. And where immaterial pixel configurations in computer simulation replace the appearance of a stable objectivity the question of a reference loses its meaning. Even our cared-for Nature, the most famous product of reflections of old European culture, can be recognised under new media conditions as a programmed environment. Under the conditions of the new media and of computer technology man has said goodbye to a world which was ordered through representations, and from a way of thinking which saw itself as a representation of the outside world. The technical media of the information society are the absolutely unavoidable *a priori* of our attitude to the world: programs have replaced the so-called natural conditions of the possibility of experiences. (1993, p. 113)

To date, no one else has worked out the breach with traditional thought in a more penetrating way. The knowledge which emerges as the result of this way of thinking moves away from many standards which were previously valid: the relevant reality, truth, causality, order through classification and representation and, finally, the traditional relationship between appearance and being, simulation and reality. Under the influence of this radical change, Bolz (1993) arrives at the following conclusion: "Digitality has replaced metaphysics." (p. 110). The latter has, according to Peters, identified an epochal change and characterized how digitalization and computerization are changing teaching and learning in multiple ways.

NOTE

1.   The first interview was conducted by Charles Schlosser and Lya Visser

REFERENCES

Bebko, S. (1998). *The application and implications of information technologies in postsecondary distance education: An initial bibliography.* Retrieved July, 2004, from http://www.nsf.gov/sbe/srs/nsf03305/secta.htm

Bolz, N. (1993). *Am ende der Gutenberg-galaxis: Die neuen kommunikationsverhältnisse.* München: Fink.

Dunn, S. L. (2000, March-April). The virtualizing of education. *The Futurist. 34,* 34-38.

Jones, R. (2003). A recommendation for managing the predicted growth in college enrollment at a time of adverse economic conditions. *Online Journal of Distance Learning Administration, 6*(1). Retrieved July 2004, from http://www.westga.edu/%7Edistance/ojda/spring61/jones61.html

Peters, O. (2003). *Distance education in transition: New trends and challenges.* Oldenburg, Germany: Carl von Ossietzky University.

Rubin, E. (2003). Speaking personally with Eugen Rubin. *The American Journal of Distance Education 17*(1), 59-69.

PART III

NATIONAL AND REGIONAL CASE STUDIES IN DISTANCE EDUCATION

CHAPTER 10

OPEN AND DISTANCE LEARNING FOR DEVELOPING COUNTRIES

Is the Cup Half Full or is it Still Half Empty?

Tony Dodds

INTRODUCTION

I entered the business of what is now called distance education in 1968 in Tanzania while at an early stage of an adult education career. I believed then, as I do now, that the main purpose of adult education, and by default, therefore, distance education, is to help to equalise educational opportunities and to provide chances of educational achievement to people who have been deprived of such chances and without adult or distance education would be likely to remain so. It is for that reason that I prefer the somewhat ambiguous phrase "open and distance learning" (ODL) or, as the South African Institute for Distance Education calls it, "open learning through distance education." It ought to be about opening up oppor-

Trends and Issues in Distance Education: International Perspectives, 117–129
Copyright © 2006 by Information Age Publishing

tunities for educational success to those who don't otherwise have them. The great advantage, or at least challenge, of using the media, both electronic and print, in adult education is that they have the potential to reach out to people who cannot make use of traditional face-to-face forms of learning.

This article identifies four significant international trends in distance education and examines them from the stand-point of the above expectation of its potential to democratise education. It raises issues related to their application in developing countries, especially in Africa. The first two are positive trends though they are littered with potential pitfalls: the growing use of modern information and communication technologies in distance learning, and the internationalisation of access to tertiary courses via the electronic media. The third trend is the increasing emphasis on independent and isolated learning embodied in such phrases as the virtual campus and the dangers that poses for two crucial uses of ODL in developing countries, namely for in-service professional and vocational education, especially teacher education and the spread of the open school movement to fill the gaps left by inadequate provision of traditional schools, especially in developing countries. The fourth trend is essentially negative: the growing predominance of advanced or tertiary education in the open and distance education world and its neglect of adult basic education.

The unifying theme of the article is the potential through open and distance learning to put in place mechanisms for lifelong learning for all adults regardless of national or educational background and the progress in developing countries towards achieving that goal. It is to a large extent summed up in a quotation, from my professional guru, Michael Young, Lord Young of Dartington, from an address he gave to the 25th birthday conference in Swaziland of the Distance Education Association of Southern Africa, DEASA, in 1999:

> Lifelong learning is all very well as a noble slogan, but it would be of little overall value if it were only lifelong learning for the few and not the many. In the fullness of time nothing less than universal learning will suffice. The educational battle between the champions of the few and the champions of the many has been joined ... It is an outflanking policy I am presenting traversing a circuitous route towards mass engagement. It is to make universities which have done so much to enlarge inequality the instruments of equality instead ... I know it will be a long time before the Universality of London is established. The Universality of Namibia, or Zimbabwe or Ghana or Delhi or Hong Kong could come beforehand, at any rate with that spirit if not the name. (Young, 1999)

THE DAZZLE OF THE NEW TECHNOLOGY

The last decade has seen the technological revolution, through the almost unbelievable spread and development of computer applications, make a major impact on open and distance learning. The generational changes come thick and fast according to recent literature on its historical development; the buzzwords of ODL in this first decade of the 21st century are "online learning," "e-learning" and "virtual learning." In some cultures, distance learning without computer technology at its core is not distance learning at all. There can be no doubt about the potential for such new information and communication technologies (ICT) to increase vastly the speed of delivery of learning materials, to allow for much more effective management and administrative structures and to enhance the frequency, the quality and the personalisation of interaction between students and their tutors and between students themselves in ODL programmes. All these features are crucial to the quality and effectiveness of such programmes and all three are areas (delivery, management, interaction) where there have, traditionally, been serious failures and setbacks in such programmes throughout the world. There is also no doubt that this revolution will continue, accelerate, and spread in both the industrialised and the developing world in the years to come. It is therefore vital that the ODL providers in developing countries become increasingly familiar with the new technologies and explore through experimentation all means to incorporate these technologies into their programmes in order to provide their students with more efficient administration, more rapid access to their learning materials, and more personal contact with their tutors and mentors in order to minimise the extreme loneliness that distance learners—especially in developing countries—so often experience.

These potential improvements in the quality of ODL through new ICT, however, must be treated with certain cautions, at least in the immediate future. I will discuss four such cautions here. First is the question of access to such technology amongst actual and potential distance learners. Three articles in an as yet unpublished collection of papers on ODL in Southern Africa highlight the low levels of such access among students of ODL programmes in Namibia and South Africa in the early years of this new century. These two countries probably are amongst the most technologically advanced countries in Africa and the students surveyed represent the solid middle classes of their populations, namely teachers, nurses, and managers. Yet, in Namibia, Mowes found that less than 10% of such students registered with the University of Namibia Centre for External Studies external degree programmes had regular access to a computer either at home, or at work; Beukes found that, among primary school teachers enrolled in diploma upgrading programmes, most had to travel several kilometres to make use of a telephone; and Beneke and Hayes concluded that for students of Vista University's distance learning programmes for teacher upgrading in South Africa, computer-based student counselling services were as yet an unreliable means of reaching their target audiences (Beukes; Hay & Beneke; Mowes, 2003). In recent consultancy work in Ghana and Mozambique I have myself observed the low levels of computer access among distance learners and the even lower level of access of such students and their providing agencies to reliable computer networks for the use of e-mail or the Internet in their programmes, whether for the delivery of materials, for management information activities, or for student tutorial interaction. If students do not have access to the new ICTs, there is no purpose served by incorporating such technology into learning programmes.

The second caution is about the mode of application most appropriate as such technologies gradually become more accessible. It appears at present that access to such technologies has to be made available to students by the providing bodies wherever that is possible. In Namibia and South Africa, and other southern African countries, several universities offering ODL courses, as well as pre-tertiary ODL institutions, are making efforts to equip study centres at least in regional centres with interactive ICT facilities such as networked computers and audio- and video-conferencing networks. It is my opinion that this is the most important form of investment in the new technology that currently needs to be made in order to increase student access in developing countries to the advantages of the technological revolution I referred to above. But such access will, for some considerable time to come, be limited and needs to be used in a group learning environment, and not, as is true in most systems in industrialised settings, as an individual learning tool. This has significant implications for the pedagogy employed through the technology.

My third caution is about the costs. I have seen no evidence that the incorporation of ICT in ODL programmes decreases their costs. In fact, what evidence I have seen is to the contrary, even in industrialised countries. A recent study has suggested that, in addition to initial installation costs for a computer laboratory, one has to calculate an ongoing annual expenditure to maintain that system of between 30% and 50% of the initial costs. The added maintenance costs of networking such a laboratory could add a further 20% (Moses in Perraton & Lentell, 2004). Every ODL provider in a developing country with which I am familiar has problems finding the funds to offer the courses it wishes to offer at the quality it wishes to provide. Such institutions must perforce consider whether such add-on costs to existing programmes in order to introduce computer-based ICTs is well-directed investment at this point in time.

My final caution relates to the phrase that has now become almost a cliché, the digital divide. My first caution highlighted the problem of accessibility to new ICT in developing countries even among the better-off sections of those societies. Any approach to ODL which allows itself to be dazzled by the new technologies as they are used in industrialised countries, regardless of whether they are the best ways to achieve the learning targets of a particular institution, or which weds itself to technology-based courses obtained from the industrialised world, may well be increasing the educational deprivation of students who would be able to use more traditional technologies for ODL. That represents the international digital divide. But, possibly more serious in my opinion, is the danger of internal digital divides within developing countries. The more ODL providers in developing countries tie themselves to new ICTs in the development and delivery of their courses in order "to keep up with the Joneses" of the industrialised world, the more they are likely to limit their provision to the better-off sections of their own societies, who undoubtedly will increasingly have access to those technologies in the near future, and the more they make themselves and their courses inaccessible to the more deprived and, almost by definition, the less-well educated sections of their communities. As I said at the outset, this moves away from the basic purpose of adult education and of open and distance education as I see it.

None of these cautions mean that developing countries should not invest in ICT for ODL or that they should stick exclusively to the old technologies. They do mean that such investment should be made and experiments carried out that explore ways whereby the new technologies can be made accessible to all levels of ODL provision and can be used effectively to promote learning among an ever-increasing proportion of those in developing countries who are most in need of education.

THE GLOBALISATION OF LEARNING BY ODL: A NEW FORM OF IMPERIALISM?

When I first visited Ghana in 1971, a quick glance in the daily national newspapers revealed any number of advertisements for correspondence courses from institutions in England and the USA. A few years later, these were largely replaced by adverts for similar courses offered by Ghanaian or Nigerian institutions. On a recent visit, I failed to find a single advert for distance education courses offered by local institutions. Earlier, such adverts were for secondary-level courses and qualifications. These seem no longer available. Today there are at least three Ghanaian universities offering external degree courses by distance learning, but they were not advertising in the newspapers while I was there. There were, however, numerous adverts from international universities, some respectable and world-famous, others largely unknown to me, offering e-learning opportunities, often at post-graduate level, through direct enrolment with the parent overseas campus, and with little evidence of local tutorial or administrative support.

No doubt such globalisation of access to courses from a wide range of international universities increases the opportunities for tertiary and post-graduate education for at least a small minority of students in developing countries who for one reason or another cannot get it through their national universities, namely those who can afford the often very high fees and can find ways of obtaining the foreign exchange with which the fees must be paid. Indeed, one of the dreams from its inception of the Commonwealth of Learning, now one of the most important international ODL agencies, with a strong commitment to its development in developing countries, has been that any student in any Commonwealth country should have access to any course offered by ODL in any other Commonwealth country. It is as yet an unfulfilled dream, but a dream well worth pursuing, so long as, in its pursuit, COL ensures that mechanisms are put in place for the accreditation and quality control of such courses and the local acceptability of the qualifications offered and for the counselling of prospective students about the quality, relevance, and required technological infrastructure for successful completion of such courses.

Without mechanisms to protect and advise students about the relevance and suitability for their own particular needs of international courses, there are serious dangers that students are tempted into enrolment and the payment of fees they can ill afford for courses they stand little chance of completing or whose qualifications will not be acceptable for local employment even if they do succeed. National and international accreditation bodies are urgently needed to stop the globalisation of university courses through ODL/e-learning becoming a new form of international educational exploitation. Perhaps a more productive form of globalisation would be for international universities to make their courses available through cooperative arrangements, "e-cooperation," with local universities, as has begun to happen in a few cases. Unfortunately, such cooperation is rarely as financially attractive to the overseas partners as is the direct enrolment of students who pay the fees directly to them.

THE VIRTUAL CAMPUS: DANGERS OF DEHUMANISING ODL FOR IN-SERVICE PROFESSIONAL EDUCATION AND IN OPEN SCHOOLS

One of the founding philosophies in distance education was embodied in the phrase "independent learning." This was particularly promoted through the University of Wisconsin, which emphasized the opportunities for students in correspondence education and later in distance education to exercise their independence of choice over the time, place, pace, and even the curricula of their studies that the media and related technologies offered, instead of the didactic, teacher-determined patterns of traditional campus studies. This drew on the andragogic principles that adults, as adults, know what they want and are individual and independent beings who cannot and should not be conscripted into pre-determined educational programmes, often initially designed for adolescent students. No one, least of all myself, should be able to deny that independent learning is a desirable goal at which all education should aim, nor that adults as adults need to exercise more control over where, when, how, how fast, and what they study than is normally allowed for in traditional face-to-face schools, colleges, and universities. There is, however, a growing recognition that students who, for one reason or another, opt for distance learning, are not by definition independent learners at the outset, but that they need to be helped to become independent learners through guided, structured, and supported educational experience. The flexibility of time, place, and pace are often essential to allow them to study, but structured expectations and encouragement to meet deadlines are often equally essential if they are to persevere in spite of their difficulties, especially the fact that study is very rarely the first priority in their lives (Mpofu, in Dodds (Ed.), in press). In today's technological world of ODL, the concept of independent and isolated (or home-based) study has been taken to its extreme in the concept of virtual campuses or universities in which the technology replaces personal contact, and where real people, face-to-face, in real classrooms and real universities, are replaced by virtual reality and technological teaching. This is possibly appropriate for advanced learners in highly industrialised societies where there are any numbers of places where such students can obtain support and study facilities. I wish to examine the issue of whether these concepts are appropriate for two forms of ODL that are increasingly important to developing countries.

Some of the earliest examples of correspondence education, perhaps the oldest ancestor of today's ODL, if we wish to play the generations game, were vocational courses in bookkeeping, accountancy, and business studies. Vocational and professional training remains a key and possibly growing sector of ODL. This is certainly true in the industrialised world, where many professions, including the legal, the teaching, and the medical professions, have either developed their own in-service training courses or have gone into partnership with ODL agencies to do so. It is also exemplified by the number of commercial and industrial companies that encourage their employees to upgrade and up-skill themselves through ODL programmes, again either developed by the corporations themselves (including, even in the UK, several corporate universities) or in cooperation with recognised ODL providers. The advantage for the employees is that such courses are increasingly available at all stages of their careers and are recognised by their employers for promotional purposes. The advantage for the employer is that such training can take place without serious loss of working hours. A characteristic of most such programmes is that the practical learning, which is an essential component, can be carried out in the workplace under the supervision of experienced practitioners. In developing countries, the most outstanding example of such in-service training through ODL is in the teaching profession. Faced with crises, both as regards quantity and quality of primary and secondary schools, many countries have turned to ODL teacher education programmes to provide the required training without taking the teachers out of their schools for extended periods. Countries have also recognised that, in order to meet the urgent demands both from their own people and from the international community to achieve universal basic education, the need for in-service training of newly-recruited untrained teachers is a long-term need. This is exacerbated in many countries by the frightening attrition rates among teachers because of the HIV/AIDS pandemic. Training teachers is, in part, an essentially human and practical process. Technology-delivered courses and virtual campuses can perhaps provide the content that teachers have to learn in order to teach the subjects concerned, but training in how to teach and how to manage classrooms and pupils, needs practice, guidance from experienced teachers, and supervision. These cannot be provided at a distance. The danger of the independent learning emphasis and the expectation of technology-delivered courses and virtual campuses is that such programmes neglect the practical aspects of teacher training and the human, face-to-face mentoring, tutoring, and supervision that those aspects require. The programmes become too heavily content-oriented, and the teachers trained in this way have not necessarily received enough training in how to become better classroom teachers.

The second form of ODL in which the independence of the learner and the effectiveness of technology-only teaching can be over-emphasised, and the need for human contact seriously underestimated, is in the use of ODL to provide substitute schooling for young adults or adolescents who are unable to find places in traditional schools. More and more countries in the developing world are turning to the so-called Open School movement to make up shortfalls in their full-time traditional school provision. In Africa, such experiments began many years ago, especially at junior and senior secondary level, where countries such as Zambia and Malawi were unable to provide places in traditional secondary schools for pupils who were completing primary school in ever larger

numbers. The correspondence education model that was proving successful in providing working adults with the secondary school qualifications
they had missed out on earlier was adopted and adapted into the supervised study-group model. Here, adolescents studied the same correspondence courses, but in groups supervised by an older person, possibly a
teacher working part-time. This model was rapidly accepted and promoted by Ministries of Education in many countries, especially in Central
and Southern Africa, to relieve the pressure for ever more expensive secondary schools to meet the demand as resources generally, and for education in particular, declined in the 1980s economic recession.
Unfortunately, such programmes were expected, on the basis of the
claims of economies of scale made by distance education generally, to be
able to expand almost ad infinitum without parallel or, in some cases, any
expansion of resources. The concept of students learning on their own
without teachers or dedicated facilities, which is where the economies of
distance learning come from, led to an assumption that, once the courses
were there, an infinite number of students could benefit from them. The
results were often dismal and led to a declining popularity among students and their parents, and a reputation among traditional education
officials as "education for failure." The lesson that distance education was
not, by itself, an adequate structure for adolescent learning had still to be
learned (Dodds & Mayo, 1996). In recent years, in response to the still
growing demand for out-of-school secondary education for such young
adults and adolescents, a new approach to the same pattern of provision
has been developed, first in Malawi where the experiment was not maintained, and then in Namibia and Botswana, in the form of para-statal,
semi-autonomous dedicated distance education institutions with this out-
of-school secondary provision as their first priority. These institutions are
the Namibia College of Open Learning (NAMCOL) and the Botswana
College of Distance and Open Learning (BOCODOL). At the heart of the
apparent initial success of these new bodies, both of which grew out of
earlier government department programmes, have been three features.
First has been the parastatal nature of their management structures. Second is the dedicated ODL professionalism that these management structures have been able to promote. Third has been the recognition that the
services they offer must be tailor-made to their various target audiences
and that, as their primary target audience is the out-of-school youth, their
programmes must be built on supportive and structured learning environments for such young people that are not exclusively media- or technology-delivered and include tutorial support made available in far-from-
virtual campuses. The resources to make this combination possible are
seen as a sine qua non for success, and figure in strenuous negotiations
for resources with their governments (Dodds, 2003).

UNFINISHED BUSINESS:
ODL FOR ADULT BASIC AND NON-FORMAL EDUCATION

My fourth and final trend is the unfortunate concentration of international ODL, and even more so of the virtual and e-learning movement, on the more advanced levels of education, mainly at university or tertiary level and the relative neglect in the ODL fraternity of adult basic and non-formal education. This neglect appears to be equally true in the developing world as it is in the industrialised world, though there is less excuse there for such neglect. More than ten years after the international conference in Jomtien set Education for All (EFA) by the year 2000 as an internationally-accepted educational necessity, the World Education Forum in Dakar had to restate, as an international educational goal, "achieving a 50% improvement in levels of adult literacy by 2015, especially for women and equitable access to basic and continuing education for adults." This was in recognition that in 2000 there were 875 million adults in the world who were illiterate, with probably at least 200 million of these in Africa. This figure was set to grow as more children who had not been to school became adults by 2015. In these circumstances, to what extent, if at all, have the successes of open and distance learning in recent decades been targeted at the failures of EFA? The answer, sadly, has to be: to a very limited extent. Can ODL afford to ignore this crying need, and is it doing so because its practitioners do not see ODL as an effective way of meeting such a need? If this is so, it is not because of evidence that it doesn't work for adult basic or non-formal education; in fact, what limited evidence does exist suggests it can be very effective (Dodds, 1995; Siaciwena, 2002; Fentiman, 2003; Wrightson, 2004). All these studies have shown that there is plenty of evidence of the successful use of ODL, usually on quite a small scale or for a limited time. The Siacewena study (2000) includes reports from participants in programs using media for basic education. Participants say that what they have learned in such programs has helped them to avoid starvation in periods of famine or promote inter-ethnic understanding in areas of civil conflict. I believe, as I said in a paper delivered to the Ministers of Education conference on Open and Distance Learning, held under the auspices of NEPAD in Cape Town (South Africa) in February 2004, that there are two overwhelming conclusions and a third one that relates to the first two, that can be drawn. The first is that it can be done: we have the technology and are rapidly getting access to new technologies that will increase our capacity to provide learning opportunities to large numbers of adults in developing countries that can enhance their quality of life. This is dramatically illustrated in the Siaciwena (2000) case-studies. At the same time, such projects can be the first stages of opening up further education possibilities for their learners if we are able to exercise the political will to make these opportunities available. The second is that we have been remarkably unsuccessful to date in persuading our political masters or our senior administrators that these opportunities are worth investing resources in at levels sufficient to make serious inroads into the educational deprivation of adults on a large enough scale so as to make an impact on overall national development indices. A third conclusion relates to both of the previous points. Our technical ability to reach undereducated adults with information, knowledge, and skills that can make significant changes in their lives can be dramatically improved if we can harness the new technologies, with all the caution I have suggested earlier in this article, to that purpose. Instant access to vital agricultural information about market prices or animal or crop disease prevention measures, for example, or to health and social information that can increase people's ability to avoid the threat of HIV/AIDS, or cope more effectively with its devastating impact when it does strike a family or a community, could be incorporated into more traditional adult education programmes (Dodds, 2004). In this way, such information could usefully be made available on a much wider scale than it is at present if computer access points or tele-centres could be set up in remote rural areas in developing countries. At present, such access is extremely scarce and there is little evidence of either commercial or political or even educational determination to pay more than lip-service towards its realisation.

CONCLUSION

I return to the question implied in the subtitle of this article: how much progress has been made in the last few decades towards using open and distance learning to overcome the problems of educational deprivation in developing countries? Of course, the question as posed is no question. If the cup is half full, it is by nature also half empty. But the phrase sums up my own conclusions. Huge strides have been made through ODL to make education available to tens of thousands of citizens in developing countries who would not otherwise have had those opportunities without these techniques. New methodologies have been and continue to be tested to make this expansion of education even greater in the coming decades. However, to move closer to the full mark, certain steps are needed that perhaps suggest philosophical and political transformations or at least attitude changes on the part of education policy-makers and practitioners. First, if the dreams of the technological revolution in education are to be realized among the more educationally deprived sections of developing societies, huge efforts have to be made in the very near future by all concerned to make the new technologies available in usable forms to potential distance learners from those sections of society; such availability will be very slow in coming if no such interventions are made. Second, the way in which such technologies are incorporated into learning structures must take into account the essentially human nature of educational experience and avoid increasing isolation and loneliness among the learners. Third, national and international accreditation structures, which protect the rights and interests of students in developing countries, must be created to promote and control the globalization of educational courses through the new technology. Fourth, and in my opinion, most crucially, serious efforts must be made to use what we now know about ODL and ICT to bring about the rapid increase in effective large-scale programmes of adult basic and non-formal education that can seriously address the curses of adult illiteracy and under-education. As Michael Young said in the quotation with which I started, in the long run "nothing less than universal learning will suffice." We have the tools to achieve this. Do we have the will?

REFERENCES

Beukes, H. A. (2003). Some environmental factors affecting the academic performance of rural distance students of the University of Namibia negatively. In T. Dodds (Ed.), *Open and distance learning in Southern Africa.* Unpublished

Dodds, T. (1996). *The use of distance learning in non-formal education.* Vancouver: COL; Cambridge: IEC.

Dodds, T. (2003). Out-of-school secondary education at-a-distance in Africa. In J. Bradley (Ed.), *The open classroom: Distance learning in schools.* London: Routledge.

Dodds, T., & Mayo, J. (1995). *Distance education for development: The IEC experience 1971 to 1991.* Cambridge, UK: International Extension College.

Fentiman, A. (2003). SOMDEL: Somali Distance Education Literacy Programme Macalliya Raddiya. IRFOL: Cambridge.

Hay, J., & Beneke, P. (2003). Student profiling in open learning for an effective student counselling model. In T. Dodds (Ed.), *Open and distance learning in Southern Africa.* Unpublished.

Mowes, D. L. (2003). Improving the quality of student learning. In T. Dodds (Ed.), *Open and distance learning in Southern Africa.* Unpublished.

Mpofu, S. (2003). What is wrong with lecturing: The case for and against. In T. Dodds (Ed.), *Open and distance learning in Southern Africa.*

Perraton, H., & Moses, K. (2004). Technology. In H. Perraton & H. Lentell (Eds.), *Policy for open and distance learning.* Oxford, England: Routledge.

Siaciwena, R. (2000). *Case studies of non-formal education by distance and open learning in Africa.* Vancouver: COL; London: DFID.

Wrightson, T. (2004). Building literacy through the SOLO Press. Unpublished report Cambridge: IEC.

Young, M. (1999). From Universities to Universalities. Address given at the 25th Anniversary Conference of DEASA, University of Swaziland. *Open Praxis, 1*.

CHAPTER 11

THE PROMISE OF M-LEARNING FOR DISTANCE EDUCATION IN SOUTH AFRICA AND OTHER DEVELOPING NATIONS

Lya Visser and Paul West

THE CHALLENGES FACING DISTANCE LEARNERS IN SOUTH AFRICA

Distance learners in South Africa are challenged on many fronts. Firstly, people living outside of the major cities (and even in the less developed suburban townships), suffer from unreliable or non-existent postal services and from poor telephone systems and other deficient communication services. Secondly, people trying to upgrade their skills to improve their standard of living must continue to work full-time while studying part-time. This adds pressure to daily living and family commitments, especially if it is compounded by living with a number of other people in the same room and working by candle light after others have gone to sleep. Thirdly, the historically poor education provided during the colo-

Trends and Issues in Distance Education: International Perspectives, 131–136
Copyright © 2005 by Information Age Publishing
All rights of reproduction in any form reserved.

nial and apartheid periods has left many people lacking the prerequisite knowledge and skills required for further study. Further, many distance learners must study in English, which may be their third or fourth language. Finally, many students do not have people to turn to for academic help.

TELECOMMUNICATIONS AND DISTANCE LEARNING

It is increasingly recognized that regular communication between the instructor and the student is critical to successful distance learning (Moore & Kearsley, 1996; Visser, 1998). In distance learning, communication between the instructor and student has traditionally taken the form of faxes, emails, face-to-face contact sessions, telephone calls, teleconferences, and sometimes even videoconferences. All these technologies are very useful in maintaining contact with the learners, given the caveat that there exist no financial restrictions on such communication.

The development and increased availability of advanced technology cellular telephones may offer excellent, affordable opportunities to increase communication between instructors and students, and among students, especially in developing countries. South Africa is one of the countries were these opportunities for m-learning (mobile learning) are currently being explored.

CELLULAR TELEPHONES IN SOUTH AFRICA

South Africa is an interesting example of the expansion of cellular telephone technology. In this nation, the tele-density (the number of landlines per population) is just over 10%. This means that only one in eleven people owns a landline telephone. In contrast with this low figure, more

Table 11.1.   Demographic and Communications Data for South Africa

Total population	44.5 million
Life expectancy at birth	50.9 years
Literacy rate % of 15 and above	85.6
Telephone landlines per 1,000 people	111
Cellular subscribers per 1,000 people	242
Internet users per 1,000 people	64.9

Source: Human Development Report of the United Nations Development Program (2001).

than 90% of the country's population has access to telephones due to the widespread use of cellular telephones. It is important to note that this does not mean that more than 90% of the population owns a cellular telephone: rather, it means that 90% of the population either owns a cellular phone, or has ready access to a cellular phone owned by someone else. Cellular telephone signals are found all over the country and even in the most remote rural areas. People who previously have not had personal access to a landline telephone can now communicate via SMS and other cellular technology at low cost.

PREPAID CELLULAR SERVICE PACKAGES AND TEXT MESSAGES IN EDUCATION

Cellular telephones have become increasingly popular as they are not prone to as much downtime as landlines. Cellular companies have been able to quickly respond to market demand by providing "prepaid" packages. These packages do not require the opening of an account and can thus be used by everyone—not just by those who have a credit card and/or a good credit rating. Another advantage is that the bill is paid upfront, so there are no surprises and no unforeseen costs.

Prepaid cellular telephone service enables users to buy the minutes in advance of using them. This kind of service typically incurs the highest per minute charges. Therefore, pre-paid cellular phone users tend to make only short, essential phone calls and use text messaging services whenever appropriate. Text messaging is frequently referred to as "SMS" (Short Message Service). SMS's are compact messages of up to about 140 characters that can be sent at very low cost. A cellular telephone call just to say: "Hello" would likely cost more than sending about 18 words by SMS. Many cellular telephone users successfully use abbreviations, which can rapidly "stretch" the word-count.

In distance education, SMS can be used for student support and for urgent messages. A tutor can send a student a personal message such as "For you to do" (13 characters) in the short form "4U2do" (5 characters). Likewise, a student who has not sent in work in time can receive an urgent reminder from the teacher using only a quick sentence: "Deadline TMA 15/2. Pls reply." This short message (signifying "Deadline tutor marked assignment was on 15 February, please reply") can have considerable impact, as it shows the interest of the tutor in the student's progress, and reminds the student to act. One can easily think of longer sentences that "save" even more characters.

An important point to consider when engaging in discussion via SMS is the length of the messages that can be sent. Messages need to be kept relatively short. Members must think about how to word their question or response carefully before sending it. The average word is about 7 characters; add a space and that makes it about 8 characters average per full word. This means that a message can comprise about 18 words if all words are fully spelled out. With abbreviations, many more words can effectively be included in one message.

A large number of cellular telephones include the capacity to transmit faxes or emails, and to store text documents. Newer phones have started to include full Internet access and introduce an "always on" cellular technology which enables the cellular telephone user to access the Internet directly and not pay telecommunications charges on a time basis (for voice calls, time is charged by the second). These data services are available in many of the countries that have GSM and cellular telephone services. These configurations provide the best opportunities for education institutions truly wanting to reach their clients.

COMMUNICATING WITH LEARNERS

Many distance education institutions allow learners to telephone in for questions, although tutors and instructors may be responsible for hundreds of learners (as is the case in South Africa), and thus may have to limit the time they allow for answering calls. In addition, tutors often also must answer written questions, grade assignments, and stay in touch with the providing institution. Learners who have questions and/or need other support should, within reasonable terms, be able to make a call whenever it is convenient for them. This may mean making calls during tea breaks, lunchtime, or after work.

In the past, innovative institutions have tried to accommodate learners' needs by setting up voice mailboxes for them. This would make it possible for learners to leave messages for their tutor and to collect the tutor's answer later. The infrastructure required had to be established and maintained by the institution, an infrastructure that has little to do with the core business of the institution; i.e. providing learning opportunities. Once cellular telephones started becoming widespread, learners started having greater access to their own voice mailboxes. Even if the student has to borrow a cellular telephone, he or she can later retrieve a message left by a tutor. Landline systems in South Africa rarely have voicemail facilities.

Cellular telephone systems also make it possible for distance education providers to set up systems to deliver a collective voice or text message to all learners who have access to cellular telephones. If learners have cellular telephone numbers registered with the institution, programs can be accessed by tutors to broadcast short text or voice messages to all learners simultaneously. This type of communication can be used for variety of important goals such as encouragement and motivation, reminders for upcoming assignments and examinations, important information such as changes to examination dates or venues, and preliminary corrections and updates related to assignments or to study notes.

Transmitting the above oral or text information can be accomplished using a regular cellular telephone. The institution carries the cost of outgoing messages. Typically, the institution can negotiate low service rates with the cellular telephone companies. Learners can send text messages to their tutors, asking simple questions or requesting a phone call.

Institutions can make significant strides in meeting learner needs by providing tutors with appropriate computer interfaces to receive and send cellular text messages. This means that tutors can receive short text messages from learners in much the same way as they receive emails, with the difference being that text messages must be kept short (usually 140 characters, which is about 35 words). This requires that the learner presents a well formulated question, which saves time and makes answering easier. Similarly, responses need to be kept brief, giving a very short answer and/or referring learners to appropriate pages in their study notes and resources.

To maximize the usefulness of text messaging for distance learning, a guide discussing how to most effectively use this technology should be included in the introductory materials sent to the learner. The guide should contain generic information on how to send and receive SMS's and the telephone numbers that should be used to get support. Distance education providers may consider the inclusion of basic telephone instruments with some study packages, along with a prepaid "starter-kit" from a local cellular telephone provider. Students should have a prepaid service with a reasonable amount of time for contact. Access numbers should be provided for direct connection to the lecturer or department, or possibly a call-center. Students can be identified at the institution through their cellular numbers.

SMS text messaging is an efficient form of asynchronous communication, as it is quicker than trying to decipher long voicemail messages. It has as an additional advantage that it offers a form of educational communication that is quick, personal, and affordable. The traditional isolation of the distance learner is greatly diminished and communication patterns are established. Learners may, with their permission, have their cellular numbers shared with other learners in the same program; in this way they can more easily communicate with each other so that peer support will be possible.

GROUP DISCUSSIONS

It is possible to have a cellular telephone provider set up a group discussion facility using cellular telephones. Each message can comprise about 150 characters and is sent to a number, much like the email address used for discussion listservs. The message is then broadcast to all the cellular telephones in the group. Members of the group can continue their discussion with no connection to the Internet. Although this way of communicating is definitely less attractive than using computer conferencing, it has the advantage of being more affordable and less complicated. Institutions have little doubt about the ability of their clients to use the technology, as it is used on a daily basis for all forms of social communication already. This form of communication suits the lifestyle of many learners (especially young adults) and could be very helpful in gaining and maintaining learner motivation.

CONCLUSION

There are rapidly growing possibilities for using cellular telephones for instant communication, Internet access, e-mail, and multimedia access. SMS is a technology that is close to the learner, offers interactivity at a low price, and is user-friendly. The effective use of SMS technology may reduce the sense of isolation (for both the learner and the tutor) typically associated with distance education. This is especially important since studies have shown that delayed feedback and lack of learner-tutor interaction are important causes of drop-out in distance learning (Visser, 1998). The initial experiments with SMS have shown encouraging results. The relatively simple interface of cellular phones, combined with the steadily decreasing communication prices, has resulted in student support possibilities that no one could have foreseen ten years ago.

REFERENCES

Human Development Report. Retrieved July 7, 2004 from http://www.undp.org/hdr2003/indicator/cty_f_ZAF.html

Moore, M. G., & Kearsley, G. (1996). *Distance education: A systems view.* Belmont, CA: Wadsworth.

Visser, L. (1998). *The development of motivational communication in distance education.* Unpublished dissertation. Enschede, The Netherlands: University of Twente.

CHAPTER 12

BRITISH DISTANCE EDUCATION

A Proud Tradition

Steve Wheeler

INTRODUCTION

This chapter examines the contribution of British scientists and technol
ogists to the current knowledge and practice of distance education.
Some significant technological contributions are evaluated and the history of distance education in the United Kingdom is traced. The chapter concludes that technology-supported distance education remains a
prevalent force in the UK, and illustrates that conclusion by providing
specific recent examples of prominent e-learning and distance education projects.

A BRITISH LEGACY

Distance education is often perceived to be the preserve of geographically
large nations. For example, countries such as Australia, South Africa and
Canada, all geographically large, are renowned for their use of distance
education to reach and teach remote students, and enjoy a long history of

Trends and Issues in Distance Education: International Perspectives, 137–161
Copyright © 2005 by Information Age Publishing
All rights of reproduction in any form reserved.

doing so. In contrast, the United Kingdom is a small country, and it would be easy therefore to assume that the British are late entrants into the field of distance education. This conclusion, however, would be erroneous. It might be surprising to discover that the British have a proud tradition of distance education that can be traced back to the correspondence courses of the Victorian era. This chapter will outline some of the contributions Britons have made to distance education, as well as the technologies that support distance education. British contributions to distance education throughout the last 150 years have been substantial; this chapter will provide some of the more recent examples of distance education in the United Kingdom. The journey begins in Victorian England.

THE FIRST POST

The Victorian era brought industrialization and change to society, and public communication was one of the areas that experienced substantial change. In 1840, the "penny post," the world's first organized mailing service, was established in England. One of the first people to recognize the tremendous communication potential of this new service was Isaac Pitman. Pitman is now credited with establishing one of the world's first organized correspondence schools, which taught shorthand to a distributed nationwide audience of office workers.

The 'Penny Black'

This was a significant advance on previous forms of correspondence courses, as the penny postal service permitted two-way communication between teacher and student, regardless of their physical locations within England. Pitman mailed via post his instructional manuals, complete with exercises for the distance students to complete. Distance learners would then send their completed exercises back to Pitman's organization for marking and feedback. Thus the correspondence course was birthed as a new form of organized education provision.

Pitman was born into a working class family in Trowbridge, Wiltshire, on January 4th, 1813. He left school when he was 13 years old. He was saddened to have to leave school and requested that he be allowed to return. After being informed that return was not possible, Pitman took a job as a clerk in a counting house. Pitman refused to give up on his education, and soon began to study at home using the little spare time he had available to him. Later, with a wealth of knowledge in his head, he was

Sir Isaac Pitman

appointed to teach at a school in the small English town of Barton-on-Humber, a significant event for someone who had himself not been permitted to return to school. Subsequently, in 1837, Pitman opened his own private school at Wotton-under-Edge. One of the subjects he taught there was shorthand. To support his learners in acquiring shorthand, Pitman wrote a small instructional book on shorthand style, which was eventually developed into a new shorthand system, and named after him.

Pitman continued to work on shorthand instruction, and eventually reduced the main principles of his shorthand system to fit onto postcards. He mailed these to his distance learners, who then transcribed short passages from the Bible into shorthand before mailing their transcriptions back to him for correction. Pitman Shorthand is now the most widely used shorthand system in the world. Although he will probably be best remembered for his shorthand notation system, it is Pitman's work establishing the first organized correspondence course that is of most interest to distance educators. Pitman's distance education system was so successful that, within a few short years, the school had enrolled more than 100,000 students across the UK.

A DEGREE OF DISTANCE

Toward the end of Queen Victoria's reign, in 1890, a Cambridge scholar by the name of Richard Moulton informed his colleagues that he was considering the feasibility of establishing an entire degree program delivered through distance education, using Pitman's correspondence techniques. Moulton's ideas were fiercely rejected by the University's Board of Regents, and so Moulton took his ideas across the Atlantic to try again. Immigration was a huge personal risk, but it ultimately paid dividends. Soon after arriving in the United States, Moulton joined the faculty of the University of Chicago and, within a few years, he was successful in establishing the world's first distance education degree.

Not long afterwards, the correspondence program was enhanced via telecommunications technology, but before this happened, the world was to be introduced to the first computer: the mechanical calculating machine known as the Difference Engine.

TECHNOLOGY-SUPPORTED LEARNING

Considering its comparatively small population, Britain has contributed disproportionately to the rise of technology-supported learning over the last two centuries. One of the most ubiquitous technologies anywhere is the personal computer. Some would argue that the computer is the single most important distance education technology today. But the origins of the computer are in 1821, in the London home of Charles Babbage, the inventor of the Difference Engine.

Babbage was born in London on the day after Christmas, 1791, and died in October 1871. He was reared in a well-to-do family, the son of a London banker. In his early years, this child prodigy taught himself algebra, and developed a keen passion for all things numerical. It was inevitable that he would eventually train formally as a mathematician, and in 1811 Babbage commenced his studies at Trinity College, Cambridge, England. He soon discovered, however, that his tutors had little to teach that he did not already know. He therefore branched out into other scholarly activities, eventually being elected to the Royal

Charles Babbage

Society in 1816. His work also contributed towards the foundation of the Royal Astronomical Society in 1820. He was appointed to the Lucasian Chair of Mathematics at Cambridge University, the prestigious position previously held by Isaac Newton.

During this period of his life, Babbage began to take an interest in the notion of the "calculating machine." He based his ideas on a number of earlier attempts at creating a device that surpassed the capabilities of the ancient abacus. One of Babbage's influences was the earlier attempt at creating a counting machine by the Frenchman Blaise Pascal, in 1694. His idea of a mechanical calculator was also based on the machines that printed logarithmic tables for naval navigation.

Babbage eventually succeeded in securing several government grants with which to build his "Difference Engine." He encountered several technical problems, however, and soon turned his attention to a more sophisticated device, the Analytical Machine, which was designed in two parts, or sections. The first section would store up to 1,000 50-digit numbers, while the second section was designed to process the "data." Punched cards, similar to those used on the Jacquard loom, were used to input instructions. Again, this project was never brought to fruition and, lacking any concrete outcomes, Babbage's work eventually stalled due to lack of interest from the British government and his academic peers.

During his life, Babbage spent more than £17,000—in his day, a small fortune—on his quest to invent. One government official was reported to have declared that the only good use for Babbage's machines was to calculate exactly how much he had spent on his folly. Babbage died a bitter and disappointed man, having invested much of his time and personal fortune into an ambitious and ground-breaking engineering project that showed little positive results during his own lifetime. His legacy and influence on modern life, however, is profound, and Babbage is today rightfully acknowledged as the "Father of Computing," as his work provided the foundation for mechanical and electronic computation in the years to come.

INSTRUCTING THE MACHINE

Another significant figure in computing history was a contemporary of Babbage. Ada Augusta Byron, who was born in 1815 and died in 1852, was the daughter of the poet, Lord Byron. It is reported that she wished to become "an analyst and a metaphysician," and that she was passionate about the advancement of science, an aspiration that women were discouraged from following in 19th century Britain.

At the age of 17, Byron was introduced to Mary Somerville, an English literature scholar. Somerville strongly encouraged her to pursue her mathematical studies, and it was at a dinner party in November, 1834 at Somerville's house that Byron heard of Babbage and his vision of the calculating machine. Babbage was trying to secure funding to build the Analytical Engine, his automatic calculating system, and the successor to his earlier invention, the Difference Engine. Babbage had conjectured that a calculating engine might not only predict, but could also act on a prediction. Byron was very impressed by Babbage's ideas and began to dream about how she could become involved in his project.

In 1843, Byron married the Earl of Lovelace. It was during this time that Byron, now Lady Lovelace, began to correspond with Babbage regarding his attempts to create the Analytical Engine. Letters between the two were reported to be filled with a heady mixture of fact and fantasy, as they both began to speculate on how such a calculating device might be used. In the year of her marriage, Lady Lovelace published an article in which she predicted that Babbage's machine might be used to perform a multitude of tasks, such as playing music, creating pictures, and composing letters. Her vision for the machine included room for both scientific and domestic use and, if one takes a very long view, she was not far off the mark.

Lady Lovelace suggested to Babbage that a plan might be formulated to enable the Difference Engine to calculate "Bernoulli" numbers using punched cards. Later, she conceived the idea that, if certain conditions were met, the machine would be able to jump from one set of punched cards to another. In this way, if the machine was required to repeat a set of instructions, it could simply "jump back" and use the previous set of cards. This concept of efficiency in programming represents the first use of a subroutine, known as a "loop," now commonly used in all computing programs. Lady Lovelace is now acknowledged by many as the world's first computer programmer. Ada Byron, in her collaboration with the genius Charles Babbage, gave the world the second part of the computer equation: the knowledge that it was possible not only to create a computing device, but to write instructions for it to follow so that it could produce a defined result. The modern computer is based upon this premise. In 1979, the U.S. Department of Defense named a computer program "Ada" as a tribute to her pioneering contribution to computing.

THE IMPACT OF THE COMPUTER

When Babbage created his Difference Engine in Victorian England, he would have had no conception of the far reaching effects of his invention. As we have already seen, Babbage's first attempt at creating a machine to mechanically manipulate arithmetic functions became the blueprint for the earliest electronic computers.

Since the end of the 1980s, the computer has entered the world's collective consciousness as a ubiquitous electronic device that affects every aspect of our daily lives. Few would doubt that the computer now strongly influences the way we live, work, communicate, and spend our leisure time. Computers govern the way we account for our finances, the traffic flow in and out of cities, and even the way we pay for our food at the supermarket. The computer is at the very heart of the information revolution, and is a central component of the industrialized world. When connected to the vast global telecommunications network of the Internet, the modern personal computer proves to be a powerful tool. In terms of distance education, the personal computer provides distance learners with opportunities to access learning opportunities they otherwise would not likely enjoy. We can say that Babbage's invention is now "grown up," offering us a multitude of destinations and experiences, and enabling us to explore previously unseen worlds. It is undeniable, therefore, that computers now enable us to work and communicate flexibly and enjoy unprecedented access to information. However, freedom of this kind comes with a price for educators.

COME THE REVOLUTION

History has shown that most revolutions have a dictatorship waiting in the wings. The information revolution is no exception, exuding an element of tyranny. The manner in which computers are employed in some classes has begun to dictate in these setting the way teachers conceptualize and develop courses, design learning materials, manage the virtual learning environment, and assess learning, and communicate with their students. Jonassen, Peck, and Wilson (1999) have responded to this trend, arguing that in order for students to learn effectively from new technology, it will first be necessary for their teachers to accept a new philosophy of teaching and learning. This new model is premised upon educators rejecting the role of the knowledge provider, and instead adopting of the role of facilitator. The "sage on the stage" is rapidly becoming the "guide on the side," and the modern computer is a prime cause of this shift in emphasis.

In light of the impact the computer revolution is having on the traditional classroom, educators are being required to radically alter their mindsets, and perhaps even forget some of the things they learned during their initial teacher training. Educators in today's technology context relinquish a certain amount of intellectual and supervisory authority to students, enabling students to construct their own knowledge structures and attach meaning to them without the influence and bias of the teacher or educational institution. Jonassen et al. believe that if this model is adopted, students will not only maximize their use of technology (including the computer and Internet), but will more freely explore the educational alternatives that will open up for them. There are signs that this is happening in some classrooms.

The personal computer and its associated communication technologies, then, are beginning to change the way teachers think about the nature of learning itself, and the changes in instructional strategy as a result of this change in thinking are occurring with astonishing speed. Babbage's brainchild is, ironically, now altering and supplanting the very education system that was started in his own era.

Another innovation as ubiquitous and, arguably, as influential, as the computer was also invented by a Briton prior to the turn of the 20th century. This invention also has a great deal of impact on the practice of distance education as we understand and practice it today.

RINGING THE CHANGES

Alexander Graham Bell

One of the most influential, and therefore often overlooked, technologies to impact the modern world was invented by a Scot, Alexander Graham Bell. Bell (1847-1922) along with his assistant, Thomas A. Watson, constructed mechanical instruments that transmitted recognizable voice-like sounds. Bell's work led to the invention of the forerunner of the modern telephone, a device which today forms the basis of many communications technologies ranging from the cellular phone to the Internet.

Bell received his official patent to design the telephone on March 7, 1876. Three days later, he and Watson, located in different rooms, tested the new type of transmission device described in his patent. Watson heard Bell's voice through the earpiece saying, "Mr. Watson, come here. I want you." Bell had had an accident with a battery, and had spilled acid over his clothes. He had inadvertently used the telephone to speak to Watson because of this emergency, but when he realized the magnitude of his achievement, the spilled acid was soon forgotten.

The first telephone company, the Bell Telephone Company, was established in 1877 to exploit the potential of Bell's new invention. During his productive career, Bell invented several other devices, but none as long-lasting and influential as the telephone. Technology-assisted distance education owes much to this Scot inventor, who changed the concept of what it meant to communicate with others over great distances. Today, we take for granted the fact that we can dial a number, and somewhere in the world, a corresponding telephone will ring, connecting us to a person whom we can communicate with in real time.

A MAN OF VISION

John Logie Baird, who was born in Helensburgh, Scotland, in 1888, was destined to make a significant impact on telecommunication. Baird is historically celebrated as a man of great vision (television!), but he was the

John Logie Baird with his Disk TV System

inventor of many new technologies, including fiber optics, a technology that looms just as large as TV in the distance education hall of fame.

Although the original term "television" (literally, "to see from a distance") was coined by scientist Constantin Perskyi at a conference in Paris in 1900, it was Baird who is credited with the creation of the first operational device that could transmit pictures. Baird successfully tested the prototype of his mechanically-scanned disk television in the laboratory in 1925, and the device was later demonstrated in public in London in 1926.

However, it was not long before Baird's mechanical version of a "television" was supplanted by electronic television, and electronic television went on to lay the foundation for today's television broadcasts, interactive television, and video conferencing technologies. Nevertheless, Baird's pioneering achievements, including his involvement in the first trans-Atlantic television transmission, were important scientific accomplishments. Baird's far-reaching innovation is exactly that: an invention that enables us to reach across distances to hear and see one another and learn together, regardless of geographic location. The combination of the computer and the television provide the basis upon which visual communication and global information access is now universally implemented.

1945 AND ALL THAT

In 1945, a young English scientist published a somewhat quirky article in the October edition of *Wireless World* magazine, in which he speculated that if three radio transmitters were placed at equidistant points at a precise altitude above the Earth's equator, they would achieve global communication coverage. The author of the article was the celebrated science

Arthur C. Clark

fiction writer Arthur C. Clark, and the article was instrumental in opening the debate about the feasibility of communication satellites. The article, befitting a science fiction author, was entitled Extra-Terrestrial Relays: Can Rocket Stations Give World Wide Radio Coverage? (Clark, 1945). Exactly 12 years later, on October 4th, 1957, the USSR succeeded in launching the world's first artificial satellite, Sputnik, and the Space Race began.

The most important aspect of Clark's theory was the placement of the satellite at a precise orbit of 22,300 miles above the equator. At this altitude, Clark speculated, the satellite would have exactly the same speed as the rotational speed (or angular velocity) of the Earth, and it would therefore appear to be stationary in the sky. This technique, now called geosynchronous orbit, has become a common means of enabling satellite users to dispense with expensive tracking devices. Communication satellites are placed into geosynchronous orbit, and the area of optimum distance above the equator is now referred to as the Clark Belt. Clark, who was knighted for his services to science, now lives in retirement on the island of Sri Lanka. The important role of satellite technology in distance education will be described in greater depth later in this chapter.

ENQUIRE WITHIN UPON EVERYTHING

Enquire Within Upon Everything was an obscure computer program designed almost 25 years ago by a software consultant named Tim Berners-Lee. The program may have been obscure, but it was also ground-breaking, as the program encapsulated the key ideas that would eventually enable Internet users to link their personal computers to a worldwide storehouse of information.

Berners-Lee was born in London in 1955. In 1976, he graduated from Queen's College, Oxford University, and eventually started work at CERN, the European nuclear research facility in Switzerland. At that time there was a need to facilitate better communication

Tim Berners-Lee

and collaboration between the scientists who were engaged in the study of high energy physics. While working as a computer software consultant, Berners-Lee began to consider this problem, pondering how scientists could access information via computer on the emerging world-wide phenomenon that was beginning to be referred to as the Internet. In 1989, Berners-Lee proposed a global hypertext project which he called the World Wide Web. Two years later, in 1991 his ideas had crystallized on the Internet when the first Web server went "live." By 1993, the principles of his browser-based system were being championed by the University of Illinois in the United States. A year later, in 1994, Berners-Lee joined the Massachusetts Institute of Technology, where he headed up the fledgling W3 Consortium.

The Web is a truly unique and all-pervasive innovation. Without the Web, it is doubtful that the Internet would be as successful as it has become. Web browsers make accessing information via the Internet much more user-friendly, and provide an intuitive navigation system that requires very little training to use. Berners-Lee has campaigned tirelessly to keep the Web open and free, and this is possibly one reason why the Web remains largely an un-policed, imaginatively fertile and unpredictable aspect of distance education.

THE BEST OF BRITISH

We have taken a historical perspective on the development of distance learning technologies and focused upon Britain's significant contributions to these technologies. The remainder of this chapter is dedicated to providing an account of some of the best practices of distance education within the United Kingdom. There is no better place to start than the establishment of a ground-breaking contribution to distance education: the British Open University.

THE UNIVERSITY OF THE "SECOND CHANCE"

When Prime Minister Harold Wilson was approached in the 1960s to ask whether his government would consider setting up a University founded on learning via broadcast technology, he quickly took up the idea and commissioned a team of experts to conduct a feasibility study. Soon afterwards, Walter Perry was appointed the University's first Vice-Chancellor (President). One of the distance education specialists invited to participate in the government's committee was the American Charles Wedemeyer of the University of Wisconsin. In Wedemeyer's view, distance education was the means by which education could be provided cheaply and accessibly for all people. This liberalized approach to education, coupled with the industrialized model of distance education put forward by German Otto Peters, became the early philosophy upon which the British Open University (OU) was founded (Moore & Kearsley, 1996).

Originally called the University of the Air due to its early basis in television and radio, the OU was eventually established as an autonomous academic institution in 1969. The OU delivers its courses through a combination of paper-based, television, and radio technologies (via the government owned British Broadcasting Company, the BBC), and is also increasingly using a range of computer-mediated communications methods to connect its distributed audience of students. The OU also makes effective use of a nationwide (and international) network of tutor/counselors, who provide the human face of the vast organization. Some of the courses offered by the OU feature summer schools, week-long events that are conducted at traditional universities around the UK during the "down time" of the summer months. In summer school, the distance education student can spend an intensive seven days in the company of like-minded students, engaging in a range of discussions, lectures, and exercises designed to enhance and support the program's distance learning materials. Courses are offered in a range of subjects including the sciences, technology, social sciences, liberal arts, business studies, and languages, from undergraduate to doctoral level. In conjunction with local schools throughout the British Isles, the OU has for some time also offered a practice-based postgraduate teacher certificate. Of the 23 major subjects offered by the OU, 17 were recently awarded an "excellent" status by the UK government's academic standards watchdog, the Quality Assessment Agency (QAA).

The British Open University is now widely recognized as one of the most successful educational institutions in the world, with distance learners on all continents. Twenty-two per cent of the UK's part-time higher education students are studying with the OU, and 70 percent of these remain in full time employment as they study. More than two-thirds of the OU's registered students are aged between 25-44 years. These statistics reveal that over the past 30 years, mature, employed students have been able to access higher education in a manner that suits their lifestyles and domestic commitments. It is not without reason that the British Open University has been dubbed the "University of the Second Chance."

TELEMATICS AND A RATIO OF SUCCESS

Distance educators in the United Kingdom are relying increasingly upon telematic solutions to connect with remote learners across geographical

distance. Telematics is the convergent action of computers and telecommunications, and is based upon a combination of networks and telephony
(Wheeler & Vranch, 2001). One project that was early to exploit the
potential of telematic technologies for distance learning was established
in 1996 in South West England.

In the early 1990s, England's last tin mine (the Wheal Jane Mine in
Cornwall) was closed due to its lack of economic viability. For many Cor-
nish folk, this was the final "nail in the coffin" for a region already suffering from a downturn in the fortunes of its principal income sources
(fishing and agriculture). The region was left with a sole industry with
which to eke out a precarious income: tourism. Economic recession
loomed on the horizon.

Economic regeneration was the subject of much discussion, and many
agreed that the best way to turn around the economic fortunes of Cornwall was to retrain people for alternative forms of employment, including
tele-working. Opportunities for retraining those who were redundant
workers were few and far between, however, due to the poor travel infrastructure and extensive rural areas. For many, the nearest college of further education was inconveniently distant, and this large-scale problem
demanded some type of innovative solution.

That innovation came in the form of a European Social Fund Grant
from the European Union. In 1995, the University of Plymouth, working
in partnership with a number of public and private organizations
throughout the South West of England, was successful in securing almost
£5 million from the European Union to develop and manage a distance
education technical infrastructure. The Rural Area Training and Information Opportunities Project (RATIO) was commissioned to establish 40
telematic distance learning centers in the remote rural areas of Cornwall,
Devon, and Somerset. The goal was that no one living in the region would
be more than ten miles from a RATIO center. Many of the courses were to
be offered freely, or at nominal fees, to encourage locals to take up the
training.

Between 1996 and 1999, and in consultation with local communities,
RATIO set up centers in community centers, wine bars, and church halls
to provide outreach facilities for the region's further and higher education providers. Each college in the region was invited to submit a portfolio of distance-delivered courses that could be offered in the centers,
using a combination of telematic technologies including videoconference,
Internet, and satellite television. Each of the RATIO centers was given a
range of networked personal computers, videoconferencing equipment,
and digital satellite television reception kits. Center managers were
appointed and, in 1997, the first RATIO center opened its doors to the
general public.

In 1997, RATIO transmitted the UK's first live digital satellite pictures from the studios of the University of Plymouth, beating the government sponsored BBC and independent satellite company British SKY Broadcasting, by over six months. Soon RATIO was broadcasting several hours of quality training live via satellite throughout the region, and distance learners at the centers were able to interact with studio experts through a combination of telephone, video link, and e-mail.

Throughout its three years of European funding, the RATIO project provided training for more than 3000 people working in small businesses in areas such as computers, languages, business, and computer-aided design. RATIO's legacy is a network of learning centers, many of which are now independent and still operational, helping to provide training updates and opportunities that contribute to a better-equipped work force, and much-needed regeneration for the faltering rural economy of the South West of England. For a more comprehensive account of the RATIO project and the use of convergent technologies (telematics), see Wheeler (1999).

MASTERING DISTANCE EDUCATION

The University of Plymouth is one of the largest in the United Kingdom, with almost 30,000 full-time equivalent students on six campuses spread over 150 miles of the South West region of England. The University's Integrated Masters Program (IMP) was created to provide flexibility in the support of continual professional development at postgraduate level and offers a modular pathway to a Master's in Arts (MA) award. Many of the students taking postgraduate courses at the University are mature students who already have a professional career, such as nursing or teaching. The University of Plymouth has developed distance education modules for this audience. One of these modules, addressing the theoretical issues of educational information and communications technology (ICT), was twice successfully delivered in 2001-2002 using Web- and videoconference-based technologies.

Master's students in the IMP are graduate educators working as primary or secondary school teachers or lecturers in further or higher education. These individuals are all employed on a full-time basis, and many have family commitments. These students therefore require flexible study routines to maximize their precious spare time. Flexibility can be measured not only in terms of the students' choice of where to study and when to study, but also by personal control over the study regime. Thus, travel is reduced to a minimum and students can choose the time of the day they study, as well as the pace of study.

The educational ICT module is presented as a blended learning program, incorporating a mix of face-to-face, online, and videoconferencing delivery methods. Students are assigned to regional clusters, and are encouraged to discuss their ideas and to work collaboratively within a managed learning environment known as MTutor. MTutor was created by the University of Plymouth's Faculty of Technology, a department specializing in research into artificial intelligence. MTutor provides a multi-screen Internet-based environment in which ill-structured problems are presented to students, who work to solve these problems at their own pace. Students place their own emphases on the problems and solve them within their own individualized professional contexts.

The designers of MTutor have incorporated an intelligent tracking system into its functionality, which enables course tutors to monitor students' progress through a series of online activities. A "meeting of minds" occurs when the students within the clusters begin to discuss their solutions online and develop a community of practice through collaborative learning. Students have reported that they value this distance learning approach greatly as it affords them access to expert solutions to authentic problems as well as enabling them to participate within a community of practice to which they would not normally have access. The technology is used to create the electronic meeting place in which dispersed groups of professionals are connected week by week as they work towards their Master's degree. For a more substantial account of the MTutor project, see Culverhouse and Burton (2001).

TAKING THE HIGH ROAD

Located in the most northerly reaches of the UK, the highlands and isles of Scotland is another predominantly rural area of the United Kingdom. It makes up approximately 20 per cent of the land mass of the United Kingdom and includes over 90 inhabited islands. Yet the highlanders and islanders, like any other part of the world, experience their own unique set of problems related to education. Rural isolation and inadequate travel infrastructures, for example, create a set of problems for the region's students similar to that of the South West of England. In addition, the region's economy is heavily dependent upon small and medium-sized enterprises (SMEs). The work force is generally low-skilled with above average numbers of self-employed, part-time, and unemployed workers. It is easy to see, therefore, that demands for access into training and higher education are high.

Against this background, the University of the Highlands and Islands (UHI) was established to provide the desired educational opportunities, opportunities which can in turn contribute toward the economic regeneration of the region. UHI is also aimed at social and cultural development of its students, and many who have visited the UHI would agree that it is an exemplar for distributed education in the 21st century.

According to the UHI Website (see below) up to 15 community "outreach centers" (similar to the RATIO centers of South West England) have been established in remote sites across the region to widen the operational base of the 13 colleges in the partnership. The UHI's courses include degree level studies in Art & Design, Business & Management, Information Science & Computing, Construction & Technology, Culture & Heritage, Health, Education, & Care, and Science & Environment. The UHI has also developed a number of collaborative distance learning programs in partnership with universities in Ireland, Norway, Iceland, and Canada. Computer literacy is a central tenet of the UHI, and each student engages in blended learning activities that focus on autonomous independent study as well as teamwork and communication skills development to prepare them for a career in industry or small business. Students engage in up to six months' placement in industry prior to completing their course, and distance education throughout a student's time at UHI is a key strategy.

UHI has suggested that it is a prototypical university for the 21st century:

> Is UHI really a prototype university for the 21st century? Very likely. It certainly represents a radical break from higher education tradition within the British Commonwealth and clearly challenges the prevailing worldwide university model. [....] Its distinguishing features are student-managed learning, mass access, flexible entry and exit, multiple partnerships, stakeholder consultation and accountability, a competencies based curriculum oriented towards regional economic and social development, substantial investment in information and communication technology, and a lifelong relationship with learners. If UHI doesn't foreshadow the future of higher education, it certainly represents a bold transitional step in that direction. (www.uhi.ac.uk, 2003)

This bold but probably prescient statement underlines the growing confidence exuding from many of the British higher education institutions in recent years. The UHI and other initiatives like it are making huge inroads into previously inaccessible areas, and providing opportunities for formerly disenfranchised individuals. Another such case is the ALPs project of the Welsh valleys, described in the following section.

VIDEOCONFERENCING IN THE WELSH VALLEYS: THE ALPS PROJECT

ALPs (Adult Learner Partnerships), is a distance education project located in the valleys of South Wales featuring the use of PC-based videoconferencing systems installed in remote community centers. These systems, together with a range of interactive "distance" tutorials, were used to create a bridge between distance students and their tutors at the University of Glamorgan. The ALPs Website relates the project's mission statement:

> The main objective of the ALPs project was to build on the University of Glamorgan's track record of developing public educational opportunities for residents of the Valleys, and to do so using 'frontline' resources. A key finding was that younger age groups found the medium more attractive to use than adults, that the PC and office-based system for videoconferencing provided greater flexibility in scheduling and initiating communication than more expensive or room-based systems, and that community partners needed considerable ongoing support in order to maintain skill levels and usability of the equipment. From a teaching point of view, the ability to share data was invaluable, and allowed us to target help to individual learners in a very positive way. (www.jisc.ac.uk/jtap/word/jtap-035.doc, 2003)

The ALPs project has achieved a high level of success because it has demonstrated a "friendly university at a distance" approach promoting informal contact via the desktop videoconferencing systems. In this way it has demystified degree-level study by using low-tech examples of distance education. The project partners discovered that PC-based videoconferencing was both inexpensive and transparent. It was easy to use, and it helped distance learners to exploit the potential of simple videoconferencing in widening access to higher education opportunities.

LONG-DISTANCE SURGERY

Training surgeons has always been an expensive proposition, and for good reason: in order to enable an individual to achieve the highest professional standards required of a surgeon, trainee surgeons must undergo intensive training, supervision, and clinical practice. In the UK, trainee surgeons spend many hours in the operating room, where they acquire and hone a comprehensive range of specialized and precision skills. Many hours are also spent in the traditional classroom to learn conceptual, theoretical, and factual information surrounding the medical field. In due course, the doctor sits a comprehensive examination, and if the examiners are satisfied, the doctor is invited to become a member of the Royal

College of Surgeons. It is at this point that the doctor is deemed qualified to specialize in a particular field of surgery. This approach has been the "tried and tested" traditional training model until just recently, when new approaches to training began to appear.

Working in conjunction with the RCS and local hospitals in the South West of England, the University of Plymouth was successful in securing a large research grant from the European Space Agency (ESA) to enable the University to set up and deliver a theory program for trainee surgeons across the South West using a powerful combination of satellite television, videoconference, and Web-based teaching and learning. This model was similar to the RATIO model, but the receiving centers in this case were located in hospitals, and the audience the trainee surgeons. Live programs from the TV studio on Plymouth Hoe were broadcast each week via satellite, and contained a mixture of transmissions of live surgery (transmitted from connected hospitals across the UK and Europe by ISDN 3 cable), expert commentary and lectures, as well as discussion and magazine style presentations.

Within a year, the training project was so successful that as many as 32 hospitals in the UK and Ireland were soon participating in the scheme. In 2002, the scheme became a subscriber-based program, and now operates largely on a commercial basis. Ultimately the program will extend the program's delivery to hospitals in other European nations (Kingsnorth, Campbell, Vranch, & Wheeler, 1999).

LONDON'S ONLINE

Established in 1836, the University of London is one of the oldest of the British Universities. Throughout its long and illustrious lifetime, the university has evolved to become a collegiate university consisting of eighteen self-governing Colleges and Institutes across the span of the nation's capital. It is recognized as a center of excellence and a University open to all regardless of race, creed, or political orientation.

Upwards of 100,000 students study at the University of London, and there are an additional 30,000 students studying through the University of London's overseas program. These students are registered through the University's External Program in over 190 countries across the world, making London one of the largest universities in the United Kingdom and a rival to the British Open University. The External Program was set up in 1858 to make University of London degrees available to students who, for one reason or another, could not come to the University to study in the traditional manner. Studying through the External Program provides an attractive option for those with financial constraints, commitments to work or family, or lack of local access to higher education. Most of the degree courses are delivered by a combination of electronic and correspondence modes.

RESEARCH INTO ADVANCED TECHNOLOGIES

The northwest of England is home to the town of Lancaster and the University of Lancaster, a smaller university, but one with large aspirations. Over the last decade, the University of Lancaster has attracted much respect from the British academic community for its research into advanced technologies, and the University has also garnered a reputation for good practice using these technologies. The Learning from Home course program is one such example of Lancaster's efforts into distance education. From the University of Lancaster's Website, we read:

> Learning from Home courses are just that—they mean that you can learn from home. Some people like the flexibility they offer, others like the independence they allow. Courses are based around a variety of media such as video recordings, texts and audio tape and some use the Internet. A number of courses offer workshops or study days to supplement your independent learning. All courses offer tutor support in some form—mainly by telephone, but also by email, web-based work space (Internet courses) and sometimes in person. Practical project work is encouraged. (www.lancs.ac.uk, 2003)

One of the most innovative aspects of Lancaster University's operations resides in the Center for Advanced Technology Research. Led by Professor Peter Goodyear, the center was instrumental in establishing a range of high profile technology-supported learning programs. One of the most highly regarded is the CSALT Project, which was funded by a UK government agency—the Joint Information Systems Committee (JISC)—an organization set up to fund research into educational technology.

The CSALT project brought a very clear focus to the issues surrounding distance education, particularly those related to the use of networked learning, and attempted to build and improve upon the current level of understanding of these issues. CSALT also set out to refine evaluation methods used in the distance context to enable researchers to better identify the needs of both distance- and campus-based networked learners. Says the project's Website:

> The domain of networked learning remains dangerously fragmented: in effect there are two largely separate "worlds" of networked learning. Most

research and practical experience has been in the areas of asynchronous text-based or synchronous multimedia communications.... These two worlds are inhabited by two distinct communities of HE practitioners. There has been little cross-fertilization of ideas and experience. (http:// csalt.lancs.ac.uk/jisc/default.htm, 2003)

Research of this nature is essential for the future development and optimization of distributed, network-based learning.

ULTRA SOLUTIONS

Based in the flatland East coast of England, Ultralab—a research laboratory in the University Polytechnic of East Anglia—holds the claim as Europe's premier learning technology research center. This claim is not without merit, as Ultralab boasts an impressive portfolio of successful technology-supported learning projects that span more than a decade. Led by Professor Stephen Heppell, Ultralab is founded on the premise that creativity and community are the key components of learning in a connected society. Its innovative streaming media project, Ultralab TV, is a prime example of its use of technologies to mediate the process of learning for remotely located students (see www.ultralab.tv for more on this project).

Ultralab has a worldwide influence based on a number of projects that are global in scale. Its focus, however, is centered primarily on the United Kingdom. Although Ultralab focuses on sustaining the teaching profession throughout the United Kingdom, it has also funded a number of innovative projects, including a partial funding of one year at the University for Industry Online Learning Network (OLN). The OLN was established in 1997, and was aimed at developing connectivity and distance learning links between higher education and industry (see www.ultralab.ac.uk/projects/university_for_industry_oln/ for more details).

Sodium is another ground breaking project from Ultralab. In its own words, Sodium is a new business start-up based at Ultralab. The 'Lab, together with the government's Creative Industries Task Force, is looking to make more effective bridges between high-tech research and the fast-emerging digital creative industries (www.ultralab.ac.uk/projects/sodium/, 2003). Sodium clearly establishes and exploits the link between industry and the power and potential of distance learning through digital media.

Two projects aimed at supporting serving teachers were inaugurated by Ultralab in 2000. The first, Talking Heads, was an online community established to support the work of 1200 newly appointed head teachers (principals). Details on Talking Heads can be found at:

www.ultralab.ac.uk/projects/talking_heads. The second project, Teacher-
Net UK, was established on similar lines to support the professional
development of newly-qualified teachers using virtual technologies.
Both projects were a great success, raising the awareness of teachers to
the potential of online technologies in the process. More on Teacher-
Net UK project can be found at: www.ultralab.ac.uk/projects/
teachernet_uk.

The Notschool.net Project is an online virtual learning community of
young people, primarily teenagers, who have been excluded for one reason or another from mainstream schooling. Notschool.net provides a virtual community of learners, teachers, and experts who share the use of
innovative learning tools. Notschool.net also supports parents and children who have opted for home schooling, and ultimately seeks to provide
a route back into mainstream education.

Stephen Heppell has the final word on the phenomenon that is
Ultralab. Focusing on his team's work in Scotland, he says:

> At this stage in the new communication age, the countries best placed to
> take advantage are those small enough to be agile, with cultural stability, a
> history of intellectual endeavour and a clear commitment to education.
> Scotland has all the potential to lead the world in this and a history that sug-
> gests that she might. (http://www.ultralab.ac.uk, 2003)

TAPPING INTO THE GRID

When the New Labour government was elected in England in May 1997,
the country's new Prime Minister, Tony Blair, appointed his first Education Secretary, David Blunkett, to the office of Secretary of State for Education. During his first few weeks in office, Blunkett began to put into a
place an ambitious plan that would result in the connecting of all of Britain's schools to the Internet by the year 2002. Known as the National Grid
for Learning (NGfL), the project was a multi-million pound operation
that changed the fabric of British compulsory education. The home page
of the project's Website is depicted in Figure 12.1.

The NGfL is a battery of electronic resources and networked infrastructures created by the UK Government to aid the process of raising education standards and to provide support for lifelong learning. In order to
optimize access to these resources, the government has helped local education authorities and schools to fund connection to the Internet. In its
election pledge in 1997, Blair's government promised to connect all pub-
licly-funded schools to the Internet by 2002, and this goal was ultimately
achieved on schedule. One of the earliest beneficiaries of the powerful

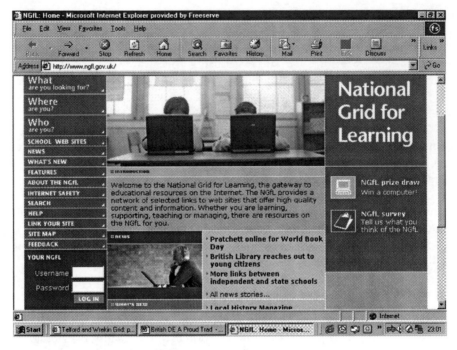

Figure 12.1.   National Grid for Learning Website.

potential of the NGfL is the Wrekin and Telford Grid project located in the West Midlands of England.

THE TELFORD AND WREKIN GRID

Children in an area of the English Midlands have recently benefited from a £12 million government education technology grant that has been used to provide an advanced educational computer network which is set to change the face of their learning experience. The Telford and Wrekin Grid is the most sophisticated e-Learning project in the United Kingdom, featuring the first secure high-speed broadband network in the country. It is also currently the largest school-based interactive video network in Europe.

Telford and Wrekin Council was awarded "pathfinder status" for NGfL by the government and as a result has adopted an innovative approach to connecting to schools to the Internet. For the past few years, it has been developing a community-based network for learning, achieved by connecting schools together into an advanced distributed server system with shared access to the Internet.

Appropriate teaching and learning resources have been developed by schools for sharing and development. School children and their teachers will also receive interactive video tuition. The project reports that 500 desktop videoconferencing systems and 15 group conferencing systems have been purchased to facilitate both individual tuition and group sessions.

Students will have the option of attending specialist lectures at a distance, and groups will be able to take part in synchronous lessons, such as virtual cultural exchanges and language learning with foreign schools. Classes can also be broadcast simultaneously to any of the schools in the network direct from a centralized service provided by the local education authority. All students have been given a personal e-mail address which they will keep throughout their lifelong learning experience.

A COMMUNITY ONLINE

Following the success in schools, the Telford & Wrekin Grid is now being extended into homes and the community at large by means of secure, digital remote access. Planners hope that this outreach will enable teachers, pupils, and parents to connect to their school at any time and from any place. This facility is expected to play a vital role in enabling parents to become more fully involved in their child's education. The network will eventually enable community members to gain access to online information and educational services from a wider range of public services, including libraries, courts, and community centers. This effort is in line with the UK government's vision of lifelong learning and career development for the whole community. (One of the key debates in schools throughout the Internet world is how to protect children from exposure to undesirable content on the Web. The Telford and Wrekin Grid provides Symantec "I" software on every networked personal computer to make the Web safer for young users.) Councillor Sue Davis, the Chair of Education and Training at Telford & Wrekin Council has declared that "This exciting initiative will allow adults and children to plug into new opportunities. By making the most of this technology, local learners of any age will be able to get in touch with people and communities in countries across the world" (www.taw.org.uk/ngflMain.htm, 2003).

BRINGING THE CLASSROOM TO THE WORLD

Multimedia was once acclaimed as the means to "bring the world to the classroom." Now, with the advent of Web-based learning, it is possible to bring the classroom to the world. One new initiative that at the time of writing is making its bid to achieve this is the UK e-Universities Initiative.

UK e-Universities (UKeU) is a British government-supported initiative that has been created to provide flexible, open access higher education opportunities and continual professional development for the global student population. Launched in the spring of 2003, the UKeU is a consortium of British universities including Cambridge, York, and Sheffield Hallam. The participating Universities will offer postgraduate qualifications predominantly through distance education (e-learning) via this initiative. The UKeU is funded through a mix of public and private monies, including an initial investment of £62 million from central government funds and a commitment of over £5 million from Sun Microsystems, with Sun providing the necessary delivery platform. The initiative's Website declares the following information to potential students:

> The UKeU platform is being built from scratch specifically to meet the needs of remote adult learners at university level. It is based on an Open Systems architecture and will be the first such platform designed exclusively for distance learning. The platform has been developed following extensive consultation with academic eLearning specialists, librarians and university administrators. (www.ukeu.com, 2003)

UKeU promises a world-class delivery platform with a secure digital learning environment for all its students, using differentiated protocols to ensure the best possible access and connectivity for all participating students, regardless of their physical location and the type of bandwidth and hardware platforms that they utilize. UKeU also promises customized courses to satisfy diverse needs of remote learners. All courses will be delivered through a combination of Internet and course textbook mailouts, with other multimedia materials in support, and with tutors available in much the same manner as the model operated by the British Open University. Students' assignments will be sent electronically for grading and will receive feedback from their tutors in what is an electronic version of the first correspondence courses implemented more than 100 years ago.

CONCLUSION AND SUMMARY

In this brief account of the current state of British technology-supported distance education, there is a great deal of history on which we might reflect. This Island Kingdom is replete with innovative educational activity, with most of the country's higher and further education institutes actively engaged in investing time and effort to exploit the new markets that continue to arise with the expansion of technology. It is interesting to note that the ethos has turned full circle for British distance education, with many contemporary education institutes returning to the roots of Pitman's correspondence course ideal.

There is, however, one major difference between Pitman's day and today: distance learners and their tutors no longer have to wait for the mailman to arrive. Now learners and tutors communicate at the speed of light.

REFERENCES

ALPS Project: Videoconferencing in the Welsh Valleys (2003). Retrieved from www.jisc.ac.uk/index.cfm?name=project_alps

Clark, A. C. (1945, October). Extra terrestrial relays: Can rocket stations give world wide radio coverage? *Wireless World*. 305-308.

CSALT Project: Lancaster University (2003). Retrieved from csalt.lancs.ac.uk/jisc/default.htm

Culverhouse, P., & Burton, C. (2001) Learning best-practice in design and problem-solving skill development: MTutor: A Web-based distance learning tool. *Quarterly Review of Distance Education, 2*(3), 221-232.

Encyclopedia Online. (2003). Retrieved from www.encyclopedia.com

Jonassen, D. H., Peck, K. L., & Wilson, B. G. (1999). *Learning with technology: A constructivist perspective*. Upper Saddle River, NJ: Merrill Prentice Hall

Kingsnorth, A., Vranch, A. T., Campbell, J., & Wheeler, S. (1999). *The digital surgeon: Training surgeons using telematics*. Paper presented at the World Conference on Open Learning. Vienna, Austria. June 1999.

Moore, M. G., & Kearsley, G. (1996). *Distance education: A systems view*. Belmont, CA: Wadsworth

The National Grid for Learning. (2003). Retrieved from www.ngfl.gov.uk

The Telford and Wrekin Grid. (2003). Online. Retrieved from www.taw.org.uk/ngflMain.htm

The United Kingdom e-Universities Initiative. (2003). Retrieved from www.ukeu.ac.uk/default.htm

The University of the Highlands and Islands. (2003). Retrieved from www.uhi.ac.uk

Wheeler, S. (1999). Convergent technologies in distance learning delivery. *Tech Trends, 43*(5) 19-22.

Wheeler, S., & Vranch, A. T. (2001). Building for the future of educational telematics: Foundations, models and frameworks. *International Journal of Engineering Education, 17*(2) 145-152.

UltraLab Project, University Polytechnic of East Anglia. (2003). Retrieved from www.ultralab.ac.uk

CHAPTER 13

TRENDS AND ISSUES IN THE DEVELOPMENT OF DISTANCE EDUCATION IN TURKEY

Ugur Demiray

INTRODUCTION

Corporations, institutions, colleges, and universities have realized that distance education, when properly implemented, is one of the most effective, economical, and productive modes of delivering instruction. This realization has motivated such institutions to use distance education to deliver high-quality training and education to their personnel, clients, and students, and do so in a cost-effective manner. The success of distance learning in corporate settings may be one of the primary reasons that distance education has received increased attention during the last two decades. It appears that the trend for the foreseeable future is that the distance education modality is going to be one of the most widely used modes of delivering instruction in virtually all teaching and learning areas, but especially in corporate training and education.

The success of distance education efforts can partly be seen by the sheer learner numbers such programs encompass. Large open universities, sometimes enrolling as many as half a million students, have been estab-

Trends and Issues in Distance Education: International Perspectives, 163–170
Copyright © 2005 by Information Age Publishing
All rights of reproduction in any form reserved.

lished all over the world, including the Chinese Radio and Television University, the Sukhothai Trammathirat Open University (STOU) in Thailand, and the Universitas Terbuka (UT) in Indonesia. The Anadolu Open University in Turkey, with more than 500,000 students in 2000, has already trained and graduated 200,000 teachers, and its programs now reach Turkish citizens living in Germany and other West European countries. The Open High School (OHS) in Turkey, which began offering distance education in 1992 with 45,000 students, now has 637,161 students and 143,000 graduates (Demiray, 2002a). Although steadily rising numbers alone do not alone tell the story of distance education, they are a partial indicator of success.

THE HISTORY OF DISTANCE EDUCATION IN TURKEY

Turkey has the unique geographic position of straddling two continents. With one foot resting in Europe (Istanbul and Thrace) and the other planted in Asia (Anatolia), modern Turkey is in a good position to learn from the successes and failures of its neighbors. Since 1923, when Atatürk founded the Turkish Republic, Turkey has used the European model for its economic, political and educational development while maintaining its cultural ties with the East. Many Turkish art forms, such as shadow theater, music, dance and literature have their roots in Asia. Similar to its Asian neighbors, Turkey, with a population of over 65 million people, is a developing country. Institutions of higher education in Turkey have traditionally modeled their programs after their British, German and American counterparts. However the educational problems facing Turkey more closely resemble those of their Asian than their European neighbors (McIsaac, Murphy, & Demiray, 1988).

Distance education in Turkey was first discussed in 1927, in a meeting at which educational problems were debated. The resultant proposal was that distance education could be used to make the people literate (Alkan, 1987). For many years, however, distance education could not be applied in Turkey for political reasons. Ankara University offered the first concrete and significant application of distance education in Turkey in 1956 for training bank personnel. Five years later, the Education Center was established under the management of the Ministry of National Education, which offered a variety of courses. Between 1975 and 1978, the Ministry of National Education started an experimental distance education program using print and television technologies. This program was coordinated by the Institute for the Diffusion of Higher Education, referred to as YAY-KUR. This attempt at distance education was not a success, likely because the program was hastily conceived and never fully integrated into the existing educational system.

In the 1970s, another institution, the Eskisehir Academy of Economics and Commercial Sciences (EAECS) was established, and was later renamed Anadolu University. It soon became a leader in the field in Turkey by organizing research areas, offering symposia, and national and international seminars and conferences.

After 1980, developments in distance education in Turkey accelerated. In 1981, it was decided that all universities should offer distance education as part of their educational offerings. Anadolu University Open Education Faculty (OEF) immediately started its distance efforts, and in 1983 enrolled 29,445 students in the Business Administration and Economics programs. In 1992, the Open High School (OHS) was established based on the OEF model. OHS' first enrollment was 44,151 students. Today, OHS has more than 600,000 students. In 1998, basic education was expanded throught the establishment of the Open Primary School (OPS). In 2002, OPS had 308,153 enrolled students (Demiray et al., 2002b). Another area where distance education is currently implemented is the Vocational and Technical Open Education School, which offers certificate programs. In 2002, this institute had more than 2,000 students enrolled.

In Turkey in 2001, a total of 479,317 of the nearly 1,500,000 candidates could enroll in university programs, while 297,971 students were placed in traditional university programs, and 181,346 students in the Open Education Faculty (OEF) programs. In 2001, the Open Education Faculty had a total of 524,494 students.

Some Notes on the Applied Programs of the OEF in Recent Years

The OEF has experienced a diverse and successful set of distance programs over the years. The OEF Teacher Training programs, for example, have enrolled more than 200,000 students from Turkey, and have also enrolled Turkish citizens living and working in a variety of European countries, including Germany, Belgium, The Netherlands, Switzerland, France and Austria. The OEF has also experienced success with its Certificate Programs in Tourism program as well as its training for Private Sector Companies, among others.

In 2003, the OEF started two-year associate degree programs for the Police Force, which falls under the responsibility of the Ministry of the Interior (42,508 male and 903 female students), and for Military Police (29,778 male and three female students), which falls under the responsibility of the Army. OEF initially supported its students through printed materials, TV, and radio programs, as well as academic counseling. Later on, OEF added video education centers, a newspaper, computer centers, a computer-supported education unit, CD-ROMs, and Internet technologies to support its course offerings.

THE ANADOLU UNIVERSITY

The Anadolu University and its distance education branch, the OEF, are financed by the Government. OEF has one dean and four vice-deans, each with different responsibilities in the areas of registration, regional offices, and organization of academic counseling, exams, course materials, media production and delivery from OEF radio and television studios, projects, and international relations and international projects. Today, OEF's programs offer more than 20 associate's degrees and three bachelor's degree programs. As mentioned above, the University has witnessed a large increase in student admissions, from 29,445 enrollees in 1982 to 636,439 in 2000.

Printed learning materials are designed by the academic staff from various universities and edited by the faculty members of Anadolu University according to the principles and techniques of distance learning. These materials are sent to the students by regular postal channels or distributed via student offices.

Table 13.1.   Examples of the Growth of Active and Passive Student Populations

Academic Year	Business, Administration and Economics Degree Programs	Open Faculty (2-year Associate Degree Progam)	Total # Students
1982-1983	29.445	n.a.	29.445
1998-1999	320.282	199.909	520.191

Source: Ozkul (2001).

Table 13.2.   Examples of Graduates per Year

Academic Year	Economics (University Degree Programs)	Business Administration (University Degree Programs)	Open Education Faculty (Associate Degree Programs)	Total
1985-1986	2,866	1,792	—	4,658
1997-1998	6,992	8,632	25,966	41,590
Total	51,387	69,770	73,651	194,808

Source: Ozkul, A. E. (2001)

The composition of students in the OEF varies from program to program. In some programs, such as the teacher training and nursing education programs, students are already working in their areas of specialization, and tend to be more mature. In the Tourism Certificate program, on the other hand, students are typically younger and are not yet working in their subject area. In the business administration and economics program, the percentage of working students increased from 30% in 1983 to 70% in 2002. Overall, the percentage of females enrolled is increasing, but males comprise 60 percent of enrollment. The age range of students across all subjects in the OEF is different from that found in traditional institutions. The students range from 17 years to 80 years old. The majority of students are married and the family average is three children.

The average duration of study is, of course, different for associate's and bachelor's degree graduates. For the two year associate's degree programs, average duration of study is 3.4 years, and for bachelor's degree graduates, 6.2 years. Approximately 70% of the students hold full time employment, and 8% work part-time.

Trends and Issues in the Open Education Faculty

Howell et al. (2004) have identified 32 trends in Turkish distance education, including student enrollment, distance learner profiles, faculty trends, changing instructor roles, technology changes, economic changes, recognition of educational needs, distance learning trends and leadership vision trends. It is interesting to note that some of these trends are identical to those found in the Open Education Faculty in Turkey. We now briefly describe each of these trends in turn.

Student Enrollment

The current Distance Education facilities at the Anadolu University and also at other higher education institutions in Turkey cannot accommodate the growing college-aged population and the increased enrollments. A proposed solution is to increase the number of distance education institutions, programs, and offerings.

Distance Learner Profiles

Turkey has witnessed a change in student profiles. For example, the percentage of female and minority learners is steadily increasing while, at the same time, enrollment age is lowering. In addition, a greater number of students are working.

Changing Instructor Roles

One of the important issues in education over the past ten years has been the changing role of the educator/instructor. In the past, Turkish instructors were viewed as both the owners and deliverers of the knowledge (the "sage on the stage"), but now, the instructor's role is shifting to that of guide and facilitator (the "guide by the side"). This change in instructor role shifts the responsibility for learning away from the instructor and toward the learner. .

As in other countries, too, Turkey has its share of faculty members who are resisting electronic course delivery. It is important that instructors be encouraged to develop positive attitudes toward distance education and its related technologies, particularly those faculty members who are participating in the delivery of distance education courses. Because instructors, staff, and tutors of distance courses who are giving their support to the distance system should not feel isolated themselves, a support community of likeminded instructors is an important role in Turkey's distance programs. Faculty training is also an important issue. Making lecturers aware that their role should be that of facilitator of learning is a challenge for distance education institutions in Turkey.

There is a growing emphasis on academic accountability in Turkey's distance education context. Academic emphasis is shifting from course *completion* to end of course *competency*. What students can actually do with the knowledge and training they have acquired is increasingly a focus in Turkey's distance education programs.

Technology Changes

There has been a huge increase in Internet usage in distance education programs in Turkey. Online course delivery is increasing. Being technologically savvy is becoming a graduation requirement for students—and is an essential requirement for the instructor.

Economic Changes

Provincial, national, and international economic trends affect all aspects of life in Turkey, including the delivery of education. The Turkish education system has close, interdependent links to the national economy. It contributes to the economy by helping to create knowledgeable, skilled, and productive people.

Education planners must have a full understanding of economic trends and education needs, and realize that funding is closely related to identified needs, economic developments, and international developments affecting Turkey. Education and training are clearly connected to, and dependent upon, economic performance and economic growth. With the ever-decreasing resources for higher education, and the increased need for additional education and training, alternative educational initiatives and offerings such as distance education are becoming a competitive necessity.

Recognition of Educational Needs

The need for more academic programs and a greater variety of courses in Turkey has influenced the growth of online learning and other distance education modalities. The realization that a vision is extremely important in the development of a learning system, the need for instructional quality, and the need for planning and evaluation of courses have strongly influenced decision-making in Turkey's educational systems. The use of the Internet and other online opportunities is becoming increasingly important in the delivery of educational material, and there is a trend to encourage the use of educational technology in courses. The distinction between distance and traditional education is increasingly disappearing. The need for effective course-management systems and Web-based technological services is growing, as is the implementation of learning and teaching strategies that exploit the capabilities of technology.

The institutional landscape of higher education is also changing. Traditional campuses are declining, for-profit institutions are growing, and public and private institutions are merging. There is a shift in organizational structure toward decentralization. Instruction is becoming more learner-centered, non-linear, and more self-directed.

CONCLUSION

In the past two decades, the number of students in the Open Education programs at Anadolu University in Turkey has more than doubled. Though this is a positive trend, an important ancillary issue is how to maintain and improve the quality of the programs while enrollments continue to increase. Imaginative and creative leadership in a favorable political environment have led to the ambitious implementation of educational reforms since the beginning of the 1980s. Continued support from the Turkish government is an important motivational factor that has made it possible to produce a large variety of distance education programs and/or projects offered by the OEF.

A number of changes in Turkey's distance community have taken place, and many challenges have already been overcome. We can now say that distance education has been established as a valid and challenging educational alternative in Turkish society. The coming decade will bring more opportunities, more challenges, and interesting trends. The role of distance education in the development of education—and of the country—

will likely continue to increase, providing more opportunities to a greater number of people to participate fully in the establishment of education for all people in Turkey. In the same way, it is hoped that international teamwork will increase, leading to better understanding and more cooperation between cultures and peoples.

The aim of this chapter has been to discuss the development of distance education and the current state of the art in Turkey. A number of challenges have been discussed and a number of trends have been identified. Some of these trends and issues are similar to those in other countries, and some are unique to the situation in Turkey. It is hoped that this chapter will contribute to a better understanding of the similarities and differences experienced by international distance education institutions and their instructors, both within and without a wide array of cultural contexts.

REFERENCES

Akyurekoglu, H. (1995). *The role of distance education in corporate training*, Unpublished Master's Thesis. The Pennsylvania State University, University Park.

Alkan, C. (1987). Acikögretim: Uzaktan Egitim Sistemlerinin Karsilastirmali Olarak Incelenmesi [Open Learning: Comperasingly Investigation of Distance Education Systems], Ankara Universitesi Egitim Bilimleri Fakultesi Yayinlari, Yayin No. 157, Ankara, Turkiye.

Demiray, U. et al. (2002a). AOL-Acikogretim Lisesi 10. Yil Etkinlikleri [10th Anniversary of Activities of Open High School], Milli Egitim Bakanligi Egitek Yayinlari Yayin No. 8, Ankara, Turkey

Demiray, U. et al. (2002b). A review of literature on the Open Education Faculty (1982-2002), Expanded 4th ed. in press.

Howell, S. L. (2003). Thirty-two trends affecting distance education: An informed foundation for strategic planning. *Online Journal of Distance Learning Administration*, *6*(3). Retrieved from http://www.westga.edu/~distance/ojdla/fall63/fall63.htm

McIsaac, M. S., Murphy, K. L., & Demiray, U. (1988). Examining distance education in Turkey. *Distance Education*, *9*(1), 106-114.

Ozkul, A. E. (2001). Anadolu University Distance Education System from emergence to 21st Century. *Turkish Online Journal of Distance Education-TOJDE*, *2*(1). Retrieved from http://tojde.anadolu.edu.tr

CHAPTER 14

A MULTIMEDIA DIGITAL LIBRARY TO SUPPORT DISTANCE LEARNING IN BRAZIL

Fredric Michael Litto

INTRODUCTION

Like many other countries in the world, Brazil is still trying to iron out the details involved in implementing distance learning in the education system. However, distance learning is an especially relevant modality in the Brazilian context due to a number of different factors. These factors include the increased demand for education (especially higher education), the relatively low levels of funding for building new education institutions, and the massive geographical expanse of the country.

This chapter discusses the development and implementation of the Virtual Library for the Brazilian Student, a Web-based system that offers free-of-charge access to multimedia resources and full-text literary materials. While the Virtual Library was originally developed to respond to the challenges resulting from the extremely low numbers of school libraries, public libraries, and bookstores in Brazil, it has now become an excellent

Trends and Issues in Distance Education: International Perspectives, 171–182
Copyright © 2005 by Information Age Publishing
All rights of reproduction in any form reserved.

resource for making intellectual and cultural materials available to distance learners at all levels of the education system. The story of the Virtual Library is inspiring, as it demonstrates how energy and creativity can allow a relatively small up-front financial investment to yield significant results, and how a resource can extend beyond its primary audience (in this case students in traditional brick-and-mortar schools) to meet the needs of new and future audiences (such as working professionals, distance learners, and researchers).

The chapter provides some contextual information on information technology and education in Brazil, an overview of how the Virtual Library was developed, and a discussion of challenges that were encountered during planning and implementation of the Virtual Library. In addition, it provides insight into the key features of the Virtual Library, the results from research conducted on the Virtual Library, and concluding remarks about the role of the Virtual Library in supporting the development of Brazil's knowledge economy.

THE FACE OF BRAZILIAN HIGHER EDUCATION

Distance learning is growing by leaps and bounds in almost all educational sectors in Brazil. However, distance learning has not seen a very high level of growth in higher education, as a centralized certification policy at the national level permits conservative forces within the educational community—unwilling to recognize the recent achievements of distance learning—to restrain its growth. It is anticipated that distance learning will gain in prominence in higher education over time. In spite of such policy issues however, higher education institutions are developing the experiential base in distance education, learning how to face the challenges and opportunities in managing distance learning programs. The complexity of monitoring educational activities in a nation as large in area (3,218,130 square miles) and in population (180 million inhabitants) as Brazil, makes national-level "fine tuning" of distance education practice extremely difficult, if not impossible.

Brazil has some 10% of its 18-24 year old population enrolled in higher education (approximately 3.5 million students). This figure is significantly lower than the figures for other countries (see Figure 14.1). Because the financial means do not exist for building a large number of new campuses for higher education in Brazil, it would behoove the country to invest in an open distance-learning university. This would provide a larger proportion of the population with access to higher education. However, there have been 30 attempts in as many years to create such an insti-

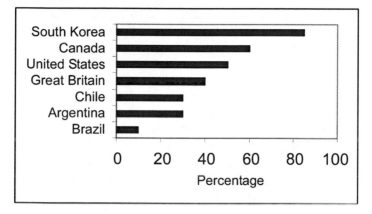

Source: Data collected by the author from among scholars attending international distance learning conferences 2002-2004.

Figure 14.1.   Percentage of 18-24 year olds enrolled in higher education.

tution, but each of these attempts has not moved beyond the planning phase (Litto, 2002).

INFORMATION TECHNOLOGY IN BRAZILIAN EDUCATION

There is a need for investment in information technology at all levels of education in Brazil. The libraries of the 1,900 higher education institutions have a total of 32.2 million volumes (not counting duplicate copies of the same work, usually acquired to compensate for students' inability to purchase textbooks). This converts to a shockingly low average of 9.2 books per student (Informativo INEP, 2004). Furthermore, there is a total of 367, 813 computers connected to the Internet in the same institutions, yielding an average of 9.5 students per computer. Were there not also computers with Internet connections in the homes of some students and instructors, we might well ask how Brazil expects to move into the knowledge society in this century (Di Cropani, 1998a; Gorini & Castello Branco, 2000).

Recent studies by UNESCO and local publishers' associations have confirmed the calamitous situation of other kinds of libraries and bookstores in Brazil. The lack of school libraries is superseded only by the lack of school science laboratories in the education system. Data on public-access libraries are similarly depressing. Most authorities informally suggest that there are only 250 institutions with free, public access to a library collection exceeding 30,000 volumes. According to the statistics, 80% of public library users are students, and most institutions lack regular funding for acquisitions. These institutions depend principally on donations and have become accustomed to a constant state of being out-of-date. Finally, the entire country has only 1,500 bookstores (the ideal would be 10,000), concentrated in the larger cities (Di Cropani, 1998a; Di Cropani, 1998b; Gorini & Castelo Branco, 2000). In fact, 89% of Brazil´s municipal districts lack bookstores entirely (Jorge, 2004; Paganine, 2002).

There were some 22 million personal computers in use in Brazil in 2004, which means that about 12% of the population uses computers. Further, there were approximately 14 million Internet users (8% of the population), less than one million of whom have broadband access. These figures, which place Brazil far behind most developed nations, are the result of two phenomena: the generally low income of the greater part of the Brazilian population, and the fact that only 0.7% of the content on the Web is in Portuguese (Brazil's national language), thereby offering little incentive for access (Litto, 2004).

The "lethargy" in information technology is also reflected in the presence—or lack thereof—of computers and Internet access in primary and secondary education institutions. There is a total of 176,880 public and private schools in the country, with a total of 48.5 million students (the school day is typically only four hours long, and many public schools have three or four shifts per day). Some of the key figures in relation to information technology in primary and secondary education are listed below (Loureiro 2004; Instituto Brasileiro de Geografia e Estatística, 2004; Instituto Nacional de Estudos e Pesquisas Educacionais, 2004):

- 80% of the schools have electricity.
- 50% of the schools have a telephone line.
- 27% of the schools have computers (a total of 276,988 machines, 80% of which are in private schools).
- 11% of the schools have access to the Internet (this represents an average of 5.7 computers in each school, and 174 students per computer).

As we survey this bleak scenario, we could conclude that most educational technology investment in both the public and private sectors is focused on hardware, software, and teacher training, rather than on content, which could be the driving force for justifying the acquisition of computers and Internet access in education at all levels. Without relevant, well-designed instructional materials written with good use of the local language (good in the sense of formal use of the language, and not just chats and other deviations from exemplary models of writing), there can only be but little motive, for most people, for bothering with computers and the Internet in teaching and learning (Litto 1998).

THE DEVELOPMENT OF THE VIRTUAL LIBRARY
FOR THE BRAZILIAN STUDENT

Given the Brazilian educational and technology situation described in the previous section, it was with great exhilaration that the School of the Future, an interdisciplinary research laboratory at the University of São Paulo, learned in 1997 that the AT&T Foundation would fund a grant for the creation of an online Virtual Library for the Brazilian Student. The proposal, which had been chosen for funding by a select panel of experts organized by the International Council for Distance Education (ICDE), provided $100,000 for the project. Shortly afterward, yet another grant of $40,000 from the State of São Paulo Secretariat of Culture permitted the initiation of a process of "cultural inclusion."

The beginning of the project clearly supported the notion that, if, in the past, one spent 20% of a project's working time on planning, and 80% on development, nowadays (due to the complexity surrounding us), the reverse is often the case: 80% for planning and merely 20% for "follow-through" on what was planned. It took the research group more than a year to organize the documental, technological and workflow aspects of the task before effectively "going live."

The goals of the Virtual Library for the Brazilian Student project were to (1) furnish complete texts of both classic and hard-to-find works of Brazilian culture, appropriate for students in schools (literary and historical works, reference materials, atlases, and so on); (2) improve the heuristic skills of students and teachers; (3) increase motivation for implementing computer and network access in schools; (4) conduct research on the usage patterns of the Virtual Library by the target audience, and (5) investigate the cost-benefit aspects of such a collection of multimedia materials for formal or informal computer-based distance learning.

The initial tasks involved in implementing the Virtual Library included forming the research team; establishing internal and external partnerships; addressing issues of intellectual property rights; acquiring hardware, software, and materials; creating collaborative working procedures conducive to productivity; constructing the user interface; and beginning the search for project sponsorship to follow through after the initial grants came to an end. Also included in the undertaking was the interchange of ideas with the institutional partner, the University of British Columbia, in the person of Tony Bates. Bates is a distinguished scholar and practitioner at UBC, who agreed to serve as formative "evaluator" of the project. The project staff consisted of a general coordinator, a specialist in networking interfaces, a specialist in graphic design, a coordinator of production, and several undergraduate assistants for data input.

An important internal partnership was established with the University´s Museum of Archeology and Ethnology, which provided the Virtual Library with valuable images of the cultural artifacts of Brazil's many Amerindian peoples. Another highly significant external partnership was developed with the Roberto Marinho Foundation of Rio de Janeiro, the "social responsibility" branch of Brazil's leading group of communications companies, Globo enterprises. The Foundation, in association with the Federation of Industry of the State of São Paulo (FIESP) and the national-level Social Services for Industry (SENAI-SESI), had developed and delivered Telecurso 2000, a complete curriculum for primary and secondary school education disseminated by open-circuit television programs and print materials. Telecurso 2000 was designed to target economically-active adults who had not completed their education (the average worker in Brazil still only has six or seven years of formal education), and who wished to do so through part-time distance learning (Oliveira, Moura Castro & Verdisco, 2003). In 2004, more than 600,000 such on-the-job, part-time students were enrolled in the Telecurso 2000 program. The Roberto Marinho Foundation gave the Virtual Library for the Brazilian Student permission to use all of the course materials already in digital form, and to this day these materials remain one of the most accessed parts of the library.

A collaborative relationship was also established with the "Vozoteca" (Library of Voices) of Luiz Kawall, an independent collector of the sounds of Brazil's past, especially the recordings of political personalities of the 20th century. These recordings, made available digitally through the Virtual Library, permit students to listen to the oratory styles of historical figures whose names have permeated textbooks, literature, popular music, and other aspects of the society.

Funding limitations prevented us from implementing a number of ideas. Nonetheless, it may be worthwhile to briefly discuss these ideas, as they may serve as suggestions for others who wish to create virtual libraries of this type elsewhere. Firstly, we had hoped to have the basic information in the Virtual Library in Portuguese, and navigation within the database in Portuguese, English, Spanish, and perhaps even French, thus permitting interested students from many parts of the world to have access to the material and learn about Brazilian culture and history. Secondly, we had hoped to create a user interface with three axes: location (click on a place and a guide to everything in the database related to it appears), time (a slide-scrolling bar), and topic (keyword access to all the files). Thirdly, we had hoped to create a frequently asked questions (FAQ) file, permitting users to find answers to their questions about the library in this easy-access format. Finally, we hoped to have a rich area of "paradidactic activities" within the Virtual Library, with reference to the audio-visual material within the collection. Such paradidactic activities would include role-playing games, peer exchange of information, soliciting expert opinions via e-mails, and conferring with other databases. There is, in fact, a useful and active ongoing exchange of ideas about curricula, classroom activities, and references among Brazilian teachers. However, we have not yet been successful in creating the powerful support system that was originally envisioned.

A number of more generic problems that could dishearten would-be virtual-library creators were encountered: 1) a lack of a tradition of teamwork in humanistic research constantly plagued decision-making and production; 2) the choice of data-inputting techniques held back development of the work—optical character recognition proved not to be practical, and digitizing almost every text anew was finally accepted as the standard; 3) addressing the problem of the many spelling changes that occurred in the Portuguese language over the last 100 years, requiring much reformatting of the texts to make them understandable to younger learners; 4) less material than was anticipated was available in the public domain, requiring the group to find new solutions; 5) instead of the "wholesale approval" expected to be received from publishers for permission to place their out-of-print works in the Virtual Library, the team only gained occasional permission on a title-by-title basis.

THE CHARACTERISTICS OF THE VIRTUAL LIBRARY

The Virtual Library for the Brazilian Student is available without charge to all interested persons at www.bibvirt.futuro.usp.br. The content is divided into several sections: a full-text collection, an images collection, a sounds collection, a "special materials" section, an activities section, and a section with suggestions for additional research sources.

The Full-Text collection includes complete literary works, historical documents, scientific journal articles, images, sounds, and software. More than 300 works of Brazilian literature in the public domain are available, and many of these are downloadable through PDAs. Literary reviews of many of the works are also available, as are some works of literature translated into Portuguese. There is also a link to the celebrated Gutenberg Virtual Library, a 30-year old digital collection now holding 3,800 international literary works in 16 different languages, all in full text. A sizable collection of scientific journals, which would otherwise be extremely difficult to find when needed, is also available in this section of the Virtual Library, made available by the publishers in the interest of aiding future generations of learners. Journals cover topics such as science education, math education, geography, digital society, writing, cinema, and educational research.

The Images section of the Virtual Library includes pictorial representations of many things of relevance to understanding Brazilian history, culture, geography, and society. Images include drawings by Jean Baptiste Debret, the Frenchman who visited Brazil between 1816 and 1831 and who left a rich pictorial account of social and economic life in colonial society. The images also include drawings and photographs of Brazilian flora and fauna and a large collection of clip art specially organized for young students.

The Sounds component of the Virtual Library includes the recordings of historical events, personalities and politicians of the past, and famous jingles and publicity spots from early media. Users can listen to the first recorded voice in Brazil, voices from the Revolutions of 1930 and 1932, sounds from World War II, an audio recording about the history of radio in Brazil, recordings of Brazil's soccer games in the World Cup, compositions of Bossa Nova, and audio explanations of the history of samba and the famous "samba schools." There is also a small but growing collection of audio books prepared for persons with visual disabilities (but available to any interested parties), including works of literature.

The "special materials" section provides access to rare treasures such as a collection of more than 80 radio interviews recorded in the period 1984-1989 with important Brazilian scientists, and several dozen downloadable video interviews with important figures such as Paulo Freire (his interviews are absolute "hits," receiving over a thousand downloads per week), Alberto Dines, Juscelino Kubitschek and leaders of the Araweté and Krenakarore tribes of the Amazon Region. Spread throughout the entire collection is ample material representing Brazil's rich folkloric traditions, in texts, images and sounds.

The Activities section stresses interactivity between developers and users of the Virtual Library, as well as among the users themselves. The focus of this section is on experiences with using the Virtual Library in the teaching/learning process. There is a message board for announcing and exchanging ideas and an annual calendar of commemorative dates, with suggestions for links to help locate pertinent information related to the commemorative dates. An area titled for "Learning and Fun" includes an annual Online Cultural Treasure Hunt, which stimulates creative information-seeking strategies within the Virtual Library, and results in the awarding of prizes (usually palmtops and books donated by local bookstores).

A final section of the Virtual Library is the Etcetera section which cites additional research sources available on the Web, as well as the addresses of "real" libraries and bookstores throughout the country, complementing the resources made available in the Virtual Library.

Taken as a whole, the content of the Virtual Library reflects its development: with the exception of the extensive and highly organized material of the Telecurso 2000, the rest is a wonderful hodge-podge of knowledge, information, and "hidden-away" wisdom. Recognizing the inconsistent funding since the completion of the initial grants, and the severe restrictions resulting from intellectual property rights, the developers of the Virtual Library have come to accept its defects and shortcomings. We await the day when the Library's virtues and strategic importance are recognized by new funding agencies, so that the needed improvements can be made. In the meantime, we delight in the Library's non-linear, exponential, eclectic growth in varied directions, and its heavy use in spite of its uneven holdings. However, being impatient as only developers of a very young library can be, we have started contemplating changing the name "Virtual Library for the Brazilian Student" to "Virtual Library for the Portuguese-Language Student," whence it will be possible to grow still further, by including educational material from the eight countries in Europe, South America, Africa and Asia where Portuguese is the principal language.

RESEARCH FINDINGS ON THE VIRTUAL LIBRARY

Some focused research on the Virtual Library has been conducted. In a study completed in 2001, an analysis was done to determine whether the Virtual Library had met its original objectives, and to evaluate the profile of its users [Salgado, 2001]. This research study found that the daily average number of discrete users exceeded 5,000 in 2001. Over the three subsequent years the daily average number of users has risen to 15,000.

In 2000, a 37-item questionnaire was placed on the Virtual Library's Web site, drawing a total of 528 user responses, of which 479 were used for the analysis. The purpose of the survey was to determine the profile of users and the level of user satisfaction with the Virtual Library. The following is a summary of the key aspects of the results regarding the attributes of Virtual Library users:

- Approximately half of the users are male and half of the users are female.
- 72% of respondents access the Internet from home, 17% access the Internet from work, 5% access the Internet from school, 3% access

the Internet from a friend or relative's home, and 3% access the Internet from a library.

- Approximately half of the users live in state capitals, and half of the users live in the "interior."
- 57% of the users live in cities with a population of over 500,000, 22% of users live in cities with a population of between 500,000 and 100,000, and 21% of users live in towns with a population of less than 100,000.
- While the Virtual Library was initially designed for use by primary and secondary school students, the actual users are somewhat older—only 28% are between the ages of 10 and 17, while 32% are between the ages of 18 and 25, and 39% are over 25 years old.
- 84% of respondents indicated that they used the Virtual Library for educational purposes, while 8% indicated they use it for pleasure and 8% indicated that they use it for work purposes.
- Primary and secondary school students comprised 38%, while university students represented 23% of the users.
- Approximately half of the students using the service attend a public school, and half of the students attend a private school.
- 57% of students responding to the survey indicated that their teachers required research on the Web but gave no orientation; 25% said teachers gave minimal orientation; 18% indicated that their teachers gave initial guidance to their Web research.

In terms of user satisfaction with the Virtual Library, the results of the questionnaire provided interesting insight into the effectiveness of the resources. For example, 57% of respondents affirmed that they "always" found what they were seeking, while 43% of the respondents found that they "normally" found what they sought. In addition, it was found that 91% of users reported having no difficulty in navigating within the Virtual Library, whereas 9% reported having difficulty with navigation. When asked whether the respondents experienced that the materials located through the Virtual Library could be found just as well in other locations, 37% said that it was possible, 34% said that "at times" they found this to be true, 14% said it was difficult, and 15% said that it was never possible. When asked to rank order the various types of resources contained in terms of their importance, it was found that the literature was of greatest importance, followed by didactic material, paradidactic material, sounds, and images. In terms of how respondents read the materials accessed through the virtual library, it was found that 28% of respondents read directly from the screen, 13% of respondents printed directly while connected to the Internet, 35% of respondents downloaded and saved the materials for later reading on-screen, and 24% of respondents down-loaded for later printing and reading.

In terms of the Virtual Library project's success in meeting its original objectives, the author of the research concluded that the original target audience had indeed been reached. In addition, the researcher found that the "free, unrestricted access" nature of the Web made the content in the Virtual Library available to a much wider audience than had originally been anticipated. University students and candidates for the university entrance exams seemed to make use of the Virtual Library as a means of having "bookless" access to required reading for which their financial resources were inadequate. The author of the research also concluded that while there was room for improvement in the interface design, users seemed satisfied with the structure and nature of access to the Virtual Library's content.

CONCLUSION

As noted at the outset, the number of school libraries, public libraries, and bookstores throughout Brazil is significantly lower than would be desirable for developing and sustaining a knowledge-based economy. With limited public funds available to rectify this situation, those concerned with Brazil's future productivity and its ability to compete globally are charged with experimenting with solutions to social problems based on the new communications technologies. Most information on the Web is in the English language and is hence of limited accessibility to learners in countries with other languages as their primary tongue. The use of mechanisms such as the Virtual Library project (as either a "stand-alone" site on the Web or as a "support system" to students enrolled in online courses) can: (1) give learners access to their own national literature, iconography and sounds of the past; (2) stimulate reading and research in online collections of national sources; and (3) help justify the expense of purchasing and maintaining computers and Web-access in schools and community centers by offering, in local languages, useful information for learning. This, in turn, diminishes the differences between learning in rural and urban settings and, in general, promotes an improved and sustainable quality of life. As more and more developing countries enter the digital age, we are bound to see a trend towards the development and utilization of collections of educational materials, organized in virtual libraries, cyber-repositories, or other Web-accessible forms and this, in turn, may be the "tipping point" of a whole new vision of how people can and should learn.

REFERENCES

Di Cropani, O. D. (1998a). As políticas do livro. Retrieved May 15, 2004, from www.minc.gov.br/textos/olhar/politicaslivro.htm

Di Cropani, O.D. (1998b). Livro, Biblioteca e Leitura no Brasil. Retrieved November 16, 2004, from www9.cultura.gov.br/textos/of01.htm

Gorini, A.P.F. & Castelo Branco, C.E. (2000). Panorama do Setor Editorial Brasileiro. Brasília, BNDES-Banco Nacional de Desenvolvimento. 2000. Retrieved November 15, 2004, from www.bndes.gov.br/conhecimento/publicacoes/catalogo/setor2.asp

Informativo INEP, Ano 2, No 38, 11 Mai 2004. Retrieved June 17, 2004, from www.inep.gov.br/informativo/informativo38.htm

Instituto Brasileiro de Geografia e Estatística. Retrieved May 15, 2004, from www.ibge.gov.br

Instituto Nacional de Estudos e Pesquisas Educacionais Anísio Teixeira. Dataescolabrasil; Edudatabrasil; Censo Escolar 2004; Sinópse Estatística da Educação Básica 2003; Sistema de Informação da Educação Superior—SiedSup; Cadastro de Cursos e Instituições da Educação Superior. Retrieved May 19, 2004, from www.inep.gov.br

Jorge, C. (2004, June). Brazil, a nation that doesn't read. *Brazzil Culture*. Retrieved May 17, 2004, from www.brazzil.com/2004/html/articles/jun04/p109jun04.htm

Litto, F. M. (1998). Culture and entropy at the interface of freedom of expression and the new communications technologies. In M. Paré & P. Desbarats (Eds.), *Freedom of expression and the new communications technologies* (pp. 201-209). Montreal, Canada: UNESCO and IQ Coletif.

Litto, F. M. (2002). The hybridization of distance learning in Brazil: An approach imposed by culture. *International Review of Research in Open and Distance Learning*, 2(2). Retrieved April 15, 2004, from http://www.icaap.org/iuicode?149.2.2.6

Litto, F. M. (2004, Fall). Digital libraries, developing countries, and continuing education: A case study in Brazil. *Continuing Higher Education Review*, 68, 78-86.

Loureiro, M. D. (2004). O Ministério da Educação e a EAD: Visão Geral e Legislação Atual. Seminário Internacional de Educação a Distância, Brasília, UNILEGIS, 9 June 2004.

Oliveira, J. B. A., Moura Castro, C., & Verdisco, A. (2003). Education by television: Telecurso 2000. In J. Bradley (Ed.). *The open classroom. Distance learning in and out of schools* (pp.133-145). London: Kogan Page.

Paganine, J. (2002). Câdê o Leitor? Retrieved June 17, 2004, from www2.univille.edu.br/biblioteca/boletim_junho2002/PAGANINE.htm

Salgado, L. (2001). *A Biblioteca Virtual do Estudante Brasileiro da Escola do Futuro da Universidade de São Paulo: Um Estudo da sua Estrutura e dos Seus Usuários*. Unpublished master's thesis, Escola de Comunicações e Artes, Universidade de São Paulo.

CHAPTER 15

ICT-ENHANCED OPEN AND DISTANCE LEARNING

A Toy for Africa's Current Elite, or an Essential Tool for Africa's Sustainable Development?

Bob Day

SUMMARY

Despite the best intentions of governments and the international community, UNESCO's *Education for All* drive is failing in Africa. Currently, Africa's educational institutions are mostly suffering severe financial constraints and are focusing on efficiency and effectiveness, competing for the minority of students who can pay. Even if the current education systems used in the developed world are working in Africa's more affluent (usually metropolitan) areas (and this is another highly contentious debate), they have failed to even begin to satisfy the learning needs of the majority of Africa's people who are becoming ever more excluded from the global information society.

Trends and Issues in Distance Education: International Perspectives, 183–204
Copyright © 2005 by Information Age Publishing
All rights of reproduction in any form reserved.

Africa has yet to experience the true, wide-ranging benefits that information and communication technologies (ICTs) have the potential to bring throughout society. Most large African institutions, including educational institutions, are importers of developed-world ICTs, but with negligible impact on the exclusion and poverty of most African people. As far as the fourth-world communities are concerned, ICTs are only just being introduced into their lives via multi-purpose community centers, school connectivity projects, and similar initiatives.

Should we be trying to inject these ICT systems (including the e-learning systems) and existing educational material—with their questionable pedagogies and embedded insensitivity to language and cultural diversity—into this fourth world? Or should we take the opportunity to open the door to as many new ICT solutions and pedagogies as may be needed now and in the future to address the learning needs of Africa's diverse, fascinating range of individuals and communities, especially the poorest and most remote?

The belief is growing that the true, wide-ranging benefits that ICTs have the potential to bring throughout African society can only be achieved by the strategic adoption of open standards, free and open source software (FOSS), and open content. Such adoption requires significant effort to build local FOSS capacity and capability across the continent, nothing less than the stimulation of genuinely indigenous ICT industries in each African nation/region.

There is a wide variety of players in the global e-learning arena. However, we should focus on education practitioners and specialists who have developed significant expertise in using FOSS, and who also appreciate the burning need to develop dramatically new pedagogies. Significant resources should be invested in bringing these visionaries together from around the world to begin to develop all aspects of these new multi-modal, multimedia-based pedagogies, as well as the associated open standards and new administrative systems that will be required for an organically-evolving free and open global education system. We cannot anticipate how significant the outcomes of such a strategy would be in Africa and the rest of the underdeveloped world.

EDUCATION IN AFRICA: A GROWING CRISIS?

Education is universally recognized as a fundamental pillar of global development and poverty eradication. Yet, many countries in Africa have been forced to undergo austere structural adjustment programs that have resulted in cuts in educational expenditure. This, together with increasing debt burdens, governance problems, an unsupportive global economic context, and the impact of HIV/AIDS, means that the basic human right of access to education continues to be denied to many

It is predicted that Africa will lose many of its teachers to HIV/AIDS in the decade to come, further complicating the problem of Africa's severe shortage of teachers. Education systems need adequate supplies of well-trained teachers, academic managers, and support staff. Of the 59 million teachers in the formal education sector globally, only 2 million are in sub-Saharan Africa (UNESCO, 2002b). To achieve education for all (EFA) in sub-Saharan Africa, it is estimated that 700,000 more teachers are needed by 2005, and 1.2 million by 2015.

Yet, national education budgets continue to be cut. The impact of budget cuts is felt mostly with teacher training, in which there is an urgent need for replacement of teachers who have died of AIDS-related diseases, as well as a need to generally improve the quality of teaching in Africa. A recent World Bank study, cited by the EFA Global Monitoring Report 2002 (UNESCO, 2002a), reported that achieving EFA goals by 2015 would require external funding of about US$2.5 billion over the 15-year period. Sub-Saharan Africa will require 85% of this funding.

Even worse, these figures neglect the millions of adults falling outside the traditional tertiary cohort; for instance, one in four adults on the planet is still illiterate. The EFA Global Monitoring Report 2002 estimates that there are nearly 862 million illiterates in the world above the age of 14, over 60% of whom are women. Some 27% of the total population in developing and underdeveloped countries is illiterate. Yet, worldwide, a disproportionately small 5% of national education budgets is spent on the much higher proportion of the population that is functionally illiterate.

The evolution of the definition of literacy is, in itself, a fundamental issue. At the 1990 EFA World Conference, the limited traditional view of literacy was broadened to include basic learning needs or competencies; that is, mastery of the "three R's" (reading, writing, and arithmetic), together with other knowledge, problem-solving, and life skills. With the advent of the United Nations Literacy Decade (2003–2013) (UN, 2002a), the International Action Plan (UN, 2002b) calls for an even broader, renewed vision of literacy, when they mention that literacy for all is at the heart of basic education for all. To achieve the established goals such as eradicating poverty and reducing child mortality, it is essential to create literate environments.

Less than 50 years ago, access to tertiary education was regarded in most parts of the world as a privilege to which ordinary families could not aspire (UNESCO, 2000). However, global access to tertiary education has grown by more than 1200%—from 6.5 million enrollments in 1950 to 88.2 million in 1997. This is attributed, at least in part, to a philosophical shift from class to mass (World Bank, 2000). In 1995, a little more than half of the world's tertiary students (47 million) lived in the developing world, with a gross enrollment ratio mostly below 15%. However, the average for sub-Saharan Africa was less than 3%. Saint (1999) points out that at least 16 countries in sub-Saharan Africa will need to double current tertiary enrollment in the coming decade just to maintain the existing and unacceptably low gross enrollment ratio. The imbalances between the global supply of tertiary education and the magnitude of the demand for access makes the imperative of providing a decent education for all one of the greatest moral challenges of our age.

Most higher education institutions (HEIs) are being asked to do considerably more in the context of shrinking resources. Inevitably, this has driven most African countries to employ cost-sharing between the student and government (only 16 countries still provide free tertiary education). While this is a common approach globally, it excludes large numbers of potential students throughout Africa, especially since few have the opportunity to work while studying. For many African countries, expenditure per student is now less than the $1000 thought to be the minimum level required to provide an acceptable quality tertiary education; so, the exclusion of the poorest is increasing while the quality of education is decreasing.

South Africa's Tertiary Sector

In South Africa, the 21 universities and 14 technikons (a South African term for technical, rather than academic, tertiary institutions) making up the current higher education (HE) institutional landscape have very different resources, management capacity, and culture. Much of this is the legacy of colonialism and apartheid, in particular the link between institutional identity and the historical provision of resources. The HE system is far from being optimally organized to meet the national human resource requirements, and confusion about its purpose and differentiation exists. The system's potential is being held back by several factors, including unproductive competition which is manifest by such trends as:

- the new managerialism,
- the volatility and expanded role of market forces in higher education,
- enhanced student mobility, and
- far-reaching changes in delivery modes.

The system is seen to be extremely wasteful and guilty of squandering valuable resources, delivering a poor return on investment measured by graduate and research output. Inequalities in access, program offerings, quality, and infrastructure are generally acknowledged. Despite a series of HE policy initiatives in the last decade to address these problems, implementation has been extremely slow and uneven. The most recent of these, the national plan on higher education (NPHE), launched in 2001, is currently dominating strategic HE thinking, and will likely continue to do so for several years.

However, because of its pragmatic, cautious approach, the NPHE may, inadvertently, be deflecting the attention of strategic HE thinkers away from the even bigger issue of the need for "education for all." The traditional, "contact-base" form of teaching, rooted in the industrial paradigm, is not seriously challenged. Exciting alternatives related to the emerging knowledge paradigm (but requiring fundamental, not incremental change) are left for later consideration. This has serious consequences for the many tens of thousands of potential students in remote and rural areas excluded from HE services.

In order to succeed in implementing the NPHE, a popular idea is that South African HEIs need to be encouraged to behave as a sector, rather than as competitors (as individual organizations or groups of organizations), to satisfy two major national imperatives:

- Teaching: instead of maintaining the traditional elitist paradigm, our HEIs need to recognize that they have been neglecting the needs of 70% of the population, and failing to provide students with the necessary qualifications in the right numbers to satisfy the current and future needs of society.
- Research and innovation: by coordinating the research outputs of each HEI to produce a sector profile aligned with national imperatives.

However, indicators are that this approach is unlikely to succeed. To date, strategic inter-HEI collaboration in South Africa has been limited (Gibbon & Parekh, 2001). Such cooperation has been most successful in areas of technical and infrastructural support and services, such as enhancing library access, strengthening ICT capabilities, and establishing a central applications office. Planning and coordination should be the main role of the consortia. Yet, this is precisely the area where they encounter the greatest difficulties. If they cannot collaborate with each other, how can they be expected to collaborate effectively and strategically with the other components of the education sector, or other sectors of society with the aim of achieving education for all?

Indeed, there is little evidence to date that either individual HEIs or consortia anywhere in the world are turning their attention to the global "education for all" initiative. Instead, the focus of both appears to be to address their existing markets more efficiently and cost-effectively (often by employing innovative ICT applications), but without breaking out of their traditional contact paradigm, and usually with the aim of enhancing their competitiveness as individual institutions.

ICTs in Africa: An Unfulfilled Promise?

The arrival of personal computers (PCs) a quarter of a century ago turned everyone into a potential computer user. It was inevitable that these PCs would be linked to the Internet, which had been established in the United States in the 1960s and '70s. In the '80s and '90s, the PC/Internet combination converted the Internet from a tool used only in military and academic circles into the global phenomenon with which we are still trying to come to terms. This, in turn, has changed the nature of the PC, as well as its most popular applications, from being predominantly a processing tool into a powerful and highly flexible communications platform.

In the context of the PC/Internet combination, three powerful trends appear to be driving the information revolution:

- *Cost of communicating:*   The transmission cost of sending digital data has decreased by a factor of more than 10,000 since 1975.
- *Power of computing:*   Computing power per dollar invested has increased by a factor of more than 10,000 since 1975.
- *Convergence:*   Analog technologies are being replaced with digital technologies capable of dealing with voice, video, and computer data over the same network.

Taken together, these trends have given rise to the merging of the computing (information technology) and communications sectors into a single sector referred to as the "information and communications technology" (ICT) sector.

The many potential roles for ICTs in development are beginning to be recognized globally (Marker, McNamara, & Wallace, 2002). International development organizations are promoting universal access to telecommunications as an integral part of their initiatives. Although ICTs can provide appropriate solutions, many of these initiatives have promoted narrow and problematic assumptions about what "access" to ICT actually means. It is well known that ICT penetration in Africa is very low compared to developed countries. Of the 818 million people in Africa, African Internet users in 2001 were estimated at 2.5 million (excluding North and South Africa). This translates to approximately 1 user in every 250-400 people, compared to the global average of 1 in 15, and a North American and European average of 1 in 2 people. The cost of Internet access (approximately $60/month) continues to be too high for the majority of the African population, being equivalent to almost 20% of GDP per capita, compared to the global average of 9%, and only 1% in high-income countries.

The New Partnership for Africa's Development (NEPAD) provides an African-owned and African-led effort to promote accelerated economic growth and sustainable development for Africa, based on partnerships between African countries themselves, but also between Africa and the developed world. NEPAD (www.nepad.org) explicitly recognizes ICT as a key priority in development efforts for the continent, as highlighted by the fact that ICT is included as one of four programs proposed for fast-tracked implementation (the other three being communicable diseases, debt reduction, and market access).

South Africa's ICT Sector

A recent study undertaken by the Department of Trade and Industry examined the rate of diffusion of ICT by eight industry sectors. With few exceptions, South African organizations in the selected sectors appear slow to adopt ICT anywhere other than in the traditional areas. In terms of the role of HEIs in the development of a knowledge society, and the use of ICT as an enabler, many of the sectors expressed the need to create a much more "ICT-aware" society. Of particular concern is that universities and technikons did not feature in any manner in any of the eight sectors. They were not seen as a source of information or training, traditional areas of activity for HEIs. In addition, the perceived low levels of innovation in most of the sectors are thought to reflect the low levels of interaction between researchers and the industry.

One of the major roles of HEIs is the output of quality graduates equipped with the types of skills that are useful to industry and society. According to the South African Human Sciences Research Council, the graduates register in 1999 revealed that less than 2% (10858) of South African graduates gained ICT qualifications, only 35% of whom were female, and 14% of whom were black. A recent study (ISETT SETA/ Department of Labour , 2002) estimates that up to 165,000 students will be needed to address ICT skills shortages in the near future. In 2000, estimates of the numbers of all categories of ICT professionals presently range between 54,000 and 74,500, of whom only about 5,000 were black

(ILO, 2001). A cause for serious concern is that no convergence is anticipated between supply and demand during the period ending in 2009.

These data provide significant evidence that growth of South Africa's
ICT industry is being seriously stunted by the insufficient supply of
appropriately qualified, trained, and/or experienced people. The existing
mechanisms established for the traditional teaching of ICTs in (South)
Africa were not designed to cope with this crucial challenge. Currently,
available ICT-related courses provide a range of accredited qualifications
primarily aimed at creating technicians, technologists, and professionals
for the long-established ICT sector and its traditional markets (e.g. military, finance, retail, etc.). These are important people, and Africa has an
immediate need for many more of them, and of world-class caliber, too.

However, there is a much broader range of ICT capabilities needed to
satisfy the growing needs of Africa's emerging knowledge economy. This
is a "chicken and egg" situation: if we do not provide such people, society
will not grow (i.e., it cannot be demand-led). Our society must, collectively, take the risk of anticipating, and thereby stimulating, the demand
for local expertise. This additional challenge is beyond the means of individual Departments of Education to face alone. Hence, there needs to be
a national strategy to address this special need; otherwise, the full potential of ICTs, particularly to alleviate poverty, is unlikely to be realized.

Three main areas of ICT teaching/learning material are widely
needed:

- *ICT Literacy/Fluency:* Most current literacy material is outdated, yet
  the dynamism of the ICT sector demands updating at least annually. In addition, much of the material has not been designed for
  the many thousands of potential learners from rural and remote
  areas. In such cases, it is essential that, for example, language and
  cultural issues are catered to if we are serious about bridging the
  "digital divide." Hence, improved ICT literacy learning material
  that satisfies these needs should be created on an ongoing basis.
- *ICT Benefits Awareness:* This needs to be created for all members of
  the leadership corps of (South) African society, including the public
  sector, private sector, civil society, academia, and rural communities. The emphasis of such material should not be on the technologies themselves, but on the potential impact of ICTs, now and in
  the future, tailored to the areas of society most relevant to each
  leader.
- *ICT Technologists and Professionals:* The theoretical content needs in
  this area for the ICT sector are being addressed by the current
  courses and material of many existing HEIs. The major concern
  from the private sector is that far from enough appropriately quali-

fied people are being produced, especially from the black community and women, and concerns are also voiced that many course components are permanently outdated, due to the years currently required to rewrite curricula, contrasted with the dynamism of ICTs. What is not being addressed, however, is the large and growing need for such ICT technologists and professionals in all other sectors of society, including private, public, development, and so on. These people need to be educated to comprehensively understand not only their sector (e.g. agriculture tourism, law, and security) but also all aspects of ICT relevant to that sector, current and future.

How Indigenous is South Africa's ICT Industry?

To date, ICT industries have not been major players in the economies of most African countries, which tend to be consumers, rather than producers to any significant degree. Africa, led by South Africa, has been importing developed-world ICTs and employing them in a variety of ways for more than two decades, but with negligible impact on the exclusion and poverty of the vast majority of its people.

In 2002, South Africa was the 20th largest country market for ICT products and services, accounting for 0.6% of worldwide revenues (SANEC, 2001). If the telecommunications market is included, the total estimated ICT market in 2000 was 79 billion rand (approximately US$79 million).

The corridor between Johannesburg and Pretoria, called Midrand, has grown into an ICT cluster (i.e., a hub of large ICT industrial organizations), but very few of the ICT cluster's products are South African in origin. The Midrand ICT cluster, like the whole South African ICT Industry, is made up of outposts (satellites, or fully dependent subsidiaries) of mostly multinational companies who find Midrand the best environment to sell American- or EU-manufactured products into the developed component of the South African market, as well as other African markets.

In the rest of Africa, much of the money used to purchase and maintain large ICT applications stems from donor funds. Hence, donor funds, which superficially appear to be "invested" in Africa, are often used to buy developed-world applications for installation in African government premises. The foreign reserves immediately flow back to the developed world, without circulating in the African economy, and the ICT "solution" seldom makes the anticipated impact, because it is a solution developed for a different problem, involving different people with different organizational circumstances and culture.

THE EMERGING IMPORTANCE OF THE FREE AND OPEN SOURCE SOFTWARE (FOSS[1]) MOVEMENT(S)

Few would dispute that the Internet is having dramatic impact on most aspects of human society, primarily in the developed world, but increasingly in the developing world. However, 15 short years ago, the Internet was far from being an accepted technology or phenomenon, and many, especially in the IT industry multinationals at that time, dismissed it as "yet another fad."

The Internet did not emerge 15 years ago, but was actually created some 40 years ago, in the 1960s. However, particularly because of the arrival of the World Wide Web (Web) in the early '90s, the Internet became accessible to much wider constituencies, each of which continue to find innovative ways of employing the system. In fact, FOSS is older than the Internet; the earliest software on the first computers was essentially open source, although the concept was not formalized until proprietary software emerged at a much later stage (Raymond, 2001). The Internet and the Web were created by the open source and open standards development processes, and it is very unlikely that they would have been produced via proprietary systems. However, these precocious offspring have set the stage for a new phase in the evolution of FOSS, which many believe is destined in the coming decade to have as much global impact as the Internet has had over the past decade.

Two years ago, FOSS was in a very similar position in South Africa as to the Internet 15 years ago, with many doubters, especially within the IT industry, and few willing to risk employing it. However, significant efforts have been made in the past two years to make FOSS adoption a priority in the public sector. South Africa's government has taken an insightful lead in adopting FOSS, and developing policies and strategies that are moving from "leveling the playing field" for FOSS, to a more pro-active approach in recognition of the need to redress the entrenched, unfair advantages that proprietary systems have inherited (OSS Working Group, 2003).

All distributed software includes the machine readable (binary) *object code*. FOSS, however, also includes the human readable form of those instructions, called the *source code*. Access to the source code offers ALL people the freedom to probe, modify, learn from, and customize the software to suit their needs. All FOSS developers claim copyright, but then use licenses innovatively to give users a variety of freedoms.[2]

Open standards in ICTs promote the freedom to access and contribute to the development of those standards, which is not the case with proprietary systems. Open standards in ICTs are critical in allowing new entrants (especially from the developing world) to participate and compete, whether at the individual, organizational, or national levels. In contrast, proprietary ICT standards are typically held by foreign enterprises that effectively relegate African engagement to a level of franchisee.

Globally, there is a growing acceptance of, and confidence in, FOSS and open standards, and this contributes to their further development. FOSS and open standards development is very distinct from that of proprietary software. FOSS programs and open standards are often produced by core groups of volunteers from all corners of the globe, linked via the Internet.[3] This process in many ways parallels the scientific method of peer review, and is producing a growing profile of robust, interoperable software, well known for its reliability.

Probably the most immediate attraction of FOSS to most people is that its use does not incur the high licensing costs associated with proprietary software. Many insist that FOSS must prove itself to be a viable alternative to proprietary software. The question most commonly posed is whether proprietary license costs are truly greater than the lifetime implementation, maintenance, and support costs associated with FOSS. The well-established FOSS products generally do well in such analyses (Blume, Bryden, Neilson, & Rotter, 2003). However, this limited focus on financial metrics is potentially dangerous, since the wider social implications tend to be ignored, even though this longer-term arena is where the greatest benefits of FOSS mostly lie, particularly for the developing world.

FOSS is currently stimulating an energetic debate regarding the global role of intellectual property rights (IPR) mechanisms (Cowan & Harrison, 2001). Recognition is growing that better understanding by a broader range of stakeholders is needed of the complex relationships between IPR, the information society in general, and the development, distribution, and services aspects of the ICT industry in particular. How far are we from an ideal balance in Africa's context?

- *In software development:* it is currently very difficult to write any major piece of software that does not infringe on a number of questionable US patents.
- *In software distribution:* throughout Africa it is extremely difficult to obtain a new PC without the Windows operating system being preinstalled, irrespective of the wishes of the user.
- *In ICT and related information services:* although ICTs have the potential to improve access to information dramatically, they also provide opportunities that were not previously practical to inhibit access to (i.e., "own") information.

In South and Southern Africa, the current copyright laws are outdated, and the legislation needs upgrading to take into account the potential benefits of the new electronic media (Van der Merwe, 1999). Properly balanced and judiciously applied, IPR promise an excellent decentralized system for the promotion of innovation, but the right balance is difficult to find. The concern is that enclosure of the information commons via the significant recent expansion of IPR may not simply hamper the non-proprietary mode of intellectual production, but runs the risk of ruling it out altogether (David, 2000).

The assertion is that FOSS is destined to have a similar impact over the next ten years as the Internet has had over the past ten years. During the recent past, when the Internet was stimulating a range of transformations across the planet, the developing world in general and Africa in particular were relegated to a following, copying, and catch-up role. History does not need to be, and should not be, repeated in the case of FOSS.

Indeed, the collaborative processes underlying the development of FOSS, open standards, and open content resonate with the processes that have been found to be most effective in socio-economic development and poverty eradication. And there is no area more appropriate for the application of these open processes and FOSS than the global obligation to provide quality education for all, especially in Africa.

ICTS IN EDUCATION IN AFRICA: WHERE ARE WE?

ICTs are disruptive, cross-cutting technologies, having the potential to impact all aspects of human society. It is generally recognized that anyone and everyone should have access to computers and the services they could be providing via global connectivity. This positions ICTs as universal support technologies, which can and should be being deployed to empower all members of society, creating a much broader and more complex "ICT Sector."

Similarly, the education sector manifests as a complex "cross-cutting" sector, impacting on individuals throughout their lives ("lifelong learning") via primary, secondary, and tertiary education, as well as adult basic education and training (ABET), and further education and training (FET) programs. In addition, each sector (public, private, civil society, etc.) has both its formal and informal education needs across a range of staff levels. Finally, there are the education needs associated with the more recent concepts of "organizational learning" characteristic of the emerging knowledge society.

So, when we talk about "ICTs in education," we are not discussing one simple issue, but we are referring to a highly complex matrix. A failure to recognize the complexity of this matrix frequently results in misunderstandings and unsatisfactory outcomes. However, by understanding this complexity rather than attempting to minimize or avoid it, we open the way to dramatic potential benefits that cannot be achieved by any other means that is "education for all."

The widespread penetration of ICTs is opening a great number of educationally and financially viable means of providing education. But, in so doing, the meaning of the term "distance" in distance education has grown less useful. This conceptual shift results from the ways in which both "contact" and "distance" provision have benefited from an increasing convergence between them, as well as recognizing that the consequent modes of teaching transcend the simplistic categorizations of "contact" or "distance." Not only are ICTs becoming increasingly essential ingredients in both modes of provision, but also their convergence is causing a long-overdue re-evaluation of the design of learning systems in which "face-to-face contact" is only one potential resource among others, and not necessarily the most important or the most effective, as generations of students at "residential" institutions can confirm.

And, in parallel, irrespective of ICT, a more mature, holistic concept of distance learning has recently emerged, i.e., Open and Distance Learning (ODL). There is an important distinction between "distance learning" and "open learning." Distance learning begins with a *method:* it is a way of teaching that does not require the teachers and learners to be in the same place at the same time. But open learning began with a *purpose:* to develop new strategies at an affordable cost, and to include all who seek the benefits of higher levels of education and training.

How can quality ODL be made available to all, when and where they need it, and in the form most appropriate to their learning needs? As described above, most of the world, and especially Africa, cannot afford to address this need via traditional face-to-face delivery. This model does not allow for provision to be scaled up to the levels required by the global demand in a manner that is capable of maintaining a sustainable balance among the tensions of Daniel's (1999) eternal triangle, to improve quality, cut their costs, and to serve more and more students.

The distinguishing pedagogical feature of HE massification (e.g., the mega-universities) is that, instead of giving individual faculty the responsibility for teaching, sophisticated learning systems have been developed based on innovative divisions of labour in which the responsibility for teaching is carried collectively by the organisation. The differentiating feature of mass provision via open learning systems is that the institution teaches, not the individual teacher. By replacing the traditional lecturer model with a total teaching system in which the functions of teaching are divided into a range of specialisations, HE massification is able to scale up the delivery of quality teaching to levels that simply are not possible in conventional campus-based or dual-mode models. (Daniel & Mackintosh, 2003).

There is a growing realization that mass provision via open learning systems represents the only viable solution to Africa's education crisis, operating as a major alternative (and additional) form of education. However, there is a grave danger that many forms of ICT-based distance education currently being experimented with are being misinterpreted as the "massification ODL solution" because, as Dhanarajan mentioned (1999), there is as much ignorance among many in education as among those outside it about what distance education can do and what it cannot do and, equally important what does and does not constitute good practice in distance education, its efficiencies, and governance.

It needs to be better and more widely understood that the use of new ICTs does not necessarily automatically constitute ODL. According to Daniel (1999) many people have a tendency today to associate educational uses of the newer information and communication technologies with distance education and then assume that technology-based teaching will foster distance learning and therefore show productivity gains over classroom methods.

ICTS, ODL AND SUSTAINABLE DEVELOPMENT: THE WAY FORWARD?

A full understanding of the mechanisms of sustainable development continues to elude mankind, but consensus is growing that both ICTs and education are essential components. The United Nations Development Program (UNDP) has produced a model (2001) of the multi-factorial relationships between skills development, education, technology and economic development, in which:

- a country's ICT investments can directly enhance the capabilities of its citizens;
- increased skill capacity can, in turn, support the further development and increase the productive use of the technological infrastructure;
- the growing sophistication of the skill base and the technological infrastructure can lead to innovation and the creation of new knowledge and new industries;
- new knowledge and innovation can support the growth of the economy that, in turn, provides resources needed to further develop the

human, economic, and technological infrastructure and the welfare of society.

In addition, in 2002 the United Nations Industrial Development Organization encouraged developing countries to take the "high road" to development, not only by building new institutions and infrastructure, but also by providing the support needed to create new skills, information, and capabilities at all levels of society. And, a recent (2002) World Bank report argues that skills needed for lifelong learning not only prepare citizens for competition in the global market, but also improve their ability to function as members of the community, thereby increasing social cohesion, reducing crime, and improving income re-distribution.

In this vision, ICTs are an integral part of an information-literate society, and personal participation in this technology-knowledge-innovation-economic development cycle begins with broader literacy. Hence, literacy includes not only the decoding and comprehension of text, but the ability to access, analyze, evaluate, communicate, and use information to solve problems and create new knowledge (OECD/Statistics Canada, 2000; ISTE, 1998). ICT, therefore, plays a much more fundamental and multi-factorial role than merely providing a delivery and instructional mechanism. This broader vision of literacy better addresses the needs and realities of youth and adult literacy learners and users within communities that can generate, share, and use knowledge for the benefit of all (Street, 1999).

Throughout Africa, however, ICT and information literacy continue, in general, to be regarded as peripheral education and training issues, especially when considering the poorest and most remote communities. This despite repeated experience that the sustainable development of these communities will not happen unless and until it is actively driven by individuals and groups from within them. In the context of UNESCO's "Education for All" challenge, which works towards the eradication of abject poverty throughout the world, this highlights the need for a fundamental paradigm change in African teaching and learning methods.

A NEW LEARNING PARADIGM FOR AFRICA?

A new paradigm aiming at mass provision of ICT-enhanced quality ODL will inevitably involve major changes in the way we use ICTs for both educational access and educational administrative systems. However, there is only room in this chapter to deal with the driving force of the new paradigm; i.e., the creation of new, appropriate, ICT-enhanced learning materials for Africa.

As we create new technology-enhanced learning materials, it must be recognized that we are only at the beginning of a long and exciting global initiative. It must not be technology that drives this development, but improved pedagogy. Over the next several years we will discover a great deal more about the innate components of each human ability, as well as the most appropriate stage in the development of each individual's brain and mind for those abilities to be built upon and mastered (Naledi 3D Factory, n.d.). However, if we take notice of what is already known, there is a great deal we can already be doing.

Much effort is being expended in digitizing existing text-based learning material and making it available electronically, particularly via the Web. This has value, since it makes this learning material more easily available to those who can make use of it. However, it does not significantly address the fundamental learning issues and, in fact, perpetuates most of the problems experienced by learners.

A crucial issue that cannot be addressed in depth here, but is central to the new learning material, is the balance between independent and interactive learning. A greater understanding will emerge of which is the more appropriate learning/teaching mode under different circumstances, but it is highly complex, as it depends on the age, preferences, and sophistication of the learner; the subject material to be learned; the availability and capabilities of teachers, lecturers, tutors, and mentors; and the possible groups of learners that can be formed. Indeed, a variety of group learning regimes (both physical and electronic) appears to have particular potential for improving learning experiences, and for improving the quality of the new learning material on an ongoing basis.

Teachers and lecturers alone cannot and should not produce this wealth of new learning material for several reasons. Most of them are already overloaded with expanding class sizes, and a growing administrative load that seems to take them ever further from their learners. More importantly, very few of them have sufficient pedagogical expertise. The process must be driven both by current pedagogy and by the major new insights that will emerge from the growing flood of relevant research. So, the primary players are most likely to emerge from the tertiary/research sector, but will need the support of teachers/lecturers, ICT experts, public and private sector stakeholders and, of course, the learners themselves.

We have already seen that at all levels, and in all African countries, the education sector is struggling to maintain the status quo, let alone make radical changes. Nevertheless, of all the levels, the tertiary sector has the best resources and capabilities. Certainly, within most of Africa's HEIs there are many individuals who have the expertise to make a significant impact if we could pool their capabilities.

The message is clear. If we in Africa are only prepared to tinker with the current bricks-and-mortar based education systems imported "as is" from the developed world, dominated by text-intensive "show-and-tell" methods, and unresponsive to our growing knowledge of how the human mind best learns, then that system will continue to deteriorate. Superficial tinkering has not worked. The changes need to be fundamental, and creating new learning materials relevant to Africa's situation using open standards and FOSS development processes is an excellent place to start.

An inevitable response is that the developing world, and particularly Africa, does not have sufficient resources to develop its own new learning materials. Instead, we should wait, observe, and take from the developed world whatever they produce over the next few years. In the meantime, we should persevere with the text-based learning material (mostly imported, usually from the old colonial powers, for language reasons), because it is "better than nothing."

However, if we examine the wide range of life-long learning needs of the broad spectrum of people in Africa, not just the elites, it becomes obvious that most imported learning materials are of little use to the many millions of excluded people for reasons of literacy, language, and/or culture (Naledi 3D Factory, n.d.).

Literacy

As discussed above, accurate figures for literacy in Africa are problematic for several reasons, including the different definitions of literacy used. Certainly, if the same measures of "functional illiteracy" for the United States used by Castells (1998) are employed for Africa, levels above 70% would be common, especially in populations outside the main cities. Hence, the pedagogical limitations of text materials are significantly amplified in Africa, which perhaps should be thought of as a "text-averse" continent for the purposes of transforming education. Instead of importing the dominantly text-based new learning materials from the developed world, materials need to be developed locally that specifically address the needs of the majority. Can materials be produced where text is replaced by the much more natural voice? Can these materials use visualization techniques, rather than text, to more accurately describe places, people, and events? Can these materials use interactive animation and simulation to allow learners to actively investigate how things dynamically happen and work? Yes, in every case; easily accessible digital multimedia tools (including FOSS) exist for all these needs.

Language

Many African people are at least bilingual, having both a local language and a colonial European language. Since most of Africa's education material is imported from the old colonial powers, their languages, rather than the indigenous language(s), dominate the education systems. This may appear reasonable in the large cities, where many youngsters are exposed to, and therefore naturally learn, both colonial and indigenous languages in their infancy, but in the remote and rural areas, where most of Africa's population lives, the picture is very different. Here, only local indigenous languages are heard and learned in infancy. The colonial languages are taught (usually not very well, by teachers who themselves are seldom fluent) to 8-14 year old learners, long after the "natural window" for language acquisition in infancy has closed. Very few reach reasonable proficiency, even for speech, whilst the much more difficult reading skills are consequently poorer. Learners in these remote, impoverished areas of Africa have enough disadvantages without being forced to read and listen in a medium which is, literally, alien to them, producing, at best, rote learning or, at worst, no learning. Therefore, much of the locally-produced new learning materials should allow the learners to choose whichever they prefer of several local indigenous languages, both for voice and text. This is already technologically possible and is being actively pursued by the African FOSS community. Also, African languages can and should be added to the now mature language technology platforms.

Culture

For quality learning, it is very important to contextualize the subject being learned: to paint the big picture first. This is particularly the case when learners are attempting to understand and master complex, often abstract, concepts, which are especially common in math, the natural sciences, and engineering. Man has always used analogies to handle such complexity, and they remain an excellent learning aid. However, analogies, like language, are often highly culturally dependent, and the analogies commonly used (especially in imported textual material) reflect the colonial, not the indigenous, culture. Using a London bus to contextualize the learning of Newton's Laws of Motion throughout much of rural Southern Africa has been failing for decades. Sadly, it has usually been the intelligence of the African learners that has been questioned, rather than the quality of the learning material and teaching. Therefore, locally-produced new learning materials should use culturally relevant analogies, often expressed via visualization, animation, or simulation, rather than text.

The conclusion is that these multimedia-based new learning environments are essential for the realization of "education for all" in Africa. It should be equally clear that little appropriate material is available for import. These materials could and should be locally produced to address the wide range of learning needs of Africa's excluded majority. So, the understanding, creation, provision, and management of these materials should be at the heart of Africa's new learning paradigm.

A BOOST TO SUSTAINABILITY

Beyond the empowerment of every individual via appropriate, quality education and training, the above ICT-based strategy is likely to have a further, more immediate impact on sustainable development. The local production of much of these ICT-based new learning materials can dramatically affect economic growth and poverty alleviation throughout Africa. Castells and Himanen (2002) state that "the next phase (of the information society) is the scientific convergence of information technology/media and social sciences (psychology, sociology, economics, etc.)" (p. 125). This poses an exciting prospect for (South) Africa.

By focusing much more strategic effort on applying ICTs to satisfy the needs (and more specifically, the education needs) of the poorest and most remote areas, Africa is not only likely to accelerate development on a broader scale, but also it is likely to emerge at the forefront of some of the social applications of ICTs. In other words, Africa could develop indigenous ICT industries that primarily address their own development needs (which imported developed-world ICTs have proven unsuitable for over the past 15 years), but which subsequently could emerge as leaders in the next phase of the global information economy, (i.e., "ICTs with a soul").

This suggests a path for the development of indigenous ICT industries in (South) Africa. The people who understand these development needs are those from the local, disadvantaged communities, not those sitting in offices in Midrand, or San Jose. The organizations that are most fit to address these needs are small, local companies working as individuals or start-ups in the SMME sector, not the multinationals. There is a wide range of explicit and implicit education needs in most disadvantaged communities; hence, there is a large set of potential solutions and markets, but there is not much investment money available in these areas. Moreover, there are few people in those communities who have the ICT skills and entrepreneurship capabilities to go with the understanding of the needs. It is unlikely that any proprietary ICT vendors, particularly multinationals, would seriously consider many, if any, of the innovative ideas from this underdeveloped, unattractive market.

However, by adopting the FOSS development processes, the local entrepreneurs and champions are immediately empowered to pilot their ideas themselves, with very low start-up costs. They do not have to reinvent wheels, but can build on what is already freely available from the global FOSS community. The biggest remaining obstacle is the lack of appropriate FOSS training and skills among the most disadvantaged communities.

As described above, that is a problem that (South) Africa can overcome relatively quickly, if approached strategically with innovative methods and the active support of the international development community.

NOTES

1. FOSS is used throughout this document to refer to both open source and free software, although proponents of free software dislike this practice. For more information, see www.gnu.org, and FLOSS (2003) "Free/Libre and Open source Software: Survey and Study: Final Report," available at: http://FLOSS.infonomics.nl/.

2. There are licenses which also include the source code that are not open source, e.g., shared source, which does not allow the user to modify and redistribute the software. Open source licenses always grant the user the freedom to use, copy, modify and redistribute the software. See http://creativecommons.org/ (Accessed 09/07/2004)

3. For an excellent overview of OSS development, see the special issue of the journal *Research Policy* (vol. 23, 2003). The seven articles in the special issue examine three major topics in open source development: (1) motivations (2) the innovation process and (3) competitive dynamics. Through these headings the implications of OSS development on areas ranging from the economics of innovation to organizational structures are explored.

REFERENCES

Blume, R., Bryden, N., Neilson, B., & Rotter, M. (2003). Designing and managing a framework for assessing results of use to OSS in South Africa: Phase 1, *BMI Tech Knowledge group Report*, No. BMI-T #SITA2003A.

Castells, M. (1998). *The information age: Economy, society, and culture, vol. 3, End of millennium*. Cambridge, England: Blackwell.

Castells, M., & Himanen, P. (2002). *The information society and the welfare state: The Finnish model*. London: Oxford University Press.

Cowan, R., & Harrison, E. (2001). Intellectual property rights in a knowledge-based economy. *MERIT-Infonomics Research Memorandum*, No. 2001-027. Retrieved July 9, 2004 from http://www.merit.unimaas.nl/publications/index.php

Daniel, J. S. (1999). *Mega-universities and knowledge media: Technology strategies for higher education*. London: Kogan Page.

Daniel, J. S., & Mackintosh, W. G. (2003). Leading ODL futures in the eternal triangle: A mega-university response to the greatest moral challenge of our age. In M. G. Moore & W. G. Anderson (Eds.), *Handbook of distance education*. Mahwah, NJ: Erlbaum.

David, P. A. (2000). A tragedy of the public knowledge "commons"? Global science, intellectual property and the digital technology boomerang. *SIEPR Discussion Paper*, No. 00-02.

Dhanarajan, G. (1999). Forward in K. Harry (Ed.), *Higher education through open and distance learning. World review of distance education and open learning*. London: Routledge and Commonwealth of Learning.

Gibbon, P. A., & Parekh, A. (2001). Uncommon wisdom: Making co-operation work in South African higher education. Johannesburg, South Africa: NEDAC

International Labour Organization (ILO). (2001). World Employment Report: Life at Work in the Information Economy: Turin, Italy: ILO Publishing.

International Society for Technology in Education [ISTE]. (1998). *National educational technology standards for students*. Eugene, OR: ISTE.

ISETT SETA/ Department of Labour. *ICT skills audit finds shortage*. ITWEB, August 29, 2002

Markcr, P., McNamara, K., & Wallace, L. (2002). The significance of information and communication technologies for reducing poverty. London: DFID.

Naledi 3D Factory. (n.d.). *Simulations (VR) as an aid to learning in Africa: An evaluation*. Retrieved July 9, 2004 from http://www.naledi3d.com/news/VR Evaluation.pdf

New Partnership for Africa's Development. (n.d.). Retrieved July 9, 2004 from http://www.nepad.org

OECD/Statistics Canada. (2000). *Literacy in the information age*. Paris: OECD.

OSS Working Group. (2003). Using Open source software in the South African government, *Government IT Officers Council (GITOC)*, Version 3.3. Retrieved July 9, 2004 from http://www.oss.gov.za/docs/OSS_Strategy_v3.pdf

Raymond, E. S. (2001). The cathedral and the bazaar: Musings on Linux and open source by an accidental revolutionary. Sebastopol, CA: O'Reilly.

SANEC – South African Netherlands Chamber of Commerce Trade Directory 2001-2002—Economic profile South Africa: The Hague: Ministry of Commerce

Saint, W. (1999). *Tertiary distance education and technology in sub-Saharan Africa*. Washington DC: World Bank.

Street, B. V. (1999). The meanings of literacy. In D. A. Wagner, R. L. Venezky, & B. L. Street (Eds.), *Literacy: An international handbook*. Boulder, CO: Westview.

United Nations. (2002a). Resolution adopted by the General Assembly: 56/116. United Nations Literacy Decade: education for all. New York: UN.

United Nations. (2002b). United Nations Literacy Decade: Education for all. International plan of action: Implementation of General Assembly Resolution 56/116. New York: UN.

UNDP. (2001). *Human development report 2001: Making new technologies work for human development*. New York: UN.

UNESCO. (2000). *World education report 2000*. Paris: UNESCO Publishing.

UNESCO. (2002). *EFA global monitoring report 2002. Education for all. Is the world on track?* Paris: UNESCO.

UNESCO. (2002). *Strategic framework for sub-Saharan Africa. In the area of teacher training and secondary education through open and distance learning.* Paris: UNESCO.

Van der Merwe, D. (1999). The dematerialization of print and the fate of copyright. *International Review of Law, Computers & Technology, 13*(3), 303.

World Bank. (2000). *Higher education in developing countries. Peril and promise.* Washington, DC: World Bank.

World Bank. (2002). *Lifelong learning in the global knowledge economy: A challenge for developing countries.* Washington, DC: World Bank.

CHAPTER 16

THE IMPORTANCE AND IMPLEMENTATION OF DISTANCE LEARNING IN TURKISH WOMEN'S EDUCATION

Emine Demiray and Sensu Curabay

INTRODUCTION

Literacy rates for women are lower than for men in many parts of the globe, and in most countries, educational opportunities for women are also generally less favorable than for their male counterparts. Unfortunately, this same inequality holds true for the nation of Turkey. Distance education, however, may hold a key in helping Turkish women to achieve an education and build a successful career. Because of the increased opportunities for learning afforded by distance education programs, it may very well be that this group will be the one most strongly turning to distance-based courses to better their lives.

This chapter focuses on the learning needs of women in Turkey. As a specific case in point, we examine the two-year Home Economics pre-

Trends and Issues in Distance Education: International Perspectives, 205–216
Copyright © 2005 by Information Age Publishing
All rights of reproduction in any form reserved.

License Program at Anadolu University's Open Education Faculty in Turkey. We begin by discussing the educational needs of Turkish women, followed by a description of the current educational status and position of women in Turkey. We then present a description of the structure of Anadolu University's Open Education Faculty and, more specifically, its distance education undergraduate program in Home Management. We conclude the chapter with an investigation of some of the enrollment statistics relating to female students in this program, and present some of these students' observations of their educational experience at Anadolu.

The Environment of the Program

The new millennium has witnessed little change in the problems faced by women in Turkey. Discrimination towards women, the marriage of young girls to husbands they have not chosen, the presence of rape, the deaths of many women over the years as victims of "honor killings," and the absence of many rights for women still form part of the fabric of life for many Turkish women.

Basic employment statistics can help provide evidence of the problems faced by women in Turkey. In Parliament, for example, only 4% of the members are female, and there is not one female governor of any Turkish province. In civil society, we see that among administrative staff, there are only three women for every 100 men, only two female employers for every 100 male employers, and only 4% of senior administrators are women. The proportion of unemployed women between the ages of 15-34 years is 82%, while a mere 6% of the female workers are union members. Only 10% of the family income in Turkey is earned by women, while a low of 14% of those receiving social security benefits are women. While 75 out of every 100 women living in rural areas work on farms, 88% of them work as unpaid laborers. In Turkey, 2500 women die in childbirth every year, while 75% of rural-based women never visit a doctor during their lifetime. The continuing discrimination against women shows itself in all areas of society (Doster, 2000).

One basic remedy to solve many of these problems is making education available to both men and women. If today's Turkish women want to develop strong personalities, become more self-confident, and enjoy an acceptable and equal status in society, they will have to become conscious, creative, productive members of the Turkish society. In today's world, the level of civilization and development of a country can be measured by looking at the educational opportunities and levels of women.

There are no laws in Turkey that prevent women from pursuing primary, secondary, technical, vocational, or higher education. However, in

Table 16.1.   Illiteracy Rate in Turkey Over the Last 65 years (%)

Year	Female	Male	Total
1935	90	70	80
1940	87	64	75
1945	83	56	70
1950	81	54	67.5
1955	74	44	59
1960	75	46	60.5
1965	67	36	51.5
1970	58	30	44
1975	50	24	36
1980	45	20	32.5
1985	32	13	22.5
1990	28	11	19.5
2000	20	6	13

rural areas, between the different geographical regions, and within the various levels of culture and civilization in cities, the educational opportunities between women and men show significant differences. Basic education has been compulsory since the foundation of the Turkish Republic; nevertheless, 20% of the female population and 6% of the male population is illiterate. Table 16.1 gives an overview of the illiteracy rates during the last six decades.

The proportion of females/males attending primary education in 1999-2000 (and compulsory since 1997) was 88.5% for females, and 99.9% for males. Attendance at secondary level was 48.4% for females and 65.2% for males in the same year. The figures for higher education in the same period were 17.4% for females and 24.4% for males. (www.die.gov.tr).

The Turkish education system, as in many countries, is divided into two main streams; formal and informal. The formal education system ranges from kindergarten to higher education. In informal education, we find basic literacy, vocational, social and cultural courses, and training apprenticeship courses (Cumhuriyet'in 75. Yilinda Turkiye'de Kadinin Durumu, 1998).

Post-primary education is divided into two main streams: general and vocational-technical. In both streams, female attendance has increased during the last decades. The same trend holds for higher education, as well. However, when viewed by discipline, there is, nevertheless an unequal distribution in the number of female and male students attending higher education, as shown in Table 16.2. The majority of female stu-

Table 16.2.   Distribution of Female and Male Students Attending Higher Education

Field of Study	# Female	# Male
Language and literature	19,798	12,669
Math and science	32,627	40,567
Medical sciences	40,898	31,410
Social Sciences	34,794	46,935
Applied social sciences	157,582	188,222
Technical sciences	29,786	101,301
Agriculture and forestry	7,617	18,187
Art	6,835	5,911
Other educational areas	639	7,015

dents are attending programs that are traditionally thought of as "suitable for women," such as Language and Literature, Art, Applied Social Sciences, and Medical Sciences (www.die.gov.tr).

There are many factors that negatively impact the education of women in Turkey, including low female employment rates, marriage at young age, late school entry, a general lack of interest in women's education, educational costs, patriarchal ideas, and the belief that education contributes nothing to a woman's future. It is true that many people recognize education as a basic factor in the development of production and the upgrading of women's status in society and in the sharing of responsibilities and participation decision-making, but women nevertheless continue to face many problems related to education (2000'li Yillar Oncesinde Turkiye'de Kadin Egitimi, 1992)

RECENT DEVELOPMENTS

There has been a more conscious and sensitive approach to the problems of women since the 1980s, when Turkey signed the international contract for the "Prevention of all Discrimination against Women." Moreover, to reduce the number of women having to leave school, family planning information has been included in school curricula. Additionally, a special unit dealing with the status of women and their problems was established with a focus on tackling specific problems of women and on improvement of the status of women. The opportunities for informal education through programs aiming at literacy and employment opportunities have been increased.

In addition to recognition of women's issues, distance education has also emerged in the Turkish education system. The Anadolu University's

Open Education Faculty, for example, began to offer distance education programs in 1982 for both degrees and post-graduate certificates. In 1992, the Open High School, which provides education at secondary school level, was established.

EXAMPLES OF PROGRAMS TARGETING WOMEN

The National Schools

The National Schools, founded in 1928, were one of the first institutions to offer informal educational opportunities aimed not only at cities, but also in rural areas where schooling is particularly difficult to achieve. The National Schools also provide learning opportunities in traditional arts for girls, mobile courses for village women, and technical education improvement programs for women. A number of programs related to women's education have been created with the assistance of UNICEF.

The Vocational and Technical Education stream and the Home Economics and Childcare stream are particularly important educational programs provided by the National Schools. The Vocational and Technical Education stream provides secondary level programs for training intermediate professional staff in Science and Technology, Vocational and Technical skills improvement, and others. The programs are in line with identified needs in various regions for purposes of contributing to the economy of the family and to the industrial development of Turkey. The Home Economics and Childcare stream offers Childcare and Education, Home Economics, Home Economics and Nutrition, Child and Pre-school Education, Decorating, Beauty Care, and Hairdressing, all aimed to provide formal education to female learners. In addition, the Home Administration Associate Degree Program (HAADP), focusing specifically on women, was established in 1992, within the Faculty of Open Education. This program seeks to develop the skills and knowledge necessary for efficient use of resources within the family unit.

The Home Administration Associate Degree Program

This two-year associate degree program admits high school graduates, or those possessing equivalency. It uses written material supported by TV programs for course delivery, with no face-to-face contact between learner and instructor. Students take two examinations—a mid-term examination

**Table 16.3.   First-Year Compulsory Courses
during the Academic Year 1999-2000**

Courses	Number Printed Units	Number TV Programs
Consumer behavior and consumer consciousness	12	6
Principles of nutrition	12	8
Health care and first aid	15	6
Etiquette dinner preparation	15	12
Home equipment	16	6
Citizenship and environmental information	15	7
Psychology	11	6
Languages		
German	25	25
French	12	27
English	30	30

**Table 16.4.   Second-year Compulsory Courses
During the Academic Year 1999-2000**

Courses	Number Printed Units	Number TV Programs
Family economics	11	7
Child care and health	18	7
History of civilization	10	9
Family structure	16	8
Knowledge of home administration	14	8
Changing technology and its effect on family life	13	8
Turkish language	15	10
Ataturk's principles and the history of revolution	30	20

and a final examination. Those students who are unable to pass the final examination may take a make-up examination. The television programs for these courses are broadcast over a 24-week period, twice per day, on specific days of the week. After the two-year course of study is up, and the mid-term and final examinations are successfully completed, the degree is awarded.

The HAADP two-year program has a number of required first-year courses. These are listed in Table 16.3, with the associated numbers of print and TV support. Compulsory courses for the second year are shown in Table 16.4.

A CLOSER LOOK AT THE HAADP PROGRAMS

Research on the effect of the program was conducted in the city of Eskisehir during the 1999-2000 academic year. The sample studied consisted of 70 female students selected from among the HAADP at the Open Education Faculty. All courses taken by these students used printed learning materials supported by television broadcasts.

An examination of the passing rate for these students finds that 16.8% of female students passed directly to the second year and 12.2% of males did the same. In addition, female students enjoyed a 19.8% first-time graduation rates (after two years), and male students enjoyed a 19.1% rate for the same, virtually an identical rate.

Focus on Female Students

Now that we have briefly looked at some general statistics for these courses, we now turn our attention to data specific to female students in this program.

Age

Most female students in this study were between 25 and 49 years of age, as is seen in Table 16.5. The fact that there were no students older than 49 years is presumed to be caused by the inability of such students to take classes because they likely had responsibility for caring for families and/or of extended families.

Marital Status

Looking at Table 16.6, we see that the twice as many students were married as were unmarried. This could be conjectured to be the result of important and often excessive duties at home, which might make distance education courses preferable over full-time, formal education courses.

Table 16.5.   Ages of Female Students (*N* = 70)

Age Groups	Number	% of Total
18-24	9	12.9
25-34	32	45.7
35-49	29	41.4
50 and older	—	—

Table 16.6.   Marital Status of Female Students (N = 70)

Marital Status	Number	% Total
Married	47	67.1
Single, divorced, widowed	23	32.9

Table 16.7.   Number of Children of Female Students (N = 70)

Number of Children	Number	% Total
None	22	31.4
1 Child	34	48.6
2 Children	14	20.0
3 or more children	—	—

Table 16.8.   Career Distributions of Female Students (N = 70)

Career Track	Number of Participants	% Total Participants
Banking	10	14.3
Police	8	11.5
Civil service	26	37.1
Teaching	12	17.1
Self-employed	5	7.1
Unemployed	9	12.9

Number of Children

In Turkey, as in many other countries, there is a close relationship between pregnancy rate and educational level. Parents whose education level is low tend to have more children, while the rate of pregnancy decreases as the level of education increases. According to a survey of population and family health, the average number of children for illiterate women is 5.1, while the number is 1.4 for university-educated women. (2000'li Yillar Oncesinde Turkiye'de Kadin Egitimi, 1992). Table 16.7 shows the number of children of the female students.

Work

Table 16.8 shows that 87% of the female students participating in the study were working. These results also reveal that 17% of these students were enrolled in programs closely related to their careers.

Personal Income

The fact that 13% of the students had no personal income is explained in that they were not working, and thus were seen as "housewives." Table

Table 16.9.   Total Monthly Personal Income Levels (N = 70)

Monthly Personal Income in US $ in 2000	Number of Participants	% Total Participants
No income	9	13%
Minimum Wage (less than $162)	12	17%
162-325	26	37%
326-488	18	26%
489-651	5	7%
652-814	—	—
815 +	—	—

Table 16.10.   Total Monthly Family Income Levels (N = 70)

Monthly Family Income in US $ in 2000	Number	% of Total
Minimum Wage (less than $162)	—	—
162-325	8	12
326-488	12	17
489-651	25	36
652-814	15	20
815-977	4	6
978-1140	2	3
1141-1302	3	4.5
1303 +	1	1.5

16.9 shows that most of the students in the Home Administration Associate Degree Program were drawn from lower income-earning groups.

The study revealed that most of the students came from middle-class families, but their individual incomes are in the low-income groups (compare Table 16.9). Table 16.10 depicts the percentages of students by monthly family income.

The reasons why students participated in the educational program are varied, but as seen in Table 16.11, more than half stated they were studying because it would give them an opportunity to get a promotion, and thus most likely, a higher income. As about two-thirds of these students were married, and of these, approximately two-thirds had children, these students did not have the chance to attend full-time formal educational courses in order to gain qualifications that would increase their salaries. Therefore, these female students chose the Home Administration Associate Degree Distance Education Program in order to achieve their financial goals.

Table 16.11.   Motivational Factors of Female Students (*N* = 70)

Reasons for Enrollment	Number of Participants	% Total Participants
Diploma	4	6
Promotion at work	44	63
Change of profession	2	3
Increase knowledge	6	8
Improve status at work	12	17
Self-actualization	-	-
No particular aim	2	3

The second motive for preferring this program (17%) was "improved status at work." The women who worked as teaching assistants (preschool, handicrafts, kindergarten, etc.) primarily made this choice. These students aimed to achieve a better position in their own careers as they saw their education as complementary to their work. As this program and their work ran parallel, they wanted to develop their own qualities and achieve better positions at work. The total rate of the "no particular aim" alternative was 3%.

Student Responses to Open Questions in Questionnaire

Three open questions were asked in the study. These open-ended questions provided students the opportunity to express more freely their concerns, challenges and feelings. For each question, a priority listing was created, depicted below.

Question 1:   Which courses are most beneficial for your daily lives?

First priority: Health Care and First Aid, Etiquette and Meal Table Preparation
Second priority: Principles of Nutrition, Child Care and Health
Third priority: Equipment at Home.

Question 2:   Which are your favorite courses?

First priority: Child Care and Health, Etiquette and Meal Table Preparation
Second priority: Health Care and First Aid, Family Economics
Third priority: Principles of Nutrition

Question 3:   Which courses are most relevant to your work?

First priority: Principles of Nutrition
Second priority: Child Care and Health
Third priority: Consumer Behavior and Consumer Consciousness
No answer: Nine students

Although only 17% of the students enrolled in this program had jobs that clearly related to the content of the program, the remainder of the students also followed the courses with great interest and benefited from them in their daily work and private life. This can perhaps be explained by the fact that participants were female and, as such, tended to prefer the subjects of home care and child care. In answer to the question, "Which courses are most relevant to your work?" the nine non-working students did not furnish a response. Seventy-seven percent of the remaining (working) students pointed out that the courses did not relate to their jobs, and that they could not use the information derived from these courses at work. The remainder of participants (23%) indicated that the courses were useful in their jobs. These results were expected, as the students who had careers differing from their fields of study thought that the courses were not useful in their jobs, while the students who worked at Public Education Centers (in areas such as child care, sewing, and handicrafts) and those who graduated from similar departments at high school, and therefore believed that the courses were useful in their jobs.

FINAL REMARKS AND CONCLUSIONS

There is a trend towards improved educational opportunities for women in this country. The shift towards improved women's education is an ongoing process. Although women participating in distance education programs evidenced a favorable view of their educational experience, they still often related those favorable views to the traditional role of women in Turkish society, including the role of a housewife and mother. In addition, although a large majority of the students thought that their studies contributed to the development of their individual personalities, the students were apparently not prepared to deviate substantially from their traditional role in society in their choice of courses, choosing disciplines of study aligned with the traditional notions of women's role in Turkish society.

Regardless, it can be seen that distance learning provides a powerful opportunity for improving the roles of females in Turkish society. Distance learning provides improved access to courses, a greater array of available disciplines of study, and the ability to fit education "into" the already busy lives of Turkish women. In real terms, this means that distance education provides a strong potential benefit to women in Turkey.

RECOMMENDATIONS

The authors make the following recommendations:

1. Higher educational programs for women should not be limited to conventional higher education programs.
2. Vocational training and carrier encouragement programs for women should be established as soon as possible.
3. Distance education programs should be designed in such a way that they stimulate the critical thinking of students and encourage reflection on the role of women in society.
4. Distance education programs should encourage female students to become self-confident, successful, and modern participants in Turkish society.

REFERENCES

"Cumhuriyet'in 75. Yilinda Turkiye'de Kadinin Durumu [The Situation of Women in Turkey on the 75th Anniversary of the Turkish Republic]", TC. Basbakanlik Kadinin Statutusu ve Sorunlari Genel Mudurlugu, Ankara, Turkey, 1998.

Demiray, U. (1999). Kurulusunun 5. Yilinda Acikogretim Lisesi ile Ilgili Calismalar Kaynakcasi [A Literature review of Open High Schools on the 5th Anniversary], MEB Egitim Teknolojileri Genel Mudurlugu, Ankara, Turkey, 1999.

Doster, N. Kadin ve Kimlik Kavgasi [Women and Identity Struggle], Sosyal Demokrat Degisim Dergisi, Sayi: 16, Istanbul, Turkey, 2000.

"2000'li Yillar Oncesinde Turkiye'de Kadin Egitimi [Women's Education in Turkey Before the Year 2000]", Birinci Uluslararasi Konseyi, Haziran 1992, TC. Milli Egitim Bakanligi Kiz Teknik Ogretim Genel Mudurlugu, Ankara, Turkey, 1992. Retrieved from www.die.gov.tr.

CHAPTER 17

"THANK YOU FOR (NOT) FORGETTING US"

A Reflection on the Trials, Tribulations, and Take-off of Distance Education in Mozambique

Muriel Visser-Valfrey, Jan Visser, and Miguel Buendia

INTRODUCTION

Over the past four decades, distance education has gradually gained a modest but increasingly prominent role within the education system in Mozambique, as well as within the overall context of the development needs of the country. However, as will be argued in this chapter, the potential of distance education is still much greater than the extent to which it is being used, particularly when compared to some of the more pressing problems that the country continues to face. Among these problems is an education system that is characterized by a relatively large base but also by high rates of drop-outs and grade repetitions (particularly among girls); huge needs in terms of human resource development for the continued economic growth of the country; and challenges posed by the continued spread of HIV/AIDS.

Trends and Issues in Distance Education: International Perspectives, 217–241

This chapter considers the development of distance education in Mozambique—a country in which distance education has played a role for over 40 years—against the background of the overall developments and needs of the country over the past decades. After a brief introduction to the country itself, a discussion of Mozambique's first post-independence distance education course (launched in 1983) will be used as an initial case study. The analysis of this experience will highlight how key contextual characteristics shaped the decision-making process around this course and how these affected subsequent achievements in distance education in Mozambique in general. Key issues and emerging trends from this first experience will be contrasted with current developments in distance education. The chapter will end with a series of discussion points that, in the opinion of the authors, need to be addressed to fully realize the potential of distance education in Mozambique.

A Brief Background

Mozambique lies on the east coast of Africa (Figure 17.1), has a surface area of 801,590 square kilometers (roughly twice the size of California). Its population is just over 18 million, of which 44% is under 15 years of age. The country is divided into 11 provinces and more than 2,400 km of coastline. This coastline plays an important role in both the tourism and fishery industries and also positions Mozambique as an important transport and trade link for the land-locked countries in the interior of Africa (such as Zimbabwe, Botswana and Malawi).

Figure 17.1.   Map of Mozambique

Table 17.1   Mozambiue—Situation Today

Total population:	18 million
Population < 15 years of age:	44%
Life expectancy	39 years
GNP per capita	US$200
People below poverty line	70%
Unemployment rate	21%
Female adult literacy rate	23%
Male adult literacy rate	64%
HIV/AIDS adult prevalence	13%
People living with HIV/AIDS	1.1 million

Source: UNDP, 2003.

The recent history of Mozambique is of a somewhat turbulent nature. Mozambique became independent from Portugal in 1975 after 500 years of colonial rule. Peace was, however, short-lived and, by the end of the 1970s, the country was racked by a war of destabilization supported by Rhodesia and South Africa that lasted more than a decade. Over one million people were killed during the war, many more were displaced within and outside the country, and a substantial part of the country's economic and social infrastructure was irreparably damaged or destroyed. The war ended in October 1992 with the signing of the General Peace Accords between the Mozambican Government and the RENAMO opposition. The country experienced peace for the first time in many years, a multi-party democracy was adopted, and the first democratic elections were held in 1994 (M. Visser, 1997).

Peace brought tremendous opportunities for development, the country-side was once again accessible, economic production (which had been brought to a halt during the war) could gradually resume, and investments in communications and industry slowly became a reality. The war had, however, left its marks on the country; industries and services had to be built up from scratch, and the levels of absolute poverty—which had grown from 15% in 1980 to 60% in 1995 (Abrahamsson, 1995)—continued to deteriorate. By 2001, 70% of the country lived in poverty (UNDP, 2003).

The erratic process of development in Mozambique since its independence had left its marks on all social sectors. In education, where incredible gains were made shortly after independence, the war provoked dramatic losses. At the end of the war in 1992, over 50% of the existing school infrastructure had been lost. Significant investments have been made in the decade since the war but, in spite of progress in terms of planning and organization, as well as in coverage and infrastructure

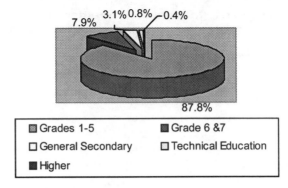

Figure 17.2.   Distribution of students in the education system (1999).

development, the education system continues to be plagued by problems of quality and efficiency. The indicators in Figure 17.2 are illustrative of the education situation in the country today.

More than 25 years after independence, the challenges to progress in Mozambique are therefore still very real, and have unfortunately been compounded by more recent developments. One of the greatest threats today is the rapid spread of HIV/AIDS. With a current adult HIV/AIDS prevalence rate of 13% (UNAIDS, 2003), the pervasiveness of the disease is rapidly growing, especially in the economically important southern and central provinces where the impact of HIV/AIDS is, over the next 10 years, expected to reduce life expectancy from 50 years in the absence of HIV/AIDS to 36 years (Ministério da Saúde, 2001). By some estimates, the impact on the economy will be substantial, with economic growth declining by up to 23% by the year 2010, resulting in a 1% annual expected decline of the GDP (Arndt, 2002). The impact on education is expected to be very substantial, with the death of large numbers of teachers and school administrators, and a potentially heavy impact on school enrollments (Verde Azul, 2000).

DISTANCE EDUCATION PRIOR TO 1975

Three distinct phases can be distinguished in the development of distance education in Mozambique. We will briefly consider the initial "pre-independence stage" and then discuss Mozambique's first post-independence distance experience, which took place in the early 1980s. This first post-independence experience will highlight some of the issues and emerging trends that prevail today.

Colonial rule by the Portuguese focused mainly on exploiting the country's natural resources. As a matter of policy, the Portuguese did little to provide social services such as health and education to the inhabitants of their colony. The education system was set up essentially to promote the advancement of Portuguese settlers and of a select few Africans who were to mediate between the colonizers and the population. The result was an astounding illiteracy rate of 93% at the time of independence (DANIDA, 1994).

Very little information exists on distance education prior to 1975. Many of the possible records, such as newspaper advertisements and archives, were destroyed. The information that remains indicates that distance education did not have a prominent role and existed mainly in the form of correspondence courses which were prepared in Portugal and sent to individual students. These courses targeted a very small section of the population, mostly consisting of Portuguese settlers who wanted to upgrade their skills while staving off the boredom of rural life. The most popular courses were in the field of electronics (especially radio and television maintenance), the arts, cooking, and photography (Franque, 1993). An exception was the courses which were offered by the railway company, C.F.M., which were locally produced and delivered to its workers by train. However, this and other courses were gradually discontinued when Mozambique attained independence in 1975.

In summary, it can be said that during the pre-independence period:

- Education in general, and distance education in particular, catered to the needs of individual students of Portuguese origin and therefore reached only a minute percentage of the population.
- Distance education had little relevance to the development needs of the country.
- Distance education was of a sporadic nature, mainly imported from outside and neither adapted to local needs nor controlled or supervised by any local authority.

Had there been the political will and the policy to do so, there would, during this period, have been room for a far more prominent role for distance education, for example by extending education to settlers and local populations in remote locations, combating illiteracy, and providing nonformal education to the local population in vital areas such as agriculture and health. Other colonies, such as Rhodesia (under British rule), were more forward-thinking in this respect and developed correspondence courses particularly targeted at children of settlers (Inquai, 1994). The Portuguese colonial policy (like that of the Spanish) was in this sense different from that of the English or the French, in that relatively little effort and money was invested in developing their colonies.

MOZAMBIQUE'S FIRST POST-INDEPENDENCE DISTANCE EDUCATION EXPERIENCE

Independence marked the beginning of a new era in all spheres of social and economic life. The formation of the first independent government in 1975, established along Marxist-Leninist principles, marked the beginning of this period. The exodus of the Portuguese from the country meant that almost no qualified human resources remained. To overcome this situation, the government of Mozambique embarked on an ambitious program to extend education to the Mozambican population through the formal education system. Faced with almost no infrastructure and very few teachers, the government chose first to expand the infrastructure and train teachers. The initial option was to focus on formal, contiguous education. Given the pressing needs, very little time was devoted to considering alternative options. It must be remembered that most activity in these early years was spearheaded by euphoria, by the need to get things done and by the drive to do away with the scars of colonial times. Reflection came much later when it became clear that in education, and other social sectors, the problems were sufficiently complex, and the country sufficiently challenged, to warrant more detailed and well-studied solutions.

The initial engagement in education rapidly began paying off, and enrollments grew dramatically. At primary level, participation doubled in six years, reaching 1.3 million students by 1982, and in secondary education the number of enrollments grew fivefold over the same period (Candido, Menete, Martins, & Ahmed, 1986). To meet the increase in demand for education, teachers were trained in crash courses and communities were involved in (rudimentary) school construction. Literacy activities were organized wherever the available infrastructure and human resources provided a minimum of possibilities—in hospitals, factories, farms, etc. The main challenge at this time was to build an education system with next to no qualified and experienced staff.

These positive developments in education did not go uncontested. As a "communist stronghold," Mozambique was seen as a threat to some of its neighboring countries. From the end of the 1970s onwards, and with the support of the neighboring regimes in Rhodesia and South Africa, a civil war raged in Mozambique which brought terrible destruction and loss of life. From its onset, the progress of this war marred the progress in all areas, including education, and posed a significant challenge to the intentions of the Government and to its ambitiously-defined development goals.

It was against this backdrop that Mozambique implemented its first major distance education experience. The first impulse for this was given during the 3rd Party Congress in 1977 when the ruling (only) party, FRELIMO, mandated that the possibilities of using distance education should be seriously studied. A small team of experts drawn from various areas of education was subsequently brought together and given the task to produce a feasibility study of the use of distance education in Mozambique (MINED, 1980).

The report of the feasibility study outlined in some detail the potential benefits that distance education could represent for the country. In terms of potential, it identified a number of possible applications, including the use of distance education for extending the formal school system, particularly at sixth- and seventh-grade level (where enrollments were severely limited because of lack of schools), but also to expand opportunities of formal secondary, higher, and technical education. Continuous upgrading of the workforce "in accordance with the economic and cultural development needs of the country" (MINED, 1980, p. 6) was also identified as a potential target, as was the training of adult literacy teachers and adult educators. However, in terms of immediate priority and as a key opportunity, the study identified the training of primary school teachers as being of foremost importance (MINED, 1980), the assumption being that other important target groups could follow.

Directives from the III Party Congress (1977)

"Priority should be given to the training of people at the grassroots, through courses for workers, through the implementation of evening classes and correspondence courses" (Relatório do CC ao III Congresso, 1977, p. 137—translation by author).

"By 1979 study the conditions for the establishment of a national centre for distance education that also uses radio broadcasting" (Directivas Económicas e Sociais, 1977, p. 100—translation by author).

This recommendation to focus on teachers as a first target group was in line with the pressing need for more (and better-qualified) teachers and the Government's priority for expanding access to education. It was also in line with the priority that was being given to developing the country's economic basis and to establishing a skilled labor force, for which high-quality education was seen as an essential prerequisite. At the time, new teachers with fourth-grade education and no professional qualification were being recruited directly into the system. It was clearly felt that the future of the education system was at risk if decisive steps were not taken to provide adequate training to this group of over 10,000 teachers. In addition, various other arguments were presented to support the rationale for choosing teachers as a first target group:

- Teachers were part of a relatively well-organized system, even at the level of districts and localities, which would make it easy to provide the necessary logistic and academic support and would facilitate the monitoring and evaluation of this first experience;
- Because many teachers had already expressed a keen and pressing interest in furthering their own academic and professional qualifications, they therefore represented a motivated target group;
- Investing in teachers made good sense from a cost-benefit perspective because of the expected spin-off effect that well-qualified teachers would have on the quality of education, and thus on the development of children and the country in general, and;
- Given their own pedagogical background, it was foreseen that teachers could be active participants in the process of continuously analyzing and improving this first experience.

An additional, interesting, characteristic of this first attempt to define distance education in the Mozambican context is that the feasibility study specifically identified distance education as an instrument/tool for advancing learning that had the potential to be integrated throughout the education system, rather than as a sub-system in its own right. With this statement, the feasibility study opened the door to using distance education as a means to promote educational access and quality in all domains, including in the informal and non-formal environment.

Following extensive discussion of the feasibility study and an extensive study visit to various countries with experience in distance education, Mozambique's first Department for Distance Education (initially called a "unit") was created. As a first step, the new Department for Distance Education selected 20 staff members who were to be trained and become the first group of distance education specialists in Mozambique. The training of this group started in 1983, with financing of the Government of Brazil and UNESCO. Course participants were trained in three key areas: production of radio programs, drafting of instructional materials, and planning and evaluation (Neeleman & Nhavoto, 2003). The course itself was developed around self-contained study materials and tutorials, and sup-

**Table 17.2.   Mozambique's First Distance Education Experience:
Profile of Participants**

Total number of students	1,224
Female students:	46.6%
Students owning a radio	53 %
Average age	30 years

Source: Candido et al. (1986).

plemented by radio programs. According to sources involved with the initiative at the time, these radio programs were so popular that they attracted an audience not only among the target group of teachers but also among the general public (Flinck & Flinck, 1988). A system of tutors was created, with study groups that held weekly meetings and a monthly meeting with the tutor. It was foreseen that the teachers who successfully completed the course would receive an academic qualification equivalent to six years of primary schooling and one year of professional teacher training and that they would subsequently be paid in accordance with their new academic qualifications.

Starting in 1984—while the civil war continued to escalate—an initial group of 1,224 teachers from six provinces was enrolled. In looking back upon this experience and before considering a number key issues and emerging trends, it is important to highlight some of the characteristics of the context in which this first experience took place:

- No prior local distance education experience or expertise to speak of.
- Emerging but as yet poorly defined educational policy framework.
- Dispersed educational network, with poor communication infrastructure.
- Escalating war and deteriorating security situation.
- Increasingly severe resource constraints.

Thus, in spite of careful preparation, the challenges to this first experience were numerous, and only 30% of the teachers were able to complete the course. Successive assessments/evaluations of this first distance education experience took place between 1986 and 1988, and attempted to make a fair assessment of its impact, its progress, and its potential (cf. Candido et al., 1986; Flinck & Flinck, 1988; Zalzman & Visser, J., 1988). Some of the specific bottlenecks and constraints that were identified include:

- Insufficient quality of materials due to hurried production and lack of experience, compounded by the problem that a substantial number of texts were too difficult for the students.
- Delays in the production of materials, forcing students to interrupt their studies for weeks on end and contributing to lowering the morale. The duration of the course ended up taking four years, rather than the planned two-year duration.
- Poor-quality support from tutors who were not well prepared, were often too far away, and did not themselves receive adequate support.
- Difficulties in accessing the radio programs, due to lack of radios and particularly batteries and occasionally caused by problems with reception (compounded by acts of sabotage as a result of the war).
- Transportation difficulties due to the war and lack of resources, which affected the contact between tutors and students.
- Emphasis on the output of the course (i.e. number of graduates) rather than on a careful monitoring of the process.

Although not specifically mentioned in any of the evaluation reports, an additional problem which affected the morale of teachers was that they never received the promised academic qualification and related salary increase. Overall, however, even though opinions of the evaluations are somewhat diverse on specific points, there was generally a very positive appreciation of the pertinence and relevance of the experience as well as of the potential that distance education could offer to the country.

Figure 17.3.   More than 10 years after the peace agreement, the scars of the war are still evident (Photo credit: Muriel Visser-Valfrey).

Nevertheless, in 1987 and as a result of a combination of factors internal and external to the system, the Ministry of Education decided to discontinue this first experience. Lack of real commitment to this innovation, political infighting within the education system, and the increasing problems caused by the war meant that the focus was placed on maintaining the status quo rather than embarking on and supporting radical innovation. As a result, the Department of Distance Education was disbanded and distance education was integrated into the recently established National Directorate for Teacher Training. This integration did not involve transferring the trained staff, the large majority of whom were assigned to other areas of education and never again worked in distance education.

An unfortunate consequence of the decision to incorporate distance education in teacher training was that the original vision of distance education as offering potential to broaden access and quality in all domains of the education system—which had been so carefully hammered out in the feasibility study—was lost and would remain so for many years. A further consequence was that the dismantling of the Department of Distance Education and the reassignment of its staff marked the beginning of a prolonged period of stagnation that ended seven years later, in 1994, with the launching of a second distance education course for primary school teachers. As a result, much of the individual commitment to the experience was squandered and proved to be very difficult to reconstitute later.

Overall, this first experience allowed Mozambique to gain valuable insight into the working of a distance education system and into the specific organizational and technical capacity required. The detailed analysis of this case makes it possible to begin pinpointing a number of key issues that affected the success of the experience at the time. We will later compare these issues to those that are important today and attempt to assess to what extent progress has been made in addressing them. Thus, key issues that emerge from that experience include:

- The inherent vulnerability of an innovation, especially in a weak policy context and/or in a context of poor educational management.
- The overriding importance of contextual factors in determining success or failure and ultimately the sustainability of an innovation. This includes the vital factor of individual commitment and vision of key persons, but also the overall organizational, political, social, and economic environment that may either encourage or stifle initiatives.
- The constant tension between the time needed to create true innovation and the political importance of demonstrating quick results.

In this example, a number of materials were hastily produced and not tested in the rush to meet deadlines.

DISTANCE EDUCATION IN MOZAMBIQUE TODAY

Seventeen years have passed since the abrupt end of Mozambique's first distance education experience. During these years, Mozambique has changed greatly. The death of Mozambique's first president in 1986 marked the beginning of political and economic changes and a movement toward a more open society and a market-oriented economy. The introduction of successive programs of economic austerity under the auspices of the International Monetary Fund (IMF) improved Mozambique's chances of receiving financing and investments to rebuild its severely damaged economy, but also brought more hardship to the poor as well as changed attitudes among the leadership in important social and economic sectors. In the area of education, the end of the war brought new opportunities for education in Mozambique. Over the years, a more coherent framework for education has developed, namely the Education Sector Strategic Plan (ESSP), which outlines objectives, priorities, and strategies, and also provides a funding framework. Funding and technical assistance for the implementation of the plan comes from a large group of multilateral and bilateral agencies as well as non-governmental organizations (NGOs). Progress has been made, in particular, in addressing issues of access to education. Various initiatives have got underway to improve the quality, including the introduction in 2004 of an ambitious new primary education curriculum. However, in spite of these initiatives, problems in access persist, and quality and equity remain two of the greatest bottlenecks within the system. Some of the problems that were evident already in the early 1980s, such as the sharply accentuated educational pyramid, and the dearth of untrained teachers, continue to be present today.

With respect to distance education, progress has been mixed. The lengthy period of stagnation brought on by the dismantling of the Distance Education Department in 1987 ended only in 1996 when the Institute for Teacher Upgrading (IAP) launched a new course for teacher upgrading. Since then, a patchwork of initiatives, ranging in size, scope, and vision, has been launched. The most notable of these initiatives are briefly reviewed below.

Teacher Upgrading

It is in teacher training that distance education has continued to leave its most important mark. Delivered entirely in print form and with considerable support from tutors, over 7,000 teachers have been able to obtain professional qualifications and upgrade their academic level since the Institute for Teacher Upgrading launched its first course in 1996. The course consists of 50 modules, each of which requires one to two weeks of study. At the end each module, the course is assessed through a multiple-choice test. In addition, to qualify for their degree, candidates have to complete an internship with a higher-qualified colleague. In implementing these courses, IAP has made much progress, compared to the 1983 initiative, in terms of organization and tutor as well as student support, which is of course greatly facilitated by the climate of peace that the country is now experiencing. The level of the modules is also better adapted to the student profile than was the case with the 1983 materials. The courses have been criticized, however, for promoting rote learning of concepts and content and for doing little to change stifling teaching practices (which also promote rote learning) in the classroom.

Providing Access to Upper Primary Education

Until 2003, distance education remained limited to teacher training and, despite some debate, very little progress was made to implement the vision of distance education as a modality for delivery in other areas of education. It took the courage of a small group of people at the Provincial Directorate for Education in Gaza Province and the individual commit-

Figure 17.4.   A display of study guides for use by students in the distance education course in Gaza Province (Photo credit: Muriel Visser-Valfrey).

ment of the staff of a local NGO called UDEBA, to launch an experimental distance education experience in formal primary schooling. Faced with tremendous problems in providing access to upper primary education (grades six and seven) for children living in severely under-populated areas (mainly because the investment needed to expand the school system does not weigh up against the small number of students), this province decided to find a local solution. Following a period of reflection and an extensive provincial study, a course was developed by local staff that uses study guides and supplementary materials (including experimental radio programs) in combination with the mandatory regular schoolbooks. Today, groups of up to 20 children meet daily in school facilities that are not used in the afternoon and study under the supervision of an adult from the community or a teacher. In addition, there are weekly sessions with a teacher. So far, the program has proven hugely popular. From a policy perspective, it is an interesting lesson in the strength of local initiative. However, it remains to be seen to what extent this course will become part and parcel of the overall strategy of the Ministry of Education.

Establishment of a National Coordinating Structure for Distance Education

The year 2001 was the first year since 1980 that the debate around distance education resurfaced in the highest echelons of the Mozambican Government. The discussion around the establishment of the new Ministry of Higher Education and the related proposal to use distance education to expand access at this level once again sparked serious discussion about the potential of distance education. In a similar fashion to what happened shortly after independence, the Government concluded that the use of distance education should not be restricted to only one sub-sector of education, but that it should be used as a means of delivery and educational improvement throughout the system (Neeleman & Nhavoto, 2003). As a result, the commission that had advanced the idea of offering higher education opportunities through distance education was restructured and sent back to the drawing board to develop a new proposal that would give hands and feet to the strategy of integrating distance education as a modality of delivery at all levels and in all areas of education.

It is too early to make decisive comments about the success of this initiative, but some important steps have been taken—including steps that, from the perspective of Mozambique, constitute an innovation and have the potential of redirecting the course of distance education. Following recommendations by the revised commission, a facilitating entity for distance education—the National Institute for Distance Education (INED)—

has been created. This institute is conceived to act as a facilitating body by providing advice and resources to distance education initiatives around the country, at different levels and for diverse purposes. In recognition of the fact that such initiatives are still few and far between, INED will also develop a number of pilot projects. The purpose of these pilot projects is to develop experience in different areas of distance education and to promote the sustainability of this modality. At present, pilot projects are foreseen in three areas: training of secondary school teachers, access to secondary education, and preparatory education for students who are planning to enter higher education.

And Finally, a Selection of Smaller Initiatives

To be complete, we conclude this section by briefly referring to other experiences—albeit of a somewhat more reduced scale—that have operated over the years. Between 1986 and 1994, the Ministry of Agriculture ran a very successful distance education course for its extension workers, covering a range of topics from livestock management and crop rotation to environmental issues and gender. Unfortunately, the restructuring of the department that supervised the course and the departure of the chief technical advisor to the project that was providing the funding put an abrupt end to this initiative. Furthermore, in the mid-1990s, radio programs were used to upgrade the level of adult literacy teachers. A worthwhile private sector initiative was put in place by one of Mozambique's largest banks. In a series of courses that focus on various aspects of financial management and accounting, this Institute has graduated over 3000 participants since 1994. Manuals from Portugal were adapted to the Mozambican context for the purpose of this course. A final example is that of the northern province of Niassa where collaboration between the Catholic Church and a local NGO resulted in the local production of materials that allow secondary school students to complete their degree at a distance (Neeleman & Nhavoto, 2003).

EMERGING TRENDS OR A PATCHWORK OF EXPERIENCES?

Forty years after distance education emerged in the Mozambican landscape, no clear patterns are discernable. On the one hand, one can conclude that throughout its recent history Mozambique has, in one way or the other, embraced distance education. Many of the developed initiatives have been characterized by enormous personal commitment of the people involved and constituted significant innovations at the time they were launched. Participants enthusiastically embraced them. On the other hand, as the analysis above has shown, these experiences are each set in very specific contexts; have so far failed to consistently live up to the expectation that they would become an integral part of policy and practice in education; and have been marked by periods of inactivity, making it difficult to draw coherent lines between them. Compounding this problem is the fact that statistics on distance education in Mozambique have been sporadically kept[1] and that because of this, any discussion of trends is based almost entirely on anecdotal observations of those education specialists who have been involved in the process in some way or the other, rather than on empirically verifiable data and careful monitoring.[2] With these observations in mind, the emerging trends that are identified below should be seen as a mere first step at identifying direction. Three main emerging trends were identified as a result of the present analysis:

- Successive courses have become increasingly ambitious in scope, particularly in terms of enrollments, and have achieved better success rates by improving organization and student support. While the number of participants as such is not a necessary indicator of success, it is indicative of a greater commitment to distance education, of greater acceptance among the public, and of more ambitious plans.
- Distance education experiences have gradually diversified over time into various areas of formal and non-formal education.
- Within the domain of teacher training, distance education has over the past two decades established itself as a legitimate modality. In terms of the professional prospects, it has achieved parity with the regular teacher education courses and has established itself as a valued and desirable means of continued education for teachers.

PUTTING TOGETHER THE PIECES: WHAT ARE THE ISSUES TODAY?

It is important to recognize the success of Mozambique's distance education experience, especially considering the adverse internal and external circumstances under which most of these have taken place. However, it is also crucial to draw critical lessons by identifying issues that continue to affect distance education today and which, if not addressed, may continue to hamper efforts.

Issues from 1987 that Remain Relevant Today

The reader will recall that the analysis of the first post-independence distance education course resulted in the identification of three main issues, namely the vulnerability of innovations, the overriding importance of contextual factors in determining the success and failure of distance education initiatives (especially in a weak policy environment), and a constant tension between the drive for results and the need to allow time for innovation. All three of these issues remain relevant and pertinent today.

Issue 1: The Vulnerability of Innovations

As was seen, distance education initiatives have emerged and subsequently been discontinued in various areas of education over the years. The ending of such initiatives is often brought on abruptly and little remains afterwards that can serve as a lesson for the future. The distance education experience for extension workers in the Ministry of Agriculture is a good example of this, as was Mozambique's first post-independence distance education experience in the field of teacher upgrading.

Issue 2: The Importance of Contextual Factors

Contextual factors too—and in particular the personal engagement of people—continue to have a decisive influence on distance education experiences. The course that was launched in Gaza Province for upper primary school students in remote areas is an excellent illustration of this point. This initiative is carried by local staff with vision and enthusiasm who are willing to take risks and work over time to develop the materials and to promote the initiative. They also happen to work in a province where the director has the courage to allow such an initiative to develop without explicit prior intervention/approval by the Ministry of Education, and where the management of the different education departments is sufficiently flexible to ensure that extra resources can be made available when needed. The existence of the UDEBA program is a further contextual factor of great importance, since the project provides both human and financial resources in support of the initiative. Should any of these contextual factors change for the worse, the future of the initiative could end up being severely challenged.

Issue 3: The Tension between the Process and the Desire to Produce Results

Finally, the tension between process and outcomes remains an issue. This is clearly illustrated by the trade-offs that have been made over the years in the distance education course for teachers that was launched by IAP in 1994. The demand for this course has been so high that the institution has been pressured from all sides (the Ministry of Education, donors, and others) to open more centers and to expand to other provinces beyond those that were initially identified as constituting a priority. Valuable time and resources that had initially been earmarked for monitoring the existing centers and for continuously revising, updating, and remodeling the course (in all its aspects) have been diverted to respond to this pressure. As a result, only minor revisions have been made to the materials, and none to the overall set-up and organization of the course, in spite of the fact that successive evaluations have indicated that certain issues—such as the focus on rote learning that was identified above—need to be urgently addressed.

Additional Issues

Additional issues have since emerged. The final section of this chapter is devoted to the task of summarizing these issues. In doing so, a number of cases (numbered 1 through 4)—drawn upon the reflections and examples provided by people who have been involved in distance education in Mozambique and who were interviewed for the purpose of this chapter—will be considered.

Issue 4: Each Experience is the First One

The teacher education course that was launched by IAP in 1994 was widely hailed as Mozambique's first distance education experience. Case 1, containing a fictitious example that is modeled on real newspaper reports, seeks to illustrate this. With each successive distance education experience, very little is done to recognize and learn from what has come before. The memory of what has gone before may be there and may even be obliquely referred to, a few of the people who participated in the earlier experiences may be recruited into the design of the new course, a cursory attempt may be made to collect and examine the (surviving) modules from the previous course, but there is rarely a systematic attempt to truly learn from the lessons of the past, to critically assess the strong and weak points of the experience, and to build in safeguards to avoid the stumbling-blocks of the past.

A consequence of this reality is, without doubt, that successive experiences are almost as vulnerable as the ones that preceded them. They are vulnerable to policy changes by government and international aid agencies because frequently they are poorly integrated into the policy and planning framework of the country, they are vulnerable to budget cuts for the same policy and planning reasons, and they are vulnerable from a

Case 1: Front page of *Noticias*, a local daily newspaper (1994)	Case 2: From the attic to the drawing table to a rural school in Mozambique (2004)
"First distance education course launched by Minister of Education"	In Fernando's attic there are three old cardboard boxes. They are nothing special to look at, and somewhat weathered and battered with age but, to members of the team working with him in the UDEBA project, they represent something of incalculable value. Inside the boxes is the only surviving full set of print materials produced for Mozambique's "first" distance education course in 1983. It is these materials that are now, in 2004, being used as a resource by writers and illustrators of the UDEBA project in designing study guides for sixth and seventh grade students from the southern Province of Gaza who have no access to upper primary school because they live in remote and sparsely populated areas of the country.
In a ceremony held in the city of Beira yesterday, the Minister of Education officially launched Mozambique's first distance education course. Amid enthusiastic clapping by various national and local dignitaries Mozambique's first study centre for primary school teachers was opened at the "A Luta Continua" primary school in Manga district. On this solemn occasion his Excellency the Minister of Education highlighted the significance of this achievement: "This course will allow teachers to upgrade their knowledge so that they may become the educational pioneers and guide our children to a better future." At the end of the ceremony, the Minister presented books and other materials to the first twenty students.	

quality perspective because design takes little account of what could have been learned from past experiences.

Issue 5: The Problem of "Institutional Amnesia"

The problem of each successive distance education experience being the first one is compounded by "institutional amnesia." Many countries, including Mozambique, have a very poor institutional memory. Archives are only sporadically kept and are easily lost in the (not infrequent) processes of institutional reorganization, which emanate from political and policy changes and (equally not uncommonly) from the conditions that are imposed on ministries in exchange for funding and loans from various organizations. The boxes in Fernando's attic (Case 2) illustrate this problem. Distance education is often especially vulnerable because many of the experiences start out as pilot projects, which (as unfortunately is often the case with pilot experiences) have a poor success rate as far as scaling up and subsequent integration into the overall educational policy and budgetary framework goes.

The potential consequences of the loss of institutional memory (be it in the form of personnel, archives, etc.) should not be underestimated. Already scarce resources are squandered re-inventing the wheel.

Issue 6: So Few Staff for so Many Needs

Setting up a distance education course/initiative goes hand in hand with extensive and specialized training of staff in areas such as management, supervision, instructional design, and quality control. In an environment such as that in Mozambique, where qualified cadres are still hard to find, it is especially these newly-trained people who are highly solicited for other jobs that offer better perspectives from a financial (and sometimes professional) point of view, including jobs in the NGO and private sector as well as among so-called donor agencies.

The lack of continuity of specialized staff is related to well-documented problems. Government employees, especially at the lower levels, receive salaries that are not competitive with the private sector. Specialized training frequently does not result in a formal degree and therefore the chances of progression on the career ladder remain slim. Where training does result in the attainment of a higher academic qualification this may also have its drawbacks, since it now becomes possible for the newly-trained specialist to seek other employment opportunities.

A quick overview of training initiatives over the past 20 years in the context of distance education in Mozambique illustrates this problem. In the case of the 1983 distance education course, 20 staff received specialized training from a Brazilian institution. This distance education experience was subsequently cut short, as was explained above, and the staff was relocated to other departments of the Ministry of Education. In the early 1990s, when the new distance education course for teachers was launched, only a handful of the original collaborators of the first initiative could be identified, and none were recruited into the newly-created Institute for Teacher Upgrading. To solve the problem of lack of technical staff, a new, even larger,

Case 3:   Diary entry of an unnamed director at an unnamed institution (1998)

"Another hard day today, feel so fed up. Afonso presented his final report today. Felt uncomfortable during the whole process. Could not help feeling resentment; he was the last head of department that was trained by the Brazilians back in 1992. Will be impossible to replace. He is also the third head of department in the past year and a half that is leaving to work for an NGO. They all go after the money. But then, who can blame them."

group of people received training, again from a Brazilian institution and with financing from another donor. Of that group, only a handful remain at the Institute for Teacher Upgrading today. The lamentations of the unnamed director at an unnamed institution (Case 3—a fictitious example) illustrate this problem.

The same problem has recently repeated itself. In the context of the creation of the National Institute for Distance Education (INED)—a recently-established institution with the mandate of coordinating and facilitating distance education initiatives in Mozambique—it once again became necessary to train specialized staff. Financing was secured for a group of 50 people in distance education. However, only a handful of the people who were selected for this course have no institutional affiliation. The majority are already working for projects or private initiatives in the field of education. The chance that these newly trained people will end up in a full-time position with the new institution—which, as a government institution cannot offer special incentives—are, according to those who have been involved in the initiative so far, very slim.

The drain of scarce resources to other areas of activity exacerbates the problem of "institutional amnesia" that was identified above, since institutional memory consists not only of physically recorded data but also of what is learned and held in memory by the people who are part of the process. With each successive reshuffling of staff, the institution and the distance education community as a whole run the risk of becoming less resistant to the whims of politicians and donors, as well as to other trials and tribulations.

Case 4: A word of welcome—A whisper from the past

Introduction to module 1: course for railway operators (1957)

"Welcome to L01, the first module of this course for railway operators. You are about to embark on a journey of learning and discovery that we expect will change your life. In this packet you will find a study book, supplementary readings, assignments with model answers, as well as instructions on how to submit your final test for the first module. Once you successfully complete the first module you will receive your next set of materials with instructions on how to use them."

Issue 7:   The Elusive Promise

For many people, the opportunity to participate in a course, to attain a degree, or to carry on studying, carries with it the promise of personal growth, of professional advancement and/or of enhanced social status. The fictitious introduction to the module for railway staff that is presented in Case 4 as an illustration speaks in this context of "a journey of learning and discovery that we expect will change your life," the Minister of Education in Case 1 refers to teachers becoming "educational pioneers [who will] ... guide our children to a better future."

As a country, Mozambique has experienced very rapid changes in its social and economic fabric over the past two decades. The liberalization of the economy and the entry of Mozambique into the world market have made it harder for people to rely on the traditional social networks for support. As a result, the concept of family has become much more narrowly defined. For many it is no longer the (extended) family that provides a basis for social and economic advancement. According to sources interviewed for this chapter, there are in Mozambique today only two ways in which an individual can realistically expect to attain the so-aspired social standing and economic comfort: by accumulating capital (sometimes in the grey and black areas of the economy) or by acquiring a degree. Both of these may provide a passport to a better job and a better future.[3]

In reality, in an increasingly competitive society in which drop-outs at all levels of the system are substantial, the chances that a degree will results in a better life are small, and so the inherent promise that (distance) education carries more often than not fails to bear fruit. It thus remains to be seen whether the hopeful participants in the distance education course for upper primary education in Gaza province, which was mentioned in Case 4, will have significantly better chances of completing their secondary education, and whether they will be able to make a better life for themselves than their friends who were not able to go to school.

The teacher upgrading course that is documented in Case 1 is, however, an exception to this phenomenon. Teachers who successfully complete the full set of modules of the course receive a formal degree as qualified primary school teachers. With this formal qualification they are entitled to be scaled in at a different salary level. Without doubt this reality has enhanced the status and legitimacy of distance education in Mozambique; it has also proven to be an incredible incentive for those who participate in the course to stay on track and complete their degree. Drop-out rates for the course are very low and in a substantial number of cases students outpace the rhythm of the course in their enthusiasm to complete the modules (Visser, M., 1999).

Issue 8: The Perpetuation of Mediocrity or an Opportunity to Innovate?

A related problem is that of quality. Unfortunately, distance education courses all too often end up replicating the mediocrity of existing courses that are offered on a face-to-face basis, the only difference being the modality of delivery and some minor, somewhat cosmetic, changes to the content. The drive for the attainment of a degree that was mentioned above makes it all the more likely that distance education courses are marketed with the purpose of satisfying (or pretending to satisfy) this need, focusing on formal output rather than substantive content. The opportunity to radically and dramatically review the very fundamentals of what it means to learn, to redefine the learning experience as a life-long activity, and to equip learners with skills (such as creativity, critical thinking, the art of asking questions) that will serve them throughout their life is easily forgotten or relegated to a back shelf in this process.

CONCLUDING REMARKS

This chapter has provided a chronology of distance education in Mozambique and has also attempted to highlight emerging trends and key issues. The analysis has shown that much has been achieved, but also that much remains to be done. At a basic level, what seems to be lacking is a clear and unambiguous answer to the question "What do we (government, social sectors, society at large) expect from education and what kind of learning environment do we wish to create?" It is the clear and unambiguous answer to this question that needs to guide every aspect of the planning and implementing process in education, as well as the decision on how distance education can play a part. What appears to be lacking for now is coherence between the vision of learning, the strategy for achieving it, and the practice in the field. There is no doubt that such coherence is very difficult to attain, but as long as compromises continue to be made at the different levels, the sustainability of distance education initiatives and the vision that is behind them will probably continue to be elusive.

NOTES

1. The Ministry of Education has made much progress in the past 10-15 years in putting in place a detailed monitoring system for education (cf. MINED, 2003). However, statistics for newer, pilot, experiences and for activities that are not directly carried out by the Ministry itself (but rather by local organizations, projects, and private entities, including the church) are only sporadically kept and get harder to trace as time goes by.

2. Such an approach to trends does not meet the criteria of a trend as defined by Ely (2004). As such, we should probably speak of "emerging trends" or "indications of trends" rather than of definite trends per se. Nevertheless a serious discussion of such emerging trends is important. To ignore what has emerged so far—even if based on evidence that does not measure up to the standard of rigorous scientific research—would take away the opportunity to draw lessons that could provide valuable pointers for future decisions.

3. This thirst for a degree is a relatively new phenomenon in Mozambique. As late as the early 1980s, the Government faced considerable difficulties just to recruit and motivate students to study abroad. Today, each scholarship

that is given out to a successful candidate leaves in the dust a long list of disappointed and dejected hopefuls.

REFERENCES

Abrahamsson, H. (1995). The international political economy of structural adjustment: The case of Mozambique. *The European Journal of Development Research,* 7(2). Frank Cass, London.

Arndt, C. (2002). *HIV/AIDS and macroeconomic prospects for Mozambique: An initial assessment.* Washington: World Bank.

Candido, A., Menete, A, Martins, Z., & Ahmed, Z. (1986). *Relatório de Avaliação da Primeira Experiência de Ensino à Distância em Moçambique para a Formação em Exercício de Professores do Ensino Primário.* Maputo, Mozambique: MINED/INDE.

Directorate of Planning (2003). 1998–2002 Period. Maputo, Mozambique: Ministry of Education.

DANIDA (1994). *Education in Mozambique: Review and perspectives.* Maputo, Mozambique: DANIDA.

Flinck, R., & Flinck, A. W. (1998). *Establishing a new distance education in Mozambique.* Maputo, Mozambique: Ministry of Education/Institute for Teacher Upgrading

Franque, A. D. (1993). *Distance education in Mozambique: Feasibility and sustainability.* MA Dissertation for the Institute of Education, University of London.

FRELIMO (1977). Relatório do Comité Central ao Terceiro Congresso. Maputo, Mozambique.

FRELIMO (1977). Directivas Económicas e Sociais ao Terceiro Congresso. Maputo, Mozambique.

Inquai, S. (1994). The development of distance education up to 1970. In *Course 2: Development of Distance Education.* London: IEC.

MINED. (1980). *Ensino a distância: A primeira abordagem.* Maputo, Mozambique: MINED.

Ministério da Saúde. (2001). *Impacto demográfico do HIV/SIDA em Moçambique.* Maputo, Mozambique: Ministry of Health, National Institute of Statistics, Ministry of Planning and Finance, and the Centre for Population Studies.

Neeleman, W. & Nhavoto, A. (2003). *Educação à distância em Moçambique.* Brazilian Review of Open and Distance Education.

UNAIDS. (2003). *AIDS Epidemic Update.* Geneva, Switzerland: United Nations Program on HIV/AIDS/World Health Organization.

UNDP (2003). Human Development Report 2003. Retrieved October 7, 2004 from http://www.undp.org/hdr2003.

Verde Azul Consult, Lda. (2000). *Draft report assessment of the impact of HIV/AIDS on the education sector in Mozambique.* Maputo, Mozambique: MINED.

Visser, J., & Zalzman, A. M. (1986). *Development prospects of the distance education system in Mozambique.* INDE, Maputo, Mozambique.

Visser, M. (1997). *Distance education in Mozambique.* Paper presented at the 18th World Conference of the International Council for Distance Education. Pennsylvania State University, University Park, PA, June 2-6, 1997.

Visser, M. (1999). *Helping learners to learn: An assessment of support to teachers studying via distance education in Mozambique.* Unpublished doctoral dissertation, International Extension College, University of London.

Zalzman, A., Dowdall, L. Hofisso, N., & Cabral, Z. (2003). *Avaliação Intermédia do Projecto Udeba Gaza.* Netherlands Embassy, Maputo, Mozambique.

PART IV

DESIGN AND DEVELOPMENT TRENDS FOR INTERNATIONAL DISTANCE EDUCATION

CHAPTER 18

A COMPARATIVE REVIEW OF ONLINE TEACHING AND LEARNING TOOLS USED IN INTERNATIONAL DISTANCE LEARNING

Wei-yuan Zhang and Lixun Wang

INTRODUCTION

With the rapid growth of the Internet, online education is establishing itself as a popular learning and teaching mode in higher education. In the early 1990s, having realized the great potential of online learning, some higher education organizations with advanced educational technology support started to develop online courses. These institutions employed highly trained Web programmers to develop course interfaces using HTML or other Web programming languages. Most other institutions lacked the technology resources for developing online courses. In the mid 1990s, some educational and business organizations developed online teaching/learning tools (learning management systems), in order to meet the increasing need for education and lifelong learning. These

Trends and Issues in Distance Education: International Perspectives, 245–259

systems were designed to enable instructors to customize their own online courses effectively, without the need for advanced Web programming skills. These tools significantly reduced the time required to develop and manage online courses, which made it possible for large-scale development and cost-effective online learning.

This chapter compares the features, functions, strengths, and limitations of 17 English and Chinese Learning Management Systems widely used around the globe: ANGEL (CyberLearning Labs Inc., 2003), Anlon (Anlon Systems Inc., 2001), Avilar WebMentor (Avilar® Technologies Inc., 2003), BlackBoard (Blackboard Inc., 2003), Blue Power (Chinese) (Beida-online.com, 2000), CentraOne (Centra Software, 2003), Click2learn Aspen (Click2learn Inc., 2002), Dianda-online (Chinese) (Dianda-online distance education technology Corp. Ltd., 2003), eCollege (eCollege, 2003), FirstClass (Open Text Corporation, 2003), FlexEducation (FlexEducation Technology Ltd., 2002), IVLE (National University of Singapore, 2002), Learning Space (IBM Lotus software, 2003), The Learning Manager (TLM Corp., 2001), TopClass (WBT Systems, 2003), Virtual Campus (Indira Gandhi National Open University, 2003) and WebCT (WebCT Inc., 2001).

AN INTRODUCTION TO LEARNING MANAGEMENT SYSTEMS

The great demand for online learning has led to the development of large numbers of online teaching and learning tools worldwide. For example, a simple query using the Google search engine uncovered 63 e-learning companies and 114 learning management systems. Through a thorough literature review it was determined that there are 17 widely-used English and Chinese online Learning Management Systems suitable for examination in the context of this study. Table 18.1 provides background information on each of these tools.

Table 18.1 illustrates that many of the learning management systems have been widely used by educational organizations around the world, with WebCT and Blackboard leading in terms of the number of institutions using their products. Also noteworthy is the Dianda-Online platform used by the Chinese Radio and Television University System. Though this platform is used only in China, the user rate is arguably comparable to other leading platforms. Under the umbrella of the China Central Radio and Television University, there are 44 provincial Radio and Television Universities and innumerable branches across the country. It is interesting to note that the University of Edinburgh, which uses the IVLE (Integrated Virtual Learning Environment) platform developed by National University of Singapore. This suggests that though the drive for e-learn-

Table 18.1.   Basic Information about Learning Management Systems

Tool Name	Version	Developer's name	Users
ANGEL	5.0	CyberLearning Labs, Inc., U.S.A.	9 universities and colleges in U.S.A.
Anlon	4.1	Anlon Systems Inc., U.S.A.	Minnesota State College, Maricopa; Community College District, etc.
Avilar WebMentor	4.0	Avilar® Technologies, Inc., U.S.A.	More than 10 customers in education worldwide
BlackBoard	5.5	Blackboard, Inc., U.S.A.	1,800 universities and colleges Worldwide
BluePower	2.0	Beida-online.com, China	Beijing University
CentraOne	6.0	Centra Software, U.S.A.	Over 40 universities and colleges worldwide
Click2learn Aspen	2.0	Click2learn, Inc., U.S.A.	36 universities and colleges in the U.S.A.
Dianda-online		Dianda-online distance education technologies Inc., China	Radio and Television University System in China
eCollege		eCollege, U.S.A.	Over 200 educational partners worldwide
FirstClass	7.0	Open Text Corporation, Canada	The Open University (U.K.); University of Texas at Austin; Singapore Institute of Management
FlexEducation		FlexEducation Technology Ltd. Hong Kong	Customers from Mainland China, Hong Kong, Taiwan, Singapore, Malaysia, Australia, etc.
IVLE	7.0	National University of Singapore	National University of Singapore; University of Philippines Open University; University of Edinburgh
Learning Space	5.0	IBM Lotus software, U.S.A.	12 universities and colleges world wide
The Learning Manager	3.2	TLM Corp., Canada	Customers from five continents
TopClass	3.3	WBT Systems, U.S.A.	14 universities and colleges world-wide
Virtual Campus		Indira Gandhi National Open University, India	Indira Gandhi National Open University (IGNOU), India
WebCT	3.8	WebCT, Inc. U.S.A.	More than 2,500 institutions in 81 countries around the world

Source: The above data were collected from the Web

ing has roots in the West, institutions from non-Western areas are emerging as reputable centers for e-learning design and delivery.

Knowing the penetration rate of these online learning management systems—and thus their importance in online education worldwide—it is worthwhile comparing the features and functions and assessing the strengths and limitations of each tool. This will help those working in the field of online distance education to consider what online tools will work best for their local needs.

COURSE DESIGN FEATURES OF LEARNING MANAGEMENT SYSTEMS

Among the most important features of online learning management systems are the course design functions, as educators rely on these functions to develop online courses effectively with little training. Based on a literature review (Hazari, 1998; Rankine, 2001; Zhang, 2001; Edutech, 2002; University of Manitoba, 2002; Zhang et. al, 2002), the course design functions may be classified into four types of features: instructional design tools, course layout templates, search capabilities, and student homepage.

The first feature refers to instructional design tools. It is essential that instructors hoping to carry out online teaching can use user-friendly instructional design tools to develop their online courses. The online learning management systems offer support to convert existing course material into an internal format used by the online course. At the same time, course structures can easily be edited, and learning modules and other resources can be managed and arranged in a flexible way. The second feature refers to the course layout templates. By using templates, instructors can create an online course simply by populating the templates with course-related materials. The software will automatically integrate the materials into a well-organized online learning environment. Different courses using the same template will have a consistent look and feel, which avoids confusion. In addition, templates can be customized according to the user's needs. The third feature refers to the search tool embedded in the learning management system. The search tool is designed to help students conveniently retrieve desired information from anywhere in the learning management system. The fourth feature refers to the student homepage. The student homepage enables students to elaborate on their course of study. The homepage also provides students with a customizable workspace that empowers them to learn simple Web design, management, and so on. Table 18.2 illustrates the course design functions of the aforementioned 17 online teaching and learning tools.

**Table 18.2.   Comparison of the Course Design Functions of
Learning Management Systems**

Tool Name	Instructional Design Tools	Course Layout Templates	Search Tool for Course Website	Student Homepage
ANGEL	✓	✓	✓	✓
Anlon	✓			✓
Avilar WebMentor	✓	✓		✓
BlackBoard	✓	✓		
BluePower	✓	✓	✓	
CentraOne	✓	✓	✓	✓
Click2learn Aspen	✓	✓	✓	
Dianda-online	✓	✓	✓	
eCollege	✓	✓	✓	
FirstClass	✓		✓	✓
FlexEducation	✓	✓		
IVLE	✓	✓		✓
Learning Space	✓	✓		✓
The Learning Manager	✓	✓	✓	
TopClass	✓	✓	✓	✓
Virtual Campus	✓	✓	✓	
WebCT	✓	✓	✓	✓

Table 18.2 demonstrates that four of the 17 learning management systems have all four course design functions embedded. All but two tools (Anlon and FirstClass) offer course layout templates for simple and quick design of online courses. It is noteworthy that Blackboard, which has a very large user group (see Table 18.1), does not provide a search tool for the course site. Six other learning management systems also lack the search feature. Nine of the learning management systems do not include the Student Homepage feature.

COMMUNICATION AND COLLABORATION FUNCTIONS IN LEARNING AND MANAGEMENT SYSTEMS

Another key aspect of online learning management systems is the communication and collaboration functions. Because of the lack of face-to-face communication between the teacher and students, online courses need to find a way to make sure that the teacher and students can interact effectively. The communication and collaboration functions of online learning management systems can be classified into five types of features;

asynchronous communication, synchronous communication, file exchange, workgroups, and whiteboard (Hazari, 1998; Rankine, 2001; Zhang, 2001; Edutech, 2002; University of Manitoba, 2002; Zhang et al., 2002).

The first feature is asynchronous communication, which includes discussion forums and internal e-mail. Students and instructors can communicate through asynchronous tools such as e-mail without having to be online at the same time as other members of the class. This provides a higher degree of flexibility for the online learners. It also gives the students and instructors more time to reflect on the messages they receive before sending replies. The second feature is synchronous communication, which includes text-based real-time chat and audio/video conferencing. To carry out synchronous communication, students and instructors log into a virtual space (such as a chat room) on the Web and interact with each other in a virtual face-to-face context. The asynchronous and synchronous communication tools provided by the online learning management systems enable students and instructors to communicate and collaborate in a virtual space, rather than relying on physical presence during communication in a classroom context. The third feature is file exchange, which helps students and instructors share information and collaborate with each other. For example, students can submit electronic assignments directly to the instructor via this function. In return, the instructor can send the graded assignment back to the student with embedded feedback. While working on a group project, students can upload their work to a common area on the course Website, where members of the group can access each other's contributions. The instructor can also upload files such as schedules, articles, and other course-related documents for students to access and download. The fourth feature is the whiteboard, which is especially popular in math and natural science courses, as students and instructors can look at—and modify—any text or graphics that are displayed on the whiteboard, without having to be in the same geographic location. Students can save the image displayed on the whiteboard for future use. Text-based chat or audio/video conferencing are often used simultaneously with the whiteboard to enhance communication. The fifth feature is the workgroup, which is a very useful feature for group projects. The workgroup feature includes a group location in the learning management system, and often has dedicated discussion areas and file exchange features inside the group location.

Table 18.3 summarizes the types of communication and collaboration functions present in the 17 learning management systems.

Table 18.3 illustrates that all 17 learning management systems provide discussion forums, and all but one (CentraOne) provide internal email for asynchronous communication. This suggests that asynchronous commu-

Table 18.3. Comparison of the Communication and Collaboration Functions of Learning Management Systems

Tool Name	Asynchronous Communication		Synchronous Communication				
	Discussion Forums	Internal Email	Text-based Chat	Audio/ Video Conferencing	File Exchange	Workgroup	Whiteboard
ANGEL	✓	✓	✓	✓	✓	✓	✓
Anlon	✓	✓		✓	✓	✓	✓
Avilar WebMentor	✓	✓	✓			✓	
BlackBoard	✓	✓	✓		✓	✓	✓
BluePower	✓	✓	✓	✓	✓	✓	
CentraOne	✓		✓	✓		✓	✓
Click2learn Aspen	✓	✓	✓	✓	✓		✓
Dianda-online	✓	✓	✓	✓	✓	✓	
eCollege	✓	✓			✓	✓	✓
FirstClass	✓	✓	✓		✓	✓	
FlexEducation	✓	✓	✓	✓	✓	✓	✓
IVLE	✓	✓	✓		✓	✓	
Learning Space	✓	✓	✓		✓	✓	
The Learning Manager	✓	✓	✓		✓	✓	
TopClass	✓	✓	✓		✓		✓
Virtual Campus	✓	✓	✓	✓	✓		
Web CT	✓	✓	✓	✓	✓	✓	✓

nication tools (discussion forums and internal emails) are considered integral to an effective learning management system.

All but two tools (Anlon and eCollege) include a text-based chat function, but only nine of the 17 tools provide audio/video conferencing services. The text-based chat function is significantly easier and cheaper to develop than audio/video conferencing, which may explain why few of the learning management systems are equipped with audio/video conferencing functions. A second reason for the lower number of learning management systems with audio/video conferencing could be that the bandwidth of most Internet connections is too restricted for smooth live video transmission. Finally, videoconferencing requires hardware (e.g., a Web cam and a headset) to be installed on the computers of all users, and this hardware can be relatively expensive to acquire. It is interesting to note, however, that many online courses in Asia (China, Hong Kong, Taiwan, India, etc.) offer video lectures online (called video-on-demand), so that students can "see" their instructor giving lectures, although they are not able to directly interact with the instructor. This is a step forward from television-based distance education, as students can now choose which video lecture to watch at a time that is convenient to them, rather than following a fixed television broadcast schedule. Video-on-demand is a different concept than videoconferencing, but it makes use of online video streaming technologies, and indicates that online videoconferencing may not be a faraway reality.

All but two tools (Avilar WebMentor and CentraOne) include a file exchange function, and all but three tools (Click2learn Aspen, TopClass, and Virtual Campus) include a workgroup function. This suggests that file exchange and small group collaboration are two cherished practices in online learning. Among the 17 tools, only nine include a whiteboard function. This suggests that the whiteboard function may not be regarded as an essential feature of online learning management systems.

COURSE MANAGEMENT AND ADMINISTRATIVE FUNCTIONS OF LEARNING MANAGEMENT SYSTEMS

Managing an online course can be very time consuming for the instructor. To minimize this, many online learning management systems have made use of database technology for semi-automatic course management and administration. The course management functions of online learning management systems may be classified into four types of features (Hazari, 1998; Rankine, 2001; Zhang, 2001; Edutech, 2002; University of Manitoba, 2002; Zhang et al., 2002).

The first feature is module management, which allows learning modules, curricula, and other resources (documents, images, URL's, etc.) to be managed and arranged in a flexible way. A course can be created as a series of modules, which can be linked together. The second feature is quiz management. The instructor can use these types of tools to create and manage assessments (and surveys). Some systems can generate individual quizzes for students by randomly selecting questions from a database, thereby minimizing opportunities for cheating. Students can get instant feedback after they finish a quiz, and statistical analyses of quiz results can be generated as well. Some online learning management systems provide the option of administering a timed assessment, in which the system gives a deadline for the amount of time the student can use to complete the assessment. The third feature is grade management. Some online learning management systems use database technology to enable automatic grading of students' assignments. Student grades are sorted and stored in a database and can be conveniently managed by the teachers. The fourth feature is student-tracking, which ensures that the interactions of the students with the various sections of the learning management system are logged by the server. The types of interactions that can be logged include pages accessed, quiz results, time exposure to content and time exposure to online assessments. The teacher can analyze the access pattern of a student and use this information to give individualized support to students. The system is able to generate meaningful statistical reports of students' study patterns with textual and graphical views.

The course administration functions of online learning management systems may be classified into two types of features: the secure login feature and the technical support feature. With the secure login feature, each student needs to register and get the access rights in order to enter a course site. Some online learning management systems provide groups of users, such as students, instructors, authors, etc., with differentiated access rights. This ensures that only people with the appropriate levels of permission can gain access to certain areas of the course Web site. Secure login and differentiated access rights play an important role in making students feel secure in the online learning environment; they know that only their instructor can get access to their personal data, and they can be assured that they will not lose any personal data stored on the course Web site. The technical support feature ensures that users can address technical problems by either checking the Frequently Asked Questions (FAQ) section of the course Web site to find out solutions to common technical problems, or get in touch with technicians who are responsible for dealing with such issues.

A comparison of course management and administration functions of online learning management systems is shown in Table 18.4.

Table 18.4 illustrates that the majority of the learning management systems include all aspects of course management and administrative functions. However, three of the systems (CentraOne, Click2learn Aspen, and FirstClass), do not provide quiz management functions, and two of the systems (Avilar WebMentor and Click2learn Aspen) do not provide student-tracking functions. The data shown in Table 18.4 suggests that course management and administration functions are regarded as an indispensable part of an online teaching and learning system. These functions facilitate course management and administration, and help students and tutors to smoothly carry out online teaching and learning.

STRENGTHS AND LIMITATIONS OF LEARNING MANAGEMENT SYSTEMS

When choosing an online learning management system, an educational institution should consider not only the price of the system, but also the respective strengths and limitations of various potential systems. In Table

Table 18.4. Comparison of Course Management and Administrative Functions of Learning Management Systems

Tool Name	Course Management Functions				Administration Functions	
	Module Management	Quiz Management	Grade Management	Student-Tracking	Secured Log in	Technical Support
ANGEL	✓	✓	✓	✓	✓	✓
Anlon	✓	✓	✓	✓	✓	✓
Avilar WebMentor	✓	✓	✓		✓	✓
BlackBoard	✓	✓	✓	✓	✓	✓
BluePower	✓	✓	✓	✓	✓	✓
CentraOne	✓		✓	✓	✓	✓
Click2learn Aspen	✓		✓		✓	✓
Dianda-online	✓	✓	✓	✓	✓	✓
eCollege	✓	✓	✓	✓	✓	✓
FirstClass	✓		✓	✓	✓	✓
FlexEducation	✓	✓	✓	✓	✓	✓
IVLE	✓	✓	✓	✓	✓	✓
Learning Space	✓	✓	✓	✓	✓	✓
The Learning Manager	✓	✓	✓	✓	✓	✓
TopClass	✓	✓	✓	✓	✓	✓
Virtual Campus	✓	✓	✓	✓	✓	✓
WebCT	✓	✓	✓	✓	✓	✓

18.5, the strengths and limitations of the 17 online learning management systems are listed. These points were drawn through reviewing each tool's company Web site and relevant online courses.

DISCUSSION

This chapter compared a number of popular online learning management systems developed around the world. As more and more tools are being developed, it is important for educational institutions to be knowledgeable of the basic features, strengths, and limitations of these tools, so that they can make informed decisions when choosing an off-the-shelf learning management system, or developing a homegrown learning management system.

It is interesting to note that literature to date suggests that scholars have held the view that Asian countries have lagged behind Western nations in adopting online learning (Sim, 2001). Further, some have

**Table 18.5   Strengths and Limitations of
Learning Management Systems**

Tool Name	Strengths	Limitations
ANGEL	1. Easy to customize 2. Automatically creates personal Web-space for all students, faculty, and staff 3. Tracks and logs information for evaluation	1. Used in the U.S. only 2. Does not provide links to external resources 3. Only runs on Windows servers
Anlon	1. Flexible learning object delivery 2. Rapid re-use of existing content 3. Intelligent testing and assessment features	1. No search feature 2. No online note-taking capacity 3. No course layout templates
Avilar Web-Mentor	1. Supports distribution of courses on CD-ROM 2. Instructor can verify student course completion and print certificates of completion if requirements are met	1. No search feature 2. No student-tracking function
BlackBoard	1. User-friendly interface 2. Strong built-in synchronous communication (chat) 3. Good teamwork support 4. Differentiated access rights and user roles 5. Powerful spreadsheet-like management of student grades	1. Very limited customizability of user interface 2. Student can only make "global" annotations for a whole course 3. Very limited hypertext features 4. No search feature
BluePower	1. User-friendly course templates 2. Effective online video function 3. Powerful student and instructor management system 4. Good collaboration and interaction support	1. Chinese version only 2. Designed for Beijing University only 3. No student homepage function 4. No whiteboard function
CentraOne	1. Strong support for group-oriented learning 2. Good support for dynamic content and multimedia	1. No internal e-mail function 2. No file sharing function
Click2learn Aspen	1. Public/private instant messaging between participants 2. PowerPoint upload and mark-up for enhanced presentation and collaboration capacity 3. Application sharing and desktop streaming	1. No workgroup function 2. No student homepage function 3. No student tracking function
Dianda-online	1. Allows large number (tens of thousands) of students to log-on simultaneously 2. Rich video-on-demand resources 3. Relatively cheap for universities	1. Designed for China Radio and TV University system only 2. No student homepage function 3. No whiteboard function

(Table continues on next page)

Table 18.5   Continued

Tool Name	Strengths	Limitations
eCollege	1. Course support—unlimited informational advice via phone and e-mail to faculty members 2. Free initial training sessions and workshops	1. No real-time chat function 2. No student homepage function 3. Few choices for customization
FirstClass	1. Easy access via client software, Web browser, phone, or handheld device 2. Minimal hardware and personnel requirements	1. No self-assessment function 2. No course layout templates 3. No whiteboard function
FlexEducation	1. Capacity to monitor and remote-control students' computers 2. Screen broadcast (instructor can broadcast his/her computer screens to students in real time).	1. Cannot search within course Website 2. No student homepage function
IVLE	1. Convenient lecture planning system 2. Powerful quiz management system 3. Comprehensive "workbin" system for file sharing	1. Cannot search within course Website 2. Does not include online chat function 3. No whiteboard function
Learning Space	1. Includes complete synchronous communication tools suite (collaboration server) 2. Relatively cheap for universities 3. Detailed tracking and reporting functions	1. Only fully functional on Windows platforms 2. No search function 3. No whiteboard function
The Learning Manager	1. Supports all phases of the instructional design cycle: course layout, curriculum development, course delivery & learner management, and evaluation 2. Strong support for online tests and assignments	1. Does not provide student homepage 2. No whiteboard function
TopClass	1. Strong quiz support—good integration to other parts of system (e.g., grading, granting access to course material) 2. Strong reporting features 3. Fully platform-independent for students and authors.	1. No workgroup function 2. Expensive 3. Advanced requirements of administrator skills and hardware
Virtual Campus	1. Comprehensive starter kit 2. Live academic sessions through teleconferencing 3. Video-on-demand capabilities	1. Developed for and use by Indira Gandhi National Open University only 2. No student homepage function 3. No workgroup function 4. No whiteboard function

(Table continues on next page)

Table 18.5   Continued

Tool Name	Strengths	Limitations
WebCT	1. Powerful resource management (e.g., Web pages, images, audio files) 2. Impressive collection of useful pre-programmed tools 3. Strong communication features 4. Flexible and powerful management of student files/student grades	1. Relatively slow response times in the authoring environment 2. Complex—sometimes clumsy—user interface for author (due to complex functionality and detailed parameters)

argued that Asian countries typically purchase online learning management systems from the West, and that the imported technology might conflict with local language and culture (Evans, 2000). Our review suggests that that many Asian nations (e.g. China, Singapore, Hong Kong, Taiwan, India, Thailand) have developed their own learning management systems, and that most of these tools are as sophisticated as those developed in the West. The IVLE platform developed in Singapore has entered the European market, and the FlexEducation platform, developed in Hong Kong, has attracted customers from Australia. Thus, Asia appears to be catching up with the Western world in learning management system development, and Asia is making an increasingly significant contribution to the technology of online teaching and learning.

It is important to keep in mind that the learning management systems remain limited tools designed to facilitate online teaching and learning. Therefore, regardless of the learning management system that is adopted, we must think carefully about how to make distance learning meaningful and effective. For instance, how do we strengthen the instructional design methods for online courses? What are the necessary elements for ensuring the flexibility of online courses? How do we set up virtual learning communities that foster a sense of belonging? What are the key strategies for effective online assessment? All these topics need to be explored in order to provide effective online teaching and learning to distance learners.

ACKNOWLEDGMENTS

This chapter represents part of the research outcomes of The Development, Validation and Use of a Distance and Open Virtual Learning Environment Scale (DOVILES) project, funded by the Education and Manpower Bureau of Hong Kong. The team members of this project include Prof. Olugbemiro Jegede, Dr. Wei-yuan Zhang, Dr. Lixun Wang, and Ms. Elaine Kwok. The authors express particular thanks and appreciation to Dr. David Murphy for his very detailed and constructive comments on this project.

NOTE

1. This article is based on a paper presented and discussed at the 21st ICDE World Conference on Open Learning & Distance Education hosted by the Open University of Hong Kong, Hong Kong, February 18-21, 2004. Some of the revisions made in the production of this article are based on discussions at the conference, for which we are very grateful to the participants.

REFERENCES

Anlon Systems Inc. (2001). Welcome to Anlon Systems Inc. Retrieved February 26, 2003 from http://www.anlon.com/

Avilar® Technologies Inc. (2003). Avilar® Technologies, Inc. WebMentor LMS. Retrieved February 26, 2003 from http://home.avilar.com/products/wm_lms.html

Blackboard Inc. (2003). Welcome to Blackboard. Retrieved February 26, 2003 from http://www.blackboard.com/

Beida-online.com. (2000). Beida-online. Retrieved February 26, 2003 from http://edu.beida-online.com/

Centra Software. (2003). CentraOne 6.0. Retrieved February 26, 2003 from http://www.centra.com/

Click2learn Inc. (2002). Click2learn: Leader in enterprise productivity solutions. Retrieved February 26, 2003 from http://home.click2learn.com/

CyberLearning Labs Inc. (2003). Welcome to CyberLearningLabs. Retrieved February 26, 2003 from http://cyberlearninglabs.com/

Dianda-online distance education technologies Inc. (2003). Dianda-online. Retrieved February 26, 2003 from http://www.openedu.com.cn/

eCollege.com. (2003). eCollege. Retrieved February 26, 2003 from http://www.ecollege.com/

Edutech. (2002). Web-based course tools: Evaluation grid. Retrieved November 7, 2002 from http://www.edutech.ch/edutech/tools/grid_e.asp

Evans, T. (2000). Researching the NET: Information and communications technology and research in distance and adult learning, Keynote paper at the 1st Conference on Research in Distance & Adult Learning in Asia, Hong Kong, 21-24 June.

FlexEducation Technology Ltd. (2002). FlexEducation Techonology. Retrieved February 26, 2003 from http://www.flexeducation.com/

Hazari, S. I. (1998). Evaluation and selection of web course management tools. Retrieved November 7, 2002 from http://sunil.umd.edu/webct

IBM Lotus software. (2003). IBM Lotus software: LearningSpace. Retrieved February 26, 2003 from http://www.lotus.com/products/learnspace.nsf/wdocs/homepage

Indira Gandhi National Open University. (2003). Virtual Campus. Retrieved February 26, 2003 from http://www.ignou.ac.in/virtualcampus%5Cindex.htm

National University of Singapore. (2002). Integrated Virtual Learning Environment (IVLE). Retrieved February 26, 2003 from https://ivle.nus.edu.sg/default.asp

Open Text Corporation. (2003). Welcome to Open Text, developer of FirstClass. Retrieved February 26, 2003 from http://www.centrinity.com/

Rankine, L. (2001). The way ahead: Blackboard or WebCT? Retrieved November 7, 2002 from http://www.sunderland.ac.uk/~usolds/webct/discussion-paper.pdf

Sim, S. (2001, September 28). *IDC: Asia slow in adopting online learning*. IDG News Service/Hong Kong Bureau.

TLM Corp. (2001). The Learning Manager: e-learning applications. Retrieved February 26, 2003 from http://www.thelearningmanager.com/

University of Manitoba. (2002). Tools for developing interactive academic web courses. Retrieved November 7, 2002 from http://www.umanitoba.ca/ip/tools/courseware/evalmain.html

WBT Systems. (2003). WBT Systems: e-Learning solutions for online learning and web based training. Retrieved February 26, 2003 from http://www.wbtsystems.com/

WebCT Inc. (2001). WebCT.com. Retrieved February 26, 2003 from http://www.webct.com/

Zhang, W. (2001). Comparative study of overseas' latest online learning development tools. *Journal of Jiangsu Radio & Television University, 12*(3).

Zhang, W., Perris K., & Poon, T. (2002). A profile of online education in selected open universities in Asia. In D. Murphy, N. Shin, & W. Zhang (Eds.). *Advancing online learning in Asia*. Hong Kong: Open University of Hong Kong Press.

CHAPTER 19

TRENDS IN DISTANCE EDUCATION TECHNOLOGIES FROM AN INTERNATIONAL VANTAGE POINT

Michael Simonson

In the 1980s, the southeast African nation of Zimbabwe was founded from the British Commonwealth country of Rhodesia after a long and painful process. Before the founding of Zimbabwe, the educational system of Rhodesia enrolled fewer than 500,000 learners, and most of these learners were located in the major cities and towns of the country. One of the first acts of the new government was to offer free and universal education to the nation's children, regardless of location. This resulted overnight in a tenfold increase in enrollment in the country's schools.

The teacher education faculty at the University of Zimbabwe in Harare and at other institutions of teacher training faced the immediate problem of preparing the thousands of teachers needed by the nation's many new and enlarged schools. The approach selected was part ingenious, and part necessity-based.

It was decided that teachers in training should attend one of the institutions of higher education for their first year of preparation. For their

Trends and Issues in Distance Education: International Perspectives, 261–285

second and third years, these teacher education students were assigned to a school where they taught classes of students.

College students functioned as regular educators with two exceptions. First, they were under the guidance of a more experienced colleague and, second, they continued their teacher education and higher education coursework at a distance. In other words, students enrolled in a full curriculum of coursework while they simultaneously functioned as novice teachers. Coursework was delivered to students from a distant, higher education institution. In their fourth year, students returned to the university or college and completed their degrees.

In Zimbabwe, distance education became the primary technique for preparing the thousands of teachers needed to staff the new country's schools. Interestingly, the technology used to connect professors, such as those of the faculty of education at the University of Zimbabwe and students located in the many cities, towns, and villages of the country was the postal system. Students received written assignments and printed resources from the university. They used, studied, and interacted with these materials to complete assignments, which then were returned to the faculty of education for evaluation. Follow-up assignments and materials were then posted back to students. This process continued until the second and third years of the bachelor's degree were completed. Periodic visits to the campus occurred, but the majority of the learning events and activities took place at a distance.

This system, born of the necessity of educating millions of students, used the most appropriate technology available: the postal system. Certainly, a major social, political and, ultimately, educational problem was solved, even though the approach was not high tech. However, it was efficient and effective. Whatever technology is used, the purpose is to promote communication (Simonson, 2003).

A MODEL OF COMMUNICATION

Communication occurs when two or more individuals wish to share ideas. Communication in a distance education environment happens when learners interact with one another and with their instructor. Communication, including communication for distance education, is possible because individuals have overlapping fields of experience. In other words, they have things in common, such as language and culture.

Communication must be based on what the senders of messages—distance educators—have in common with the receivers of messages—distant learners. Effective instructional messages are designed according to the situation, experiences, and competencies of learners.

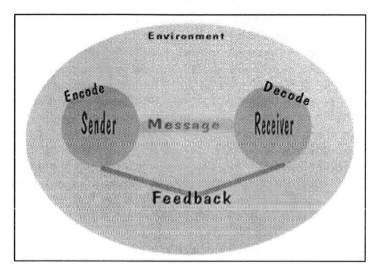

Figure 19.1.   Model of communication.

In order to communicate, instructional ideas are encoded into some transmittable form, such as spoken words, pictures, or writing. The instructional message is then sent to the learner over a channel. If the receiver of the message is nearby, such as in the same classroom, the sender (the teacher) may speak or show pictures in order to communicate. If the learner is at a distance, then the instructional message will need to be sent over a wire (e.g., the telephone), hand-delivered (e.g., the mail), or broadcast through the air (e.g., television). In other words, media are used to communicate to distant learners. In fact, media extend the senses, so instructional messages can be sent over long distances, or stored for learning at different times.

When the distant learner receives the message, it must be decoded. This means that the words spoken must be heard and defined, or the pictures shown must be seen and understood. If communication is successful, the receiver (the learner) will have the same idea or understanding as the sender (the teacher).

Effective communication requires an active audience. The response of the learners who receive messages is called feedback. Feedback allows the sender and receiver, the teacher and learner, to determine if the message was understood correctly. Feedback in distance education systems is often referred to as interaction. Feedback permits those involved in communication in a distance education system to evaluate the process.

Noise is also part of the communication process. Any disturbance that interferes with or distorts the transmission of a message is called noise.

Audible static is one form of noise. Classroom distractions are noise, as is ambiguous or unfamiliar information.

The model of communication has been widely used to describe the interaction between message designers and audiences—teachers and learners. It is also quite relevant for distance education. Specifically, instruction must be designed in a way to capitalize on what learners already know and what they have already experienced—their fields of experience. Then messages should be encoded so they can be effectively transmitted to distant learners.

Channels of communication, the media that connect the teacher and the distant learner, should be appropriate for the learner and the instruction. In other words, the media used to connect the learner, teacher, and learning resources must be capable of conveying all necessary information.

When instruction is designed and when feedback and interaction are planned, efforts should be made to minimize anything that might interfere with the communication process (e.g., noise). One way this can be accomplished is by sending information through multiple channels.

Models of communication provide a general orientation to the process of distance education. The model described contains the elements to be considered when instructional messages are communicated.

THE CONE OF EXPERIENCE

One long-standing method of categorizing the ability of media to convey information is the "cone of experience," introduced by Edgar Dale (1946), which helps organize the media used in distance education systems. Children respond to direct, purposeful experiences, not only because they are young, but also because they are learning many new things for the first time. Real experiences have the greatest impact on them because they have fewer previous experiences to look back on and refer to than do older learners. Real experiences provide the foundation for learning.

As learners grow older and have more experiences, it is possible for them to understand events that are less realistic and more abstract. Dale first stated this basic idea when he introduced his cone of experience. Dale proposed that for students to function and learn from experiences presented abstractly (those at the higher levels of the cone), it was necessary for them to have sufficient and related experiences that were more realistic (those at the lower levels). Learners need to have direct, purposeful experiences to draw upon in order to successfully learn from more abstract events. For example, if children are to look at pictures of flowers

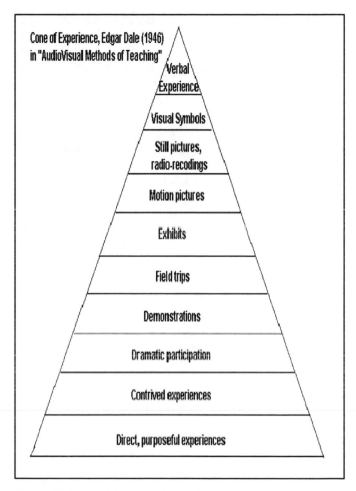

Figure 19.2.   Dale's cone of experience.

and know what they are, they must have first seen, smelled, and touched real flowers.

Media permit the educator to bring sights and sounds of the real world into the learning environment—the classroom. However, when new information is presented, it is important that it be as realistic as possible. Similarly, when younger learners are involved, more realistic instruction is needed. Still, one misunderstanding about the cone of experience is the belief that "more realistic" is always better. This is definitely not true. More realistic forms of learning are considerably less efficient in terms of uses of resources, and are often less effective because of the many distractions of realistic instruction.

The critical job of the educator, especially the designer of distance education materials, is to be only as realistic as needed in order for learning to effectively occur. If instruction is too realistic, it can be inefficient. It may cost too much, it may have too much irrelevant information, or it may be difficult to use. Similarly, learning experiences that are too abstract may be inexpensive, but may not contain enough relevant information and may not be understood.

To clarify the conflict between realistic and abstract experiences, Edgar Dale told a story about the life of a Greek sponge fisherman. The most realistic way to learn about the fisherman's life was to go to Greece and work on a sponge boat. This approach to learning would be very realistic, effective, and authentic. It would also take a long time and cost a great deal, both in money and in learning time. An abstract way to learn about the life of a sponge fisherman would be to read about it in a book. This would take only a few hours and would cost little, even though the experience would not be overly authentic. Today, most would opt for something that is in the middle of Dale's cone, such as a 28-minute video on cable television's Discovery Channel titled "A Day in the Life of a Greek Sponge Fisherman."

A TAXONOMY OF DISTANCE EDUCATION TECHNOLOGIES

In distance education it is imperative that educators think about how communication will occur and how to apply experiences that will promote effective and efficient learning. Most likely, a variety of techniques will be needed to provide equivalent learning experiences for all students, including:

- Correspondence
- Prerecorded media
- Two-way audio
- Two-way audio with graphics
- One-way live video
- Two-way audio, one-way video
- Two-way audio/video
- Desktop two-way audio/video

Correspondence Study

The simplest and longest-lived form of distance education is generally considered to be correspondence study. This approach to distance education uses some kind of mail system, such as regular post office mail or electronic mail, to asynchronously connect the teacher and the learner. Usually, lessons, readings, and assignments are sent to the student, who then completes the lessons, studies the readings, and works on the assignments, which are mailed to the instructor for grading. For a college-level course worth three credits there are often 10 to 12 units to be completed. Each is finished in turn, and when all are completed satisfactorily, the student receives a grade.

Sophisticated forms of correspondence study have used techniques of programmed instruction to deliver information. Linear programmed instruction is most common, but for a period of time there was an effort by a number of correspondence study organizations to develop print-based branched programmed instruction. Programmed instruction normally has a block of content, followed by questions to be answered. Depending on the answers students give, they move to the next block of text (linear programmed instruction) or to another section of the programmed text (branched programmed instruction). Sometimes remedial loops of instruction would be provided to help students through difficult content, or content that supposedly had been covered in previous courses or blocks of instruction. Advanced students do not need to study remedial loops. In this manner, the rate and route of instruction are varied for students of correspondence courses.

Correspondence study is relatively inexpensive, can be completed almost anywhere, and has been shown to be effective. Correspondence study has been used by millions of learners of all ages since the 19th century.

Prerecorded Media

The next logical step in the development of distance education technologies, both historically and conceptually, was the incorporation of media other than print media into correspondence study systems. First, pictures and other graphics were added to correspondence study texts. Then, audiotapes and finally videotapes were added to the collection of materials sent to distant learners. Usually, the correspondence study guide would direct the learner to look at, listen to, or view various media, in addition to assigning more traditional readings.

One interesting approach used by distance educators was borrowed from advocates of individualized instruction. This approach used audiotapes to guide the distant learner through a series of learning events, very similar to how a tutor would direct learning. This audio-tutorial approach was quite popular for a number of years, and still is used by commercial organizations that present self-help materials for individual study.

Two-Way Audio

Correspondence study filled a terrific void for those who wanted to learn when they could and wherever they were located. However, many wanted direct, live communication with the teacher, especially for those in pre-college schools.

The first widely-used synchronous form of distance education used two-way audio with either a telephone hookup, a radio broadcast with telephone call-in, or short wave radio transmission. In all cases, the distant learner and the instructor are linked with some form of live, two-way audio connection. Teachers lecture, ask questions, and lead discussions. Learners listen, answer, and participate. Often, print and non-print materials are sent to distant learners, similar to correspondence study.

The key to this approach is the participation of the teacher and learners in a class session at a regularly scheduled time, or a set period of time, over a predetermined number of weeks or months, such as a semester. For example, a high school class in French might be offered by telephone, radio broadcast, or shortwave signal every weekday from 10:00 a.m. until 10:50 for nine weeks. Students would tune in at home, assignments would be made, and activities completed. In other words, this form of distance education models the traditional classroom, except the teacher and learners can only hear one another. They cannot see each other.

Two-Way Audio with Graphics

Recently, an embellishment of the two-way audio form of distance education has incorporated electronic methods of sending graphics information synchronously to distant learners. Two general approaches are used. The first incorporates a special display board that looks like a whiteboard but that actually transmits whatever is drawn on it to a similar display board at a distant site. Because the electronic boards are connected to one another, whatever the students at the distant site draw is also seen by the instructor. The main disadvantage of this approach is the limited visual capability of the system and the difficulty in connecting more than two locations.

A modification of this approach uses personal computers that are connected to one another, either through a central bridge computer or by using special software. For these systems, the instructor sends graphics, visuals, pictures, and even short video clips to desktop computers located at distant sites. Members of the class are connected by telephone or some other two-way audio system, so they can discuss the visual information being sent via the computer.

This approach is relatively inexpensive and permits the visualization of the teleclass. The major problem is the availability of powerful, networked computers at distant learning sites.

One-Way Live Video

This approach is often referred to as broadcast distance education, popularized in the 1950s by programs such as Sunrise Semester, which was broadcast over commercial television stations. Presently, most broadcast television approaches to distance education are offered by public television stations or are broadcast in the early morning hours by commercial stations.

Programs are broadcast in installments over a 12- to 15-week period. Often, each program is about 60 minutes in length and is accompanied by packets of printed materials and readings. Sometimes, instructors are available for telephone office hours, but most commonly students watch the programs on television and respond to assignments that are described in the course packet. Completion of the assignments depends on viewing each television program, which is often broadcast several times. For those students who miss a broadcast, videotape versions are available, or students can tape the program with their own videocassette recorder.

One advantage of this approach is the relatively high quality of the video broadcasts. Public television stations offer excellent productions of important historical, political, and social events. Educational institutions use these broadcasts as the basis for high school and college courses related to the topics of the television shows. The Civil War series and the Lewis and Clark series are examples of public television programming that was modified into distance education courses.

Two-Way Audio, One-Way Video

In the last few decades, a number of organizations have begun to use live television to broadcast high school and college courses. Initially, this approach used microwave transmission systems, instructional television fixed service (ITFS), or community cable television networks.

Recently, satellite communications systems have become widely available. In these systems, the courses are offered synchronously (e.g., live) to students in as few as two to as many as hundreds of locations. Students are given a toll-free telephone number to call to ask questions of the instructor both during class and after class. Normally, students have a packet of instructional materials, including interactive study guides that they use and complete during the class presentation. Interaction between instruc-

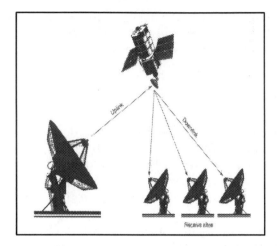

Figure 19.3.   One way video using a satellite.

Figure 19.4.   One way video—two way audio.

tor and students is stressed in these kinds of courses, even ones in which hundreds of students are enrolled.

In the last decade, as satellite uplinks and downlinks have become more prevalent, the concept of the teleconference has become popular. Teleconferences are short courses on specialty topics such as copyright, classroom discipline, sexual harassment, due process, or funding strategies that are offered by an organization to individuals or small groups spread throughout a wide geographic area. Because one satellite in geo-

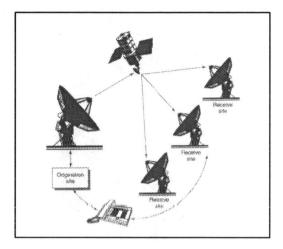

Figure 19.5.   One way video—two way audio.

synchronous orbit above the equator can transmit a video signal to nearly one-third of the earth's surface, it is possible to offer satellite programming to literally thousands of learners.

A number of educational organizations have used satellite broadcast coursework to offer entire high school and college curricula. The TI-IN Network, from San Antonio, Texas, has offered an entire high school curriculum since the mid-1980s.

Two-Way Audio/Video

Recently, especially in the United States, distance education is being widely practiced using live, synchronous television employing one of several technologies. The prevalent technology is called compressed video. This approach, commonly applied in corporate training, uses regular telephone lines to send and receive audio and video signals. The approach is called compressed video because fewer than the normal 30 video frames per second are transmitted between the sites. In the compressed video form, usually 15 video frames per second are transmitted using what is called a T-1 connection. This level of quality is quite acceptable for most instruction, except when some kind of rapid motion or movement is part of instruction.

Compressed video systems are often used in teleconferences for corporate training. Increasingly, schools and colleges are installing compressed

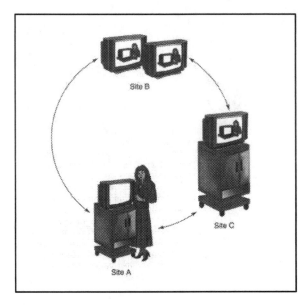

Figure 19.6.   Two way audio and video—compressed video.

Figure 19.7.   Compressed video console.

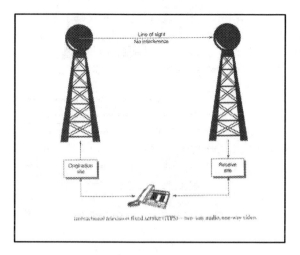

Figure 19.8.   An ITFS system.

Figure 19.9.   Desk top system.

video networks. For this approach, a special classroom is needed that has video and audio equipment to capture the sights and sounds of instruction. The video and audio signals are manipulated by a device called a CODEC (coder/decoder) that removes redundant information for transmission to the distant site. At the receive site, another CODEC converts the compressed information back into video and audio signals. Camera control information is also transmitted between sites, so it is possible for the instructor to pan, tilt, and zoom the cameras.

One major advantage of compressed video systems is their portability. Many systems are installed in movable carts that can be set up in almost any classroom or training site where there is a telephone connection. Recently, the size of the classroom systems has been reduced significantly. The best selling systems are called "set-top" systems because they are placed atop a television monitor. Set top systems contain a camera, microphone, and the electronics necessary to compress and decompress outgoing and incoming transmissions. Set top systems are less than one-quarter the cost of traditional compressed video systems, yet are of similar quality. The Digital Dakota Network (DDN) in South Dakota is a compressed video network that links more than 200 educational sites for live two-way video and audio instruction. The DDN uses traditional "roll-around" and "set-top" systems.

A second, more technically sophisticated, approach to two-way audio/video instruction uses fiber-optic cable to connect sites. Fiber optic cable is the telecommunications medium of choice for new and updated telephone, video, and computer networking. Fiber's cost inhibits its installation in all situations, but fiber's high capacity makes it possible for one fiber (sometimes called a DS-3 connection) to carry full-motion video signals, in addition to high-quality audio signals and almost unlimited amounts of other voice and data information. One exemplary use of fiber optics for distance education is Iowa's publicly owned Iowa Communications Network.

An Example: Two-Way Audio/Video in Iowa

In Iowa, distance education is being redefined on a statewide basis. Iowa's approach to distance education is based on the belief that live, two-way interaction is fundamental to effective learning. The Iowa Communications Network (ICN) makes high-quality interaction possible in the state. The ICN is a statewide, two-way, full-motion interactive fiber-optic telecommunications network with hundreds of connected classrooms. It is designed to be used by teachers and students in learning situations where they can and expect to see and hear each other. Distant and local students function together and learn from and with one another.

A key to Iowa's successful distance education system is the concept of sharing. Iowa's vision for distance education is being built around the development of partnerships of schools that share courses and activities. For example, a physics class originating in Jefferson, a small town in west central Iowa, may have students in Sac City and Rockwell City, schools in two other counties. French students in Sac City have distant classmates in Jefferson and Rockwell City, and a calculus class that originates in Rockwell City is shared with students in Sac City and Jefferson.

All three schools provide courses to partner schools and receive instruction from neighbors. Classes are small, with enrollments of 30 to 35 or less, and are taught by teachers prepared in the skills needed by distance educators.

The use of fiber-optic technology, because of its extensive capacities and flexibility of use, provides unique opportunities for augmenting the instructional process beyond what is possible with other distance delivery technologies. The Iowa approach demonstrates the use of a system that emphasizes:

- Local control of the distance education curriculum
- Active involvement by educators from local school districts
- Interactive instruction
- Statewide alliances and regional partnerships
- Pre-service, in-service, and staff development activities to support teachers
- Implementation using existing organizations and expertise
- Research-based instructional decision-making

The Iowa Communications Network

Central to distance education in Iowa is the Iowa Communications Network. The ICN is a statewide, two-way, full-motion interactive fiber-optic telecommunications network with at least one point of presence in each of Iowa's 99 counties. The ICN links colleges, universities, and secondary schools throughout the state and was constructed entirely with state and local funds. Part 1 of the Iowa Communications Network connected Iowa Public Television, Iowa's 3 public universities, and Iowa's 15 community colleges to the network. Part 2 connected at least one site in each of Iowa's 99 counties. Most Part 2 sites were high schools. Part 3 of the system is still under construction and is being expanded constantly. Currently it connects an additional 700 schools, libraries, armories, area education agencies, and hospitals.

The plan for the ICN was completed and adopted by the Iowa legislature in 1987. Construction of Parts 1 and 2 of the network was completed during 1993. In addition to the capability of transmitting up to 48 simultaneous video channels, the ICN carries data and voice traffic and, as demand increases, the system can be easily expanded without the need for "opening the trench" to lay more fiber.

In Iowa and South Dakota, and in many other states and regions, traditional education works. Educators in these two states adopted distance education, but wanted to preserve their beliefs about effective education. The fiber-optics-based Iowa Communications Network and the compressed video Digital Dakota Network permit this since both are live, two-way audio/video networks.

Desktop Two-Way Audio/Video

One disadvantage of the video telecommunications systems described in this chapter is their cost and cumbersomeness. In order to provide video-based distance education, special electronic devices are needed, satellite or telephone network time must be reserved, and equipped classrooms are required. Desktop systems often reduce the need for special high-cost equipment or special networking. Desktop systems use personal computers and the Internet to connect local and distant learners.

Increasingly, the Internet and Internet II have the capacity to connect personal computers for the sharing of video and audio information. Inexpensive servers that function as reflector sites for connecting multiple sites are also available.

Early systems used CU/SeeMe technology that was free and used very inexpensive video cameras. These systems permitted two sites to connect and to share video and audio. Multiple sites could be connected if a reflector computer was available. The CU/SeeMe approach was relatively low-quality and was used mostly for conferencing and meetings. However, it pioneered the use of desktop systems. Now higher quality cameras and even complete classrooms can be connected to a personal computer for transmission of instruction to distant learners. Certainly the desktop personal computer will be the telecommunications tool of the future.

There are four categories of desktop video/audio systems: analog, high speed, medium speed, and low speed. These systems permit sharing of video and audio from the instructor's computer to a student's computer.

Analog systems use existing telephone wiring in buildings, commonly called twisted-pair wires. The major advantage of this approach is the high quality of the video and audio. Because existing wiring is used, connections are limited to relatively short distances—several thousand feet. Analog systems are limited to a campus, or a building, which significantly reduces this application in distance education.

High-speed videoconferencing sends video at millions of bits per second. Even at this high rate, the video signal is compressed using a compression protocol such as MPEG or motion JPEG. The H.310 protocol is used for high-speed desktop videoconferencing. Currently, high-speed videoconferencing is used primarily with dedicated networks within individual schools or businesses.

Medium-speed desktop videoconferencing is currently the primary approach used today. This type of desktop video transmits at speeds of

128,000 or 256,000 bits per second. The video signal is compressed so it can be transmitted over the Internet (using the H.323 protocol). There are both hardware and software methods to compress and decompress the video signal. Because the Internet is used, medium-speed systems have considerable promise for distance education.

Low-speed desktop video includes all systems that transmit at speeds lower than 56,000 bits per second (56 kbps). This category permits conferencing using the Internet and modems at speeds of 28.8 kbps. A V32 model modem with v.80 extension is generally what is needed for low-speed desktop video. Once again H.323 protocols are used, and software and hardware compression systems are readily available. Very inexpensive systems are already in use, but the quality is quite poor, and the video signal is usually limited to a small window on the computer screen. Low-speed systems are widely used for limited types of instructor/student conferencing, rather than for course delivery.

When the Internet is used, rather than a special or dedicated network, the H.323 standard is used. The primary problem with desktop videoconferencing using the Internet is the poor quality of the video and the limited capacity of the Internet to carry video signals. Because the Internet is a "packet-switched" network, a video signal is broken into packets that are disassembled and then sent to the distant site where the packets are reassembled into a signal. Obviously, this approach is a limiting factor when live, interactive video is sent.

Video streaming is a growing subset of this category of distance education. Video streaming is usually defined as the progressive downloading of a video file (Mallory, 2001). A storage space (i.e., a buffer) that is much smaller than the video file is identified on the computer's hard drive. The video file begins to download into the file location and the file begins to display on the computer screen. The file continues to download from the origination site somewhere on the Internet to the buffer and onto the local computer screen. Often the video file is a pre-recorded event, but live video can be streamed, also.

The three most popular video file types are Apple QuickTime (using .mov files), Microsoft Windows Media Player (using .avi files), and Real-Networks RealPlayer (using .rm files). QuickTime's .mov files are very popular for standard movie downloads, but are not used as much for streamed video and audio. The most widely used format is perhaps the RealPlayer .rm file format (Mallory, 2001). A commonly used strategy is to store video segments on a CD or DVD and ship them to the distant learner to use as part of a course or lesson. CDs can store approximately 650 Megabytes (approximately one hour of video), and DVDs can store about 1.6 gigabytes, or about two hours of movie-quality video.

Desktop videoconferencing is a critical area for growth in distance education. Increasingly, the Internet will be used to connect learners for sharing of video, in addition to data (text and graphics). Before this happens, however, advances in compression standards, network protocols, and transmission media will need to be made.

DISTANCE EDUCATION CLASSROOMS

Two-Way Video/Audio Classrooms

Video-based distance education requires a classroom or studio that is equipped with the technology needed for recording and displaying video and listening to sound. Initially, studios were used as distance education classrooms. Then, as distance education became more widespread, regular classrooms were converted into distance education receive-and-send sites.

Video classrooms need recording, instruction, and display equipment. Recording equipment includes video cameras—typically three—for showing the instructor, the students, and an overhead camera mounted above the instructor console to display printed graphics materials. A switching system is needed to permit the instructor to switch between cameras and instructional equipment, such as a computer, a videocassette recorder, and a video slide projector. Several companies offer devices that attach to video cameras and cause them to follow the action in the classroom. For example, when its activation button is pushed, the student camera automatically pans and zooms to the appropriate microphone location to show the student who is talking. Also, the instructor camera has sensing

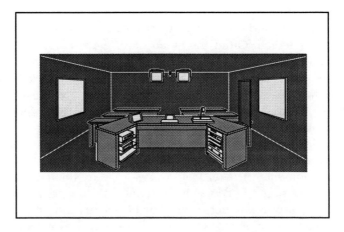

Figure 19.10.   A distance education classroom—front view.

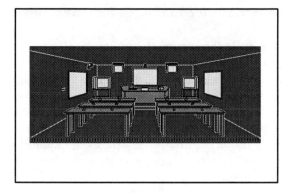

Figure 19.11. A distance education classroom—student view.

devices that, when activated, automatically direct the camera to follow the instructor's movements in the classroom.

Additionally, audio equipment is needed. Audio tends to cause more problems than video in distance education classrooms. Early classrooms used voice-activated microphones, but push-to-talk microphones are now most common.

Instructional media often found in distance education classrooms include a computer and a videocassette recorder. Student equipment includes desktop computers that are networked and that can be displayed for others to see both in the local classroom and at remote sites.

Display equipment includes large television monitors and audio speakers. Most often three display monitors are mounted in a classroom—two in the front of the room for students to view and one in the rear for the instructor. Audio speakers are connected to a volume control.

Sometimes classrooms are connected to a control room where technicians can monitor action and even control the recording and display equipment. Increasingly, however, classrooms are teacher- and student-controlled. In other words, the teacher is responsible for equipment operation and use, or students in the class are assigned these responsibilities.

CLASSROOM TECHNOLOGIES FOR ONLINE INSTRUCTION

The key to success in an online classroom is not which technologies are used, but how they are used and what information is communicated using the technologies.

Selecting Appropriate Technologies for Online Instruction

Step 1: Assess Available Instructional Technologies

Instructional technologies can be organized into two categories: tele-communications technologies and instructional technologies. Since tele-communications means to communicate at a distance, telecommunications technologies are electronic methods used to connect the instructor, students, and resources. Obviously, this chapter discusses online technologies, which means a computer and network. However, embedded within computers and networks are capabilities permitting the delivery of instruction using a variety of media.

Instructional media are ways that messages are stored, and for most online applications, include verbal symbols (words spoken and written), visual symbols (line drawings and graphics), pictures, motion pictures, real-time video, and recorded/edited video.

This list is similar to the one proposed by Edgar Dale discussed earlier in this chapter. The bottom levels of the Cone listed realistic experiences, such as actually doing something in the real world; for example, going to Greece. Realistic experiences are the most difficult to make available to students. It takes a great deal of time and extensive resources to always provide totally authentic, real-world learning experiences.

Dale implied when discussing his Cone that the tension between efficiency (abstract experiences) and effectiveness (realistic experiences) is at the core of instructional design. The professor should pick learning experiences that are no more realistic than necessary in order for outcomes to be achieved. Overly abstract learning experiences require the student to compensate or to learn less effectively. Overly realistic experiences waste resources. When the professor who is designing online instruction selects the correct media, it maximizes efficiency and makes available more resources for other learning experiences.

Assessing available technologies often requires that the instructor determine the level of lowest common technologies (LCT). This means that the sophistication of the computer and software of all learners and the instructor should be determined. Also, this means that the capabilities of the telecommunications technologies must be identified. Often, LCT is determined by having students complete a survey on which they clearly identify the technologies that are available to them.

Another strategy is to require a minimum computer and telecommunications capability before students are allowed to enroll in a course. For example, an 800 MHz, Pentium III computer with 128 MB of RAM, a 30 GB hard drive, a sound card, video card, video camera, speakers, microphone, and 56KB modem or DSL connection might be required of students. Either option has its advantages and disadvantages. Most likely, a minimum technology level needs to be required in order for online instruction to provide experiences equivalent to traditional instruction.

Step 2: Determine the Learning Outcomes

Learning outcomes are those observable, measurable behaviors that are a consequence of online instruction. When learning activities are designed, it is important that some expectations for students be identified in order to guide the selection of appropriate technologies.

Because online environments should be media-rich and strive for authenticity, it is critical that many technologies be used when teaching at a distance. It is also important that students demonstrate learning outcomes by using a variety of technology-based activities. Students may be expected to take a test to demonstrate their competence, but more likely they will be expected to offer some kind of real-world project that gives an authentic assessment of what they learned. Rubrics, which are specific, pre-determined standards for how assignments are to be graded, should be available for students to use to guide the development of the outcome materials they produce.

One strategy used by developers of online instruction is to collect student projects and use these materials as models for subsequent students. If this strategy is used, a thoughtful and comprehensive critique of the student projects should be included so mistakes are identified and not repeated. Some developers of instruction advocate that students should begin with existing materials produced previously and redesign them to eliminate weaknesses, build on strengths, and add new concepts. Specifically, text used in a lesson could be analyzed and replaced with graphics or word pictures (combinations of text and graphics that represent teaching concepts). Still pictures could be modified and upgraded to animations, and synchronous chats could be made more effective by including a threaded discussion strategy that involves asking questions, collecting answers, asking follow-up questions, and selecting most appropriate final responses.

Traditionalists identify learning outcomes in terms of behavioral objectives with specific conditions under which learning will occur, a precise behavior to be demonstrated that indicates learning, and an exact standard to measure competence. Recently, learner-identified objectives have become popular; students are expected at some point during the instructional event to identify what changes they feel are important indicators of learning. Whatever approach is used, it is critical that outcomes of instructional events be clearly identified at some point.

Step 3: Identify Learning Experiences and Match Each to the Most Appropriate Available Technology

Usually, the content of a course is divided into modules or units. Traditionally, a module requires about 3 hours of face-to-face instruction and 6 hours of student study, and a three-credit college course would consist of a total of 12 to 15 modules. In an online course, the classical approach of organizing content around teaching and study time is no longer relevant. One approach would be to simply convert a classroom-centered course's content into online modules. For totally new courses, this approach will obviously not work.

An alternative approach is to organize a course around themes or ideas that directly relate to student activities or learning activities. For example, a history course about the reconstruction period following the American Civil War might have 12 modules, each with 5 learning activities, for a total of 60 activities. The learning activities would be content-centered experiences such as reading assignments, PowerPoint presentations, and audio recordings, or learner-centered experiences, such as threaded discussions on specific topics, research assignments utilizing Web-based search engines, or even self-tests.

One example for a module dealing a topic such as the economic redevelopment of the South in the first five years after the end of the Civil War might begin with a reading assignment from the textbook about economic conditions in the South. This reading assignment would be prescribed by a Web-based assignment. The reading would be followed by participation in an online discussion with a small group of classmates. This discussion would be to identify the five impediments to effective economic development. When the group agreed to the list, it would be posted to the course's bulletin board for grading by the instructor. The third learning experience in this module would be a review of a PowerPoint presentation with audio that was prepared by the instructor that discusses what actually happened economically in the South after the Civil War. Finally, the student would be expected to write a two-page critique of the period of economic development according to a rubric posted on the Web. This assignment would be submitted electronically to the course's instructor for grading.

Subsequent modules in this course would be designed similarly. At several points during the course, benchmark projects would be required of students, such as an individual online chat with the instructor, or the submission of a major project that synthesized work completed for module assignments.

Once the course's content is organized into modules, the next design requirement is to match learning experiences to technology-delivery strategies. The reading assignments could be delivered using the textbook, or posted as files to be downloaded, or even read directly from the computer monitor. PowerPoint presentations could be handled the same way, and used directly from the computer, or downloaded and studied later. E-mail attachments could be used for assignment submission and chat rooms or e-mail could provide ways to hold threaded discussions.

In this example, the instructional media are relatively simple formats. What is sophisticated is the design and organization of the activities and content facilitated and delivered by the media.

Step 4: Preparing the Learning Experiences for Online Delivery

There are four strategies for organizing instruction for online delivery: linear programmed instruction, branched programmed instruction, hyper-programmed instruction, and student programmed instruction.

In each case, the content of the course is subdivided into modules. The modules consist of topics that relate to one another, or have some sense of unity or consistency, such as the economic condition of the South after the Civil War. The modules themselves, and the learning activities within the modules, are organized according to one of the four delivery strategies listed above.

Linear programmed instruction, a long-standing approach to individualized instruction, requires that all content be organized into concepts that are presented in blocks or chunks. Students review content, take a self-test and, if successful, move to the next chunk/block of information. This happens sequentially until the content blocks are completed. Students move in the same order through the sequence of concepts. The teacher determines the order of the concepts/chunks.

Branched programmed instruction is similar, except the self-tests are more sophisticated so that students can branch ahead if they are exceptionally proficient, or move to remediation if they are floundering. Similarly to linear programmed instruction, the order and sequence of instruction, including branches, is instructor-determined.

Hyper-programmed instruction, widely advocated for Web-based online instruction, also organizes content into modules and concepts, but permits the student to move through the learning activities at their own rate and pace, in a route they determine themselves. In other words, learning experiences are identified and mediated, and students use them until either an instructor- or student-determined outcome is met. Often, each module has a terminal, or final, activity that must be completed before the student moves to the next course module.

Finally, the student-programmed approach uses an extremely loose structure in which only the framework of the content is provided to online learners who are expected to provide the structure, outcomes, and sequence of learning activities. For example, students who enroll in a course about Reconstruction would be required to organize and sequence the modules and activities, and during the course to identify personal outcomes and activities to be accomplished.

When teachers attempt to make instruction equal for all students they will fail. Rather, the teacher of online instruction should provide a wide collection of activities that make possible equivalent learning experiences for students using an approach that recognizes the fundamental differences between learners, distant and local. Equivalency is more difficult, but promises to be more effective.

SUMMARY

The technologies used for distance education fall into two categories: telecommunications technologies that connect instructors to distant learners, and classroom technologies that record, present, and display instructional information. Increasingly, video- and computer-based systems are being used to support both categories.

The effective utilization of distance education classrooms and their associated technologies requires a new set of skills for most educators and learners. Teaching with technology to learners who are not physically located in the same site as the instructor requires a different set of skills and competencies than traditional education. Technologies are tools that must be mastered to be optimally effective in the distance context.

REFERENCES

Dale, E. (1946). *Audiovisual methods in teaching*. Hinsdale, IL: Dryden Press.

Baumgarn, K. (1995). *Classrooms of the Iowa Communications Network*. Ames, IA: Research Institute for Studies in Education.

Cyrs, T. (1997). *Teaching at a distance with the merging technologies*. Las Cruces, NM: Center for Educational Development.

Kemp, J., & Smellie, D. (1994). *Planning, producing, and using instructional technologies* (7th ed). New York: HarperCollins.

Mallory, J. (2001). Creating streamed instruction for the deaf and hard-of-hearing online learner. *DEOSNEWS, 11*(8), 1-6.

Moore, M. G., & Kearsley, G. (1996). *Distance education: A systems view*. Belmont, CA: Wadsworth.

Richardson, A. (1992). *Corporate and organizational video*. New York: McGraw-Hill.

Simonson, M., Smaldino, S., Albright, M., & Zvacek, S. (2003). *Teaching and learning at a distance: Foundations of distance education*. Upper Saddle River, NJ: Prentice Hall.

Simonson, M., & Volker, R. (1984). *Media planning and production*. Columbus, OH: Merrill.
Zettl, H. (1995). *Video basics*. Belmont, CA: Wadsworth.

CHAPTER 20

DYNAMISM AND EVOLUTION IN STUDENT SUPPORT AND INSTRUCTION IN DISTANCE EDUCATION

Implications for International Distance Education

Yusra Laila Visser

CONTEXT

Those of us who live in the United States, where Web-based instruction appears to have become the norm for distance education, can easily forget that distance education often does not take the same modality in less wealthy regions of the world. In fact, many regions of the world have had a long-standing tradition of delivering distance education courses and programs through technologies other than the Internet (e.g., print-based materials, audio technology, etc.).

To place the purpose of this chapter in context, it is important to understand the situation in which many of the world's distance education

Trends and Issues in Distance Education: International Perspectives, 287–307

programs and institutions are functioning. As a case in point, consider some of the educational issues surrounding a region like Africa. This geographically expansive continent struggles with many challenges for meeting the needs for education at all levels. Literacy rates in many countries in Africa remain low, and access to tertiary education continues to be a significant challenge.

Nevertheless, human and economic development remains a key objective for educational programs and projects throughout the continent. A World Bank (2002) report argues that "knowledge has become, more than ever, a primary factor of production through the world economy" (p. ix). One positive development is that communication technology is expanding through all parts of the world, including the developing world. The World Bank (2002) thus argues that "tertiary education, in its training, research, and information role, is vital" (p. x).

There are some 140 tertiary education institutions in sub-Saharan Africa that are offering courses and programs through distance education (Saint, 2000). These distance education programs typically rely on an approach in which information is typically sent to students through print-based media, and in which students submit written assignments to demonstrate mastery of instructional objectives. These programs may also provide face-to-face tutoring by having students and mentors work collaboratively in study centers (Saint, 2000). Beyond print-based technology, some programs also use radio, audio cassettes and, in recent years, email, to facilitate the learning process (Saint, 2000). According to the World Bank, an increasing number of tertiary-level distance education program are only now beginning to make the first systemic forays into the integration of the Internet in distance education.

Africa's state of affairs in terms of tertiary-level distance education makes that continent's situation far from the exception. In fact, one might argue that, with only a minority of the world's population living in the wealthiest nations, the vast majority of countries where distance education serves higher education needs have conditions similar to those in Africa. Distance education programs in these countries are to an ever-greater degree in the process of adjusting the delivery of instruction to integrate Web-based instruction. This transition in delivery mode places special demands on the distance education programs in general, but perhaps even more so on mentors and students.

What is the principal distinction between *correspondence*-based, mentor-supported distance education programs and those that are *web*-based and mentor-supported? In correspondence-based distance education, communication and transmission of knowledge occurs on the basis of discrete, point-to-point interactions (e.g., communication between one mentor and one student). In Web-based distance education, however, the modalities for communication and instruction are expanded beyond those of correspondence-driven distance education to include opportunities for distributed communication in any number of configurations between multiple points (e.g., communication between one instructor and multiple students, and communication among multiple students). These opportunities offer great potential for qualitatively improving the quality of the learning experience. However, these environments also generate new challenges. As Saint (2000) notes, success in such an environment requires careful management of distance education programs, which deal with "scattered students, dispersed part-time tutors, far-flung logistics, unreliable communication services, time-sensitive production and distribution of learning materials, and detailed student records" (p. 12).

The purpose of this chapter is to describe how mentoring can be conducted in Web-based distance education so that instructional gains are greatest, and in a manner that most fully takes advantage of the possibilities provided by the Web-based format. To this end, the chapter covers the following topics: the tasks associated with mentoring in distance education in general; the tasks uniquely associated with mentoring in a Web-based distance education format; strategies that can be employed in redefining the role of the student to allow for a distributed responsibility in mentoring; and tactics that mentors can use to improve the efficiency and effectiveness of their mentoring. Ultimately, the intent of this chapter is to provide some guidelines that may play a role in helping the many tertiary education institutions that are in the process of redesigning their educational systems to increasingly integrate Web-based distance education.

FOUR KEY AREAS OF MENTOR PERFORMANCE IN EFFECTIVE DISTANCE EDUCATION

The mentor is a fundamental presence in the distance learning environment (Moore & Kearsley, 1996). This is true regardless of whether the program delivers instruction through a correspondence-based or Web-based approach. There are several important responsibilities that the mentor is required to fulfill in any well-designed distance education program. These responsibilities can be categorized into four key areas (see Figure 20.1). Although these areas are generally distinct, some of the mentor's roles, as we shall see, may appear in more than one area. A description of the four areas follows below.

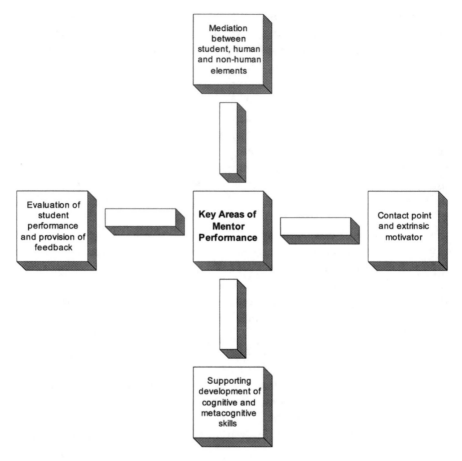

Figure 20.1.   Four key areas of distance education mentor performance.

1.   Meditates between Student, Human, and Non-human Elements of the Distance Learning Environment

A variety of sources suggest that one of the primary roles of the mentor is in functioning as an intermediary between the distance learner and other entities (human and physical) within the learning context. Let us first examine this critical role of the mentor in the distance context.

In the facilitative role, the mentor is often presented as a link between the learner and physical entities; for example, the course materials (Lewis, 1995). In some contexts, this role is designed to complement the learning materials as well as to extend the learner's understanding of the learning materials (Lewis, 1995). Bates (1984) emphasizes the human side of the presence of the mentor, emphasizing the importance of the mentor as "humanizing" the hardware and "shaping" the hardware to the needs of the students through the development of shared understanding. In this sense, the mentor is seen as giving contextual and personal relevance to the learning materials (Bates, 1984). The physical attributes of the learning environment are seen as being potentially alienating to the learner, and the mentor is presented as a mechanism in the learning environment to prevent such alienation.

Thorpe (1979) sees the mentor as an intermediary between the student and other human entities in a course, such as peers. As such, the role of the mentor is to interpret the learner such that the dialogue between the learner and the course members may be enhanced (Thorpe, 1979). This view of the intermediary role of the mentor suggests that the mentor's role is as a necessary interface between two human entities in the learning system, who otherwise might fail to communicate effectively.

2.   Serves as Contact Point and Extrinsic Motivator

While the roles and responsibilities of mentors may be defined differently (as dictated by different modes of communication and different learning institutions), the role of the mentor as a learner's point of contact, a human "dimension," appears to have remained constant. The mentor is presented as the first "port of call" for the distance learner. As such, mentors are typically expected to initiate and sustain communication with individual learners throughout the learning process (Daniel & Meech, 1978). The mentor is considered to have a direct relationship with students, which is based on reciprocity and flexibility (Bates, 1984). He or she is often charged with determining the learner's readiness to learn and to identify any difficulties learners are experience (Beaudoin, 1990).

Although successful distance learners are typically found to have high levels of intrinsic motivation (Rowntree, 1992), mentors are also expected to operate as extrinsic sources of motivation for learners in some contexts (Bates, 1995, 1996). They are often charged with stimulating the learner to continue through the full extent of the course (Beaudoin, 1990). Indeed, the general presence of the mentor as advisor and resource may be considered extrinsically motivating in and of itself. Prior research (Visser, Plomp, Amirault & Kuiper, 2000) has found that incorporation of systematic motivational design elements in the job responsibilities of the mentor has resulted in positive effects on the performance and achievement of learners.

3. Evaluates Student Performance and Provides Feedback

The role of the mentor as assessor of learner performance places an emphasis on the mentor's subject-matter-expertise and critical and analytical thinking abilities. In conducting assessment of student work, the mentor is expected to grade assignments (Beaudoin, 1990), provide meaningful feedback on student work (Daniel & Meech, 1978), monitor students to determine if course objectives are being met, evaluate the extent of the student's learning, and assign grades (Beaudoin, 1990). As noted previously, the assessment role of the mentor is further enhanced in some contexts to include the responsibility for identifying learners who are in need of academic support and assistance, and reporting the names of these students to the central administrative office of the distance learning institution (IEC, 1998).

4. Supports the Development of Cognitive and Metacognitive Skills

The mentor is charged with supporting the learner's development in terms of critical thinking, analytical thinking, and the formulation of alternative theories and hypotheses (Bates, 1984; Visser, Visser, & Schlosser, 2003). In addition, the mentor is charged with supporting the learner's development of metacognitive skills and communication skills. In a survey administered to students in three international distance education programs, a third of students reported that "help in the area of study methods" was most the most important type of academic support that a mentor could provide (Visser & Visser, 2000). In some distance education programs, the learner is the initiator of communication pertaining to cognitive and metacognitive skills development, and the mentor is expected to only offer such guidance on an as-needed basis. As a source of guidance on cognitive and metacognitive skills development, the mentor provides insight that may be of critical importance to the learner's achievement, not only in the distance course, but also in other areas of his or her life.

IMPACT OF WEB-BASED DISTANCE EDUCATION ON KEY AREAS OF MENTOR PERFORMANCE

The use of Web-based distance education significantly changes the role of learners and mentors within the distance education context (Wellburn, 1999). Indeed, Moore and Kearsley argue that mentor involvement in Web-based distance education can enhance student learning in ways not possible in correspondence-based distance education (1996). For distance education institutions transitioning into Web-based distance education, there are opportunities and responsibilities for redefining the role of the mentor and the student.

Perhaps the key difference between correspondence-based and Web-based distance education is the change in the nature of interaction with regard to learning. This change has significant implications for the task of the mentor in Web-based distance education. According to Collins & Berge (1996), there are two type of interaction for learning: "One is a student individually interacting with content. The other is social activity: a student interacting with others about the content. Both types of interaction are necessary for efficient, effective, and affective learning" (p. 5). Clearly the majority of learning-oriented interaction in correspondence-based distance education involves the interaction of the learner with the content. In Web-based distance education, both type of interactions for learning are enabled and encouraged. The result is that mentors in Web-based distance education programs must develop new competencies and acquire new responsibilities in order to best serve their students.

Beyond addressing the issue of supporting the two levels of interaction for learning, mentors transitioning from correspondence-based distance education to Web-based distance education will likely quickly realize that they face a myriad of new challenges in managing the learning process. Mentors struggle with the diversity of learner experiences, expectations, and learning cultures that are simultaneously present in Web-based distance education (Bullen, M., personal interview, March 1998). The ease of communication between all points within the learning system, as well as the students' demand for expediency in feedback (Paulsen, 2000), results in mentors spending unprecedented amounts of time communicating with individual learners and groups of learners. Learners unfamiliar with the Web-based applications look to the mentor for guidance and technical support, placing expectations on the mentor for high personal comfort levels with the technology being employed. Thus, the mentor who is transitioning from correspondence-based to Web-based distance education will face a plethora of new tasks and responsibilities, particularly if a decision is made to simply "pile on" the new roles in addition to the roles that he or she fulfilled in correspondence-based distance education.

In order to more systematically consider how the transition to Web-based instruction affects the expectations placed on mentor performance, let us once again consider the four key areas of mentor performance, this time describing these key areas in terms of new functions that the mentor may be expected to fulfill once he or she transitions to Web-based distance education. These additional functions do not replace the functions described earlier; they supplement the functions listed in the previous section.

1.   Meditates between Student, Human, and Non-human Elements of the Distance Learning Environment

When operating in a Web-based distance education context, both mentors and students experience new challenges in dealing with the non-human elements in distance education. Most notable, of course, is the requirement that the mentor be capable of assisting learners in achieving comfort with computer- and software-based technology (Berge, 1995). Mentors are required to be prepared to assist students in using a variety of different software applications, such as discussion boards, chat programs, learning management systems, search engines, email, and online registration systems. Indeed, some argue that one of the key roles of the mentor is to assist in making the technology transparent to the learner (Berge, 1995). Depending on the audience characteristics, a mentor may find that there is considerable variability in the level of proficiency that learners have with technology, thereby creating unique challenges for the mentor in maintaining a sense of "cohesiveness" among the students.

In terms of the human elements, the focus in correspondence-based distance education is on generating a comfortable, individual relationship between the student and the mentor, since communication by students with peers tends to be limited. When transitioning to Web-based distance education, the mentor is likely to find that he or she has many new responsibilities in regards to human interaction. Significant energy will have to be dedicated to promoting human relationships in the Web-based medium to ensure that there is a sense of group cohesiveness (Berge, 1995). A useful technique, for example, is to require the mentor to provide to the learners guidelines for communication, to ensure that the communication between learners is culturally and emotionally sensitive. In addition, the mentor should moderate content-related communication between students, and initiate and manage online discussions (Berge, 1995). In moderating online discussions or exchanges, the mentor often has to remain vigilant of online discourse to ensure that contributions made by students are accurate from the standpoint of subject matter expertise, and to gently correct misinformation as the need arises.

2.   Serves as Contact Point and Extrinsic Motivator

As contact point and extrinsic motivator, the mentor must dedicate careful attention to assessing learner readiness when undergoing the transition from non-Web to Web-based distance education modalities. Learner readiness includes the willingness to operate in new and innovative technological settings, as well as readiness to operate as knowledge resource and mentor. The mentor is in a unique position to facilitate these processes.

There are many time-consuming tasks associated with serving as contact-point in Web-based distance education. These tasks often appear deceivingly small or simple. Experienced mentors in Web-based distance education will be quick to refer to the significant amount of time that is dedicated to responding to individual student inquiries, supporting students with performance anxiety, recommending additional resources outside of those included in the course study materials, supporting students with lower literacy levels, and supporting learners with less keyboarding experience. In the case of regions where technology infusion has been slow, it is likely that mentor support will be especially crucial for assisting with the technical aspects of the distance education experience.

3.   Evaluates Student Performance anjjd Provides Feedback

Practice, feedback, and assessment are critical aspects of instructional effectiveness. In correspondence-based distance education, the technologies used for the transmission of student and instructor documents (e.g., postal services) are relatively slow. This constrains the amount of exchange that can take place between the mentor and the student for purposes of assessment and evaluation of student performance. In Web-based distance education, efficiency in communication provides the tutor with many opportunities to provide feedback on students' formative and summative products. Given the important of feedback in effective instruction, this is perhaps one of the most important affordances of Web-based distance education. However, with the efficiency in communication, the expectations for high levels of interaction increase, too. In light of this, several authors (e.g., Berge, 1995; Collins & Berge, 1996; Paulsen, 2000) provide recommendation for how to manage these expectations for increased communication.

4.   Supports the Development of Cognitive and Metacognitive Skills

In correspondence-based distance education, the mentor is typically given a copy of the instructional materials for the course, as well as a set of notes that are intended to assist in fulfilling the mentoring responsibilities. Communication with (and among) students in such settings is greatly limited due to restrictions imposed by the medium. In Web-based distance education, however, this factor significantly changes. Mentors in

Web-based distance education find that they will also have to take a significantly more active role in the day-to-day operation of the course. Mentors are often expected to implement (and sometimes design) learning activities (Collins & Berge, 1996). The mentor's role in supporting the development of cognitive and metacognitive skills becomes significant in this situation. The design and management of interactive, Web-based learning activities must be conducted in a manner appropriate to the medium and the learner attributes, especially in terms of needs for learner cognitive and metacognitive development.

Successful students in distance education tend to show evidence of high levels of self-directedness. For many students who have not previously experienced distance education, there is a significant adjustment involved in becoming more self-directed in their learning experiences. The mentor can thus encourage increased levels of self-direction (Collins & Berge, 1996) by helping students "ease into self-directed modes of study, rather than presuming that this capability already exists" (Beaudoin, 1990). As Beaudoin points out, "Students may have only vague notions of what self-directed study means and their own capacity for working within such a format" (Beaudoin, 1990).

There are new opportunities for the mentor working in the Web-based environment to play an active and significant role in the development of social negotiation and collaborative learning skills. Correspondence-style distance education typically involves information being manually delivered from mentor to learner and learner to mentor. Web-based distance education yields opportunities for meaningful, *continuous* interaction between mentor and learner as well as among learners themselves. To capitalize on this, learners must develop key skills for social negotiation and collaboration. The mentor is in a critical position for supporting the development of such skills. In order to maximize the benefits yielded from interactivity inherent in the Web-based instructional format, mentors must develop expert skills in both asking questions and in providing answers (Collins & Berge, 1996). This is a change from correspondence-based distance education, in which the mentor is largely responsible for disseminating his or her content knowledge through feedback on assignments and student questions. The skills and subject matter knowledge required for generating meaningful questions are qualitatively different from those required for being able to answer questions.

In Web-based distance education, the mentor often also serves as a filter for information and knowledge, such that information gathered elsewhere is assessed for validity and relevance. The uncontrolled nature of the Internet has resulted in the unprecedented growth of resources that are available to the learner through this medium. However, there are no universal mechanisms for validation of the information distributed through the Internet. Mentors possessing rich subject matter expertise and critical thinking skills may serve the dual role of raising learner awareness of the importance of identifying valid sources of information, and validating actual sources that are identified by learners. Present trends in the growth of the Internet as learning resource suggest that the mentor's role in this capacity should be expanded considerably (Harasim, Hiltz, Teles, & Turoff, 1997; Sammons, 2003).

CONCERNING THE CUMULATIVE IMPACT OF MENTOR PERFORMANCE EXPECTATIONS ON WEB-BASED DISTANCE EDUCATION

The previous two sections of this chapter have painted two pictures of the mentor's job in distance education. The first section covered the key tasks that would apply to mentoring regardless of the specific delivery system used for distance education. The second section addressed the additional tasks that are likely to be added to the mentor's performance expectations when the decision is made to move to a Web-based format.

In considering the impact of the Web-based format on expectations placed on mentors, it seems evident that one cannot reasonably assume that mentors can fulfill all the tasks associated with the general mentoring role as well as the additional tasks that result from operating in a Web-based format. Without somehow addressing the scope of mentor tasks in the Web-based environment, significant problems for the mentor, the students, and therefore for the distance education program as a whole, would be the result.

One of the attractions of distance education for many higher education institutions is the potential for scalability of courses. Whereas there are limits imposed on the number of students that can be accommodated within the physical constraints of a face-to-face classroom, this specific constraint does not exist in distance education. Indeed, many large distance education institutions, such as the British Open University, have successfully delivered classes to very large numbers of students (Bork, 2001). However, this can only be accomplished by substantively changing how distance education is implemented, so that mentoring tasks are distributed over a number of different support functions in the program.

Mentors are generally paid only modest compensation for their work, thereby raising important ethical considerations if mentors are asked to work at levels that they cannot sustain. In addition, distance education programs would likely find it difficult to convince potential mentors to work for them if the workload seems unmanageable. The mentors may quickly become overburdened, resulting in a potential increase in the turnover rates among mentor staff. In turn, this would generate increased costs for the distance education program (due to the need to recruit and train new mentors), as well as threatening the quality of the program (by causing experienced mentors to leave the program).

Students in Web-based distance education programs would also be negatively affected if mentors are tasked with a job that is larger than they can reasonably be expected to handle. If the mentors are overburdened with some of the tasks they are expected to carry out (answering technical questions, responding to individual inquiries, motivating students, providing continuous feedback, etc.), other tasks will fall to the wayside, and the student will only receive a portion of the support and guidance that is needed. Learning and performance gains among students may be compromised as a result, and students may opt to discontinue their studies, or to seek instruction through another modality.

The net result of overburdening the mentor, therefore, is that the potential opportunities emerging from Web-based distance education are not brought to fruition. Indeed, it is these very opportunities that the Web-based format offers that are likely to be lost. It therefore becomes imperative that distance education programs, instructional designers, mentors, and students alike develop creative approaches for redefining roles and allocation of resources to successfully realize the benefits of the Web-based format. The next section of the chapter briefly discusses how mentor and student roles can be adjusted to ease the burden otherwise placed on the mentor.

REDEFINING THE ROLE OF THE STUDENT

In Web-based distance education, the learner can be involved in the learning process in new ways that enhance the learning experience of the student and reduce reliance on the established mentor roles. Interestingly, one of the things that make learners in Web-based distance education particularly valuable to each other as resources is their diversity. This diversity goes beyond the conventional differences in demographic and cultural composition of the learning group. Diversity in learner experience refers to how students differ in terms of things such as expectations for the course, prior experience with the subject matter, contexts in which students have experienced things related to the subject matter, learning and educational contexts in which students have participated previously, experiences with distance education and other modalities, and expertise in technology. The variation of learners in this regard, coupled with opportunities for interaction among all members of the class, presents opportunities for learners to mentor each other in a number of areas that would otherwise fall exclusively within the realm of the mentor's role. Below is a list of some of the ways in which students can enrich each others' learning experiences can enrich each others' learning experiences:

- *Students can share and discuss the diversity in experiences and expectations present in the class.* This discussion can create opportunities for learners to become sources of what Baltes, Dittmann-Kohli, & Dixon (1984) refer to as rich factual and procedural knowledge that is understood as content-rich and culture-dependent knowledge.
- *Students can take an active role in providing evaluative feedback on the work of their peers.* The mentor might provide guidelines for providing substantive feedback while maintaining a constructive tone. Such an approach meets the need for regular feedback while also giving learners experience in critically and constructively evaluating content related to the subject of instruction.
- *Students can become sources of motivational support for one another.* Prior research has shown that the integration of motivational design in distance learning positively impacts retention rates and student satisfaction (Visser, Plomp, Amirault, & Kuiper, 2000). By providing students with a basic introduction to Keller's ARCS model (1987), students can learn to identify the motivational needs of their peers and to respond to those needs by writing each other messages that employ recommended motivational tactics.
- *Groups of students can build mutually beneficial collaborative relationships.* For example, one student may have an extensive technical background but little experience in writing academic papers, while another student may have developed sound writing skills but be lacking confidence in his or her ability to deal with the technological aspects of the course. If these students were to develop a collaborative relationship, the potential gains for each would be significant.
- *Students with greater experience in distance education can be encouraged to serve as a resource for students who are at risk of dropping out or falling behind.* Often, novice distance learners are poorly prepared for dealing with the unique challenges faced in distance education. Experienced distance learners can, with relatively little additional effort, share some of the strategies that they have developed to function effectively in a distance education environment. Such support could make the difference between success and failure for the novice student.

An important cautionary note is warranted here. In order for students to successfully participate in ensuring the success of a Web-based distance education course, it is necessary for several conditions to be met. First, the students should be made aware of their mentors' expectations at the beginning of the class. Second, if high levels of participation are expected of students, it is advisable to increase the amount of the final course grade that is accounted for by student participation. Third, the course designer(s) and mentor need to ensure that the course is developed and implemented in such a way that the logistical aspects of the course encourage students to support each other. Fourth, the inherent benefits of the redefined role of the student should be clear to the students. Finally, both the mentor and the students should realize that the redefined role is intended to make it possible for the students to share *some* of the mentoring tasks. In other words, when students take on responsibilities to support one another in the learning process, it should not result in the mentor withdrawing from those tasks. The students' assistance and support can alleviate some of the pressure otherwise placed on the mentor, but cannot, and should not, result in students being left without the benefits of an active mentor. Rather, the redefined role of the student should generate value-added benefit for both the learner *and* the mentor.

STRATEGIES FOR INCREASING EFFICIENCY IN MENTORING

As has been noted above, the role of the student can be significantly adjusted in Web-based distance education to accommodate an approach to mentoring that is distributed among the many members of the distance-delivered course. In addition, however, there are a number of different strategies that have been proposed for helping the mentor to function in a more efficient manner and to maximize the amount of time that the mentor can invest in sharing expertise and experience related to the subject matter of the course. The latter is an important consideration. As Beaudoin (1990) notes, one of the key tasks of the educator working in a distance learning context is to enable students to engage in an increasingly self-directed manner. He observes that

> Because the concept of self-directed learning implies empowerment of learners through lessened dependency on teacher direction, skeptics assume this mode of teaching is less time consuming than the traditional lecture-discussion format. However, instructional tasks associated with self-directed learning are generally more time consuming than working with standardized curricula and learning formats. (p. 3)

With this in mind, let us consider some relatively simple and affordable strategies that can be employed to increase efficiency in mentoring such that mentors can dedicate more time to enabling and supporting effective self-directed learning.

Design

- *Employ deliberate, systematic course design and evaluation.* Perhaps the most important consideration in ensuring efficiency in instruction and learning is to carefully design the course. Paulsen (2000) argues that, for certain courses, "the interactive workload could be decreased through proactive design and preparation" (p. 129). In terms of evaluation, Bork (2001) notes; "The designers are not perfect, and will miss some details. So extensive evaluation and improvement with typical intended users is important" (p. 143).

- *Design course calendar to chunk submission of assignments.* One option in the design of an online course is to chunk together a series of assignments for submission as a single unit. This allows the mentor the limit the frequency with which he or she must provide feedback on assignments. Note, however, that careful thought should be given to learner characteristics and the nature of the instructional content, to assure that this strategy does not negatively affect the quality of the learning experience.

- *Design activities that embed software learning so students can adjust to the LMS.* Student queries about the use of the learning management system or of software used to deliver an online course can yield large amounts of queries to which the mentor must respond. In order to avoid this situation, the course activities at the beginning of the semester can be designed so that they include a gradual orientation to the various facets of the software being used for the course.

- *Design group assignments or activities.* By having students collaborate on assignments and submit group products, the amount of time the mentor spends on assessment can be reduced significantly (Paulsen, 2000). However, such an approach should only be selected if the nature of the content merits it. In addition, students should be given careful guidelines for working collaboratively, since group work can generate logistical problems for students if such activities are not well-designed.

- *Create external administrative and technical support.* Questions of an administrative or technical nature can consume much of a mentor's time, as these questions are often highly idiosyncratic in nature (because students have different software and hardware configurations, and because a variety of specific support issues can arise, for example, with registration and admission questions). It is therefore highly desirable to shift responsibility for these kinds of questions away from the mentor, to external experts in each of these areas (Berge, 1995, Paulsen, 2000).

Development

- *Refine and reuse instructional materials.* If materials have been designed carefully and have been found to be largely effective once implemented, it is highly desirable to refine and reuse such materials to the extent possible. This not only reduces the cost of course development, it also removes potential inefficiencies for the mentor when he or she has to learn to develop a comfort level with new and uncomfortable material.

- *Develop clear assignment and activity directions.* This is a must for every instructional setting, but it is especially important in the online distance learning setting. If the procedures for an assignment or activity are not clear, it can generate a significant amount of lost time for students, and it also increases the amount of "on-the-spot" guidance that the mentor must provide to compensate for unclear instructions.

- *Identify outside resources for student support.* Paulsen (2000) notes that one of the distinct features of teaching online is that mentors and students have access to a vast amount of online resources. In the process of course development, it can be beneficial to identify accurate online resources that students can be referred to for guidance on the course content, pre-requisite skills and knowledge, or technical issues. Creating an annotated webliography will ensure students know what resources to refer to when they are in need of additional information or practice.

- *Develop self-assessments and peer assessments where possible* (Paulsen, 2000). Self-assessment guidelines can be developed to allow students to critically determine whether they have met the requirements for an assignment. Peer assessment guidelines can be used by students to evaluate and provide feedback to their peers' work. Both self-assessment and peer-assessment can be used so that students can get formative feedback without increasing the burden on the mentor. Such assessments can also be used as a "quality check" prior to submission of an assignment to the mentor. The latter approach benefits the mentor (by reducing chances of receiving assignments that require exhaustive feedback) and the students (by increasing the chance of receiving a good grade, since a preliminary analysis of the quality of the work has been done prior to submission of the assignment).

- *Use self-correcting quizzes* (Paulsen, 2000). Many of the current Learning Management Systems include course features for creating fixed-response assessments, coding the correct response, and automatically comparing the coded correct response to the student's response to determine the student's performance. There are also quiz and survey generators available online, independent of the commercial learning management systems. If assessment items are created using sound educational measurement principles, self-correcting quizzes can play an important role in measuring student performance without intense mentor effort.

- *Create FAQs and tutorials* (Paulsen, 2000). If the course developers have a sense of common questions that students are likely to ask, they can develop a repository of Frequently Asked Questions (FAQs). Students can refer to this repository *before* contacting the mentor if they are having difficulties. Likewise, if it is anticipated that students will have difficulty determining procedures for using certain aspects of the online learning system, self-contained tutorials can be developed so that students can get independent practice, instead of having to ask the mentor for assistance. Both of these resources can be refined and reused from semester to semester. In addition to helping to reduce the mentor workload, providing FAQs and tutorials helps the students feel less reliant on the mentor for answers to procedural questions.

Implementation

- *Send group emails.* A sense of isolation is one of the key challenges faced by students in distance education. A feeling of isolation not only affects the student's motivation in a class, but also affects the completion rates in a distance education class. Many of these feelings of isolation can be reduced if the instructor remains in consistent contact with the students. This can be efficiently accomplished by sending emails to the class as a whole. Using a conversational style in those messages is usually recommended. Group messages can be used to motivate students, as well as to remind students of important issues in the logistics of the course (e.g., upcoming deadlines).

- *Define a clear process for handling student questions.* When students contact the mentor with questions, the answers to those questions are often of relevance to others in the class. It is therefore advisable to set up a process for student questions that encourages students to post general questions in a location where other students can view the questions and the answers. Use of informative subject lines for question messages is also helpful. Any expectations in this regard (i.e., questions that should not be publicly posted on a course Web site) should be communicated to the students at the beginning of the class, and should be reinforced as needed during the semester. The process for student questions might include a statement to specify that questions of a personal nature, or questions about assigned grades, should be sent to the mentor's personal email.

- *Provide sample products for highly complex assignments.* If the course requires students to complete large-scale assignments that are in an advanced subject area, it may help if you share complete or partial sample assignments with the students. This will give students a picture of the goal to which they are working, and will reduce the amount of time that a mentor has to spend providing feedback on assignments that have not "met the mark." However, exercise should be cautioned with this approach to avoid help prevent students from mindlessly mimicking the approach used in the sample assignments. One strategy that can be used to avoid this is to upload a variety of sample assignments, of varying levels of quality, without identifying which sample assignments are the most or least positive examples.

- *Provide general class feedback on assignments.* Feedback is an essential part of learning, and one of the mentor's roles is to provide a rationale for the score that a student receives on an assignment. Generally, students will commit similar mistakes when working on their individual assignments. One strategy that mentors can use to reduce the amount of time dedicated to providing feedback is to write messages to the class as a whole, identifying what common mistakes accounted for students losing points, asking students to make sure that that they understand their individual grades, and encouraging students to contact the mentor if there are any additional questions.

- *Create support groups or dyads.* One of the strongest impacts of the Web on distance learning is the opportunities it creates for collaboration among students. Mentors can assign students to groups and charge the members of the groups with providing certain types of support to each other. For example, students can be charged with reviewing each other's work prior to submission, helping each other out with technical problems, or figuring out practice activities. If the mentor conducts a short learner analysis at the beginning of the semester, students can be assigned to groups with a greater amount of planning. For example, each group could contain one highly technical person, one person with extensive distance learning experience, and one person with experience in the subject of instruction.

- *Restrict mentor communication with individual students and small groups* (Paulsen, 2000). Several of the recommendations listed involve focusing on communication between the mentor and the class as a whole. To the extent possible, mentors should limit their communication with individual students to only those topics that are of a truly personal nature. Mentors will have little time to work on other tasks if their students have high expectations for personalized communication. And, research (Visser, Plomp, Amirault, & Kuiper, 2002) has found that motivational benefits are yielded as much with group communication as with individualized communication in distance education.

- *Share moderating roles with students* (Berge, 1995). Online distance education courses tend to make ample use of small-group and large-group discussions. The moderator of these discussions has several responsibilities, including identifying prompts for discussion, setting guidelines for participation, initiating and maintaining discussion, enforcing guidelines for participation, checking for inaccurate contributions, and summarizing the content covered in the discussion. If a mentor models effective moderating strategies for the first few online discussions, the mentor can then assign individual students or groups of students with the task of moderating future discussions. To effectively assign students to such tasks, students should be given adequate time to immerse themselves in the subject matter, and the mentor should set guidelines for moderating and participation.

One might ask if the strategies described in this chapter will compromise the quality of the instruction by cutting corners. Most individuals who have used such techniques and strategies might argue that the opposite is likely to be true. Such strategies as described in this chapter increase the amount of accountability placed on both the mentor and the learner, thereby yielding a more effective instructional experience for both. In addition, such strategies increase the extent to which students reflect on their own work and the work of their peers. This, in turn, enables learners to develop meta-analytical skills, consider a greater number of varying perspectives, and engage in increasingly higher levels of critical thinking. In addition, these strategies will likely "free up" the mentor's time, increasing the available time and effort towards ensuring quality in both the process and the outcome of Web-based courses (Baltes, Dittmann-Kohli, & Dixon, 1984; Bates, 1984, 1995, 1996; Beaudoin, 1990; Berge, 1995; Bork, 2001; Collins & Berge, 1996; Daniel & Meech, 1978; Harasim, Hiltz, Teles, & Turoff, 1997; Hodgson, Mann, & Snell, 1995; Keller, 1987; Lewis, 1995; Martin, 1997; Moore & Kearsley, 1996; Paulsen, 2000; Rowntree, 1992; Saint, 2000; Salmi, 2002; Sammons, 2003; Visser, Visser, & Schlosser, 2003; Visser & Visser, 2000; Wellburn, 1999).

REFERENCES

Baltes, P. B., Dittmann-Kohli, F., & Dixon, R. A. (1984). New perspectives on the development of intelligence in adulthood: Toward a dual-process conception and a model of selective optimization with compensation. In P. B. Baltes & O.G. Brim, Jr. (Eds.), *Life-Span Development and Behavior* (Vol. 6, pp. 33-76). New York: Academic Press.

Bates, A. (1984). *The role of technology in distance education.* London: Croom Helm.

Bates, A. (1995). *The future of learning.* Retrieved February 25, 2005, from http://bates.cstudies.ubc.ca/learning.html

Bates, A. (1996). *The impact of technological change on open and distance learning.* Retrieved February 25, 2005, from http://bates.cstudies.ubc.ca/papers/brisbane.html

Beaudoin, M. (1990). The instructor's changing role in distance education. *The American Journal of Distance Education, 4*(2), 21-29.

Berge, Z. L. (1995). Facilitating computer conferencing: Recommendations from the field. *Educational Technology, 35*(1), 22-30.

Bork, A. (2001). What is needed for effective learning on the Internet? *Educational Technology and Society, 4*(3), 139-144.

Collins, M., & Berge, Z. L. (1996). *Facilitating interaction in computer mediated online courses.* Retrieved March 1, 2005, from http://www.emoderators.com/moderators/flcc.html

Daniel, J., & Meech, A. (1978). Tutorial support in distance education. *Convergence*, XI, 93-99.

Harasim, L., Hiltz, S. R., Teles, L., & Turoff, M. (1997). *Learning networks.* Cambridge, MA: MIT Press.

Hodgson, V., Mann, S., & Snell, R. (Eds.). (1995). *Beyond distance teaching: Towards open learning.* Milton Keynes: Open University.

Keller, J. M. (1987). Development and use of the ARCS model of motivational design. *Journal of Instructional Development, 10*(3), 2-10.

Lewis, R. (1995). The creation of an open learning environment in higher education. *Innovation and Learning in Education, 1*(2), 32-36.

Martin, R. R. (1997). *Key issues in transitioning from distance education to distributed learning.* Retrieved April 1, 1998, from http://fcae.nova.edu/~kearsley/online.html

Moore, M. G., & Kearsley, G. (1996). *Distance education: A systems view.* Belmont, CA: Wadsworth.

Paulsen, M. F. (2000). *Online education: An international analysis of web-based education and strategic recommendations for decision makers.* Bekkestua: NKI Forlaget.

Rowntree, D. (1992). *Exploring open and distance learning.* London: Kogan Page.

Saint, W. (2000). *Tertiary distance education and technology in sub-Saharan Africa.* Washington, DC: World Bank.

Salmi, J. (2002). *Constructing knowledge societies: New challenges for tertiary education.* Washington, DC: The World Bank.

Sammons, M. (2003). Exploring the new conception of teaching and learning in distance education. In M. G. Moore & W. G. Anderson (Eds.), *Handbook of Distance Education* (pp. 387-397). Mahwah, NJ: Erlbaum.

Thorpe, M. (1979). *The Student Special Support Scheme: A Report.* Milton Keynes: Open University.

Visser, L., Visser, Y., & Schlosser, C. (2003). Critical thinking in distance education and traditional education. *Quarterly Review of Distance Education, 4*(4), 401-407.

Visser, L., & Visser, Y. L. (2000). Perceived and actual student support needs in distance education. *Quarterly Review of Distance Education, 1*(2), 109-117.

Wellburn, E. (1999). Educational vision, theory, and technology in virtual learning in K-12. In C. M. Feyten & J. W. Nutta (Eds.), *Virtual Instruction* (pp. 35-64). Englewood, CA: Libraries Unlimited.

ABOUT THE AUTHORS

Ray Amirault, PhD, is assistant professor in instructional technology at Wayne State University. He teaches courses on a variety of subjects, including knowledge management, trends and issues in instructional technology, learning management systems, and foundations of instructional design. Ray's research agenda is focused on the study of learning in technical domains, particularly in terms of mental models, conceptual development, learner motivation, and expert performance. Prior to joining the faculty at Wayne State University, Ray was a member of the faculty at Florida Atlantic University. He has worked on a variety of instructional design, performance improvement and distance learning projects, serving clients such as the U.S. Navy, Pearson PCS, Verizon Wireless, Motorola, IBM, and Florida State University. Ray holds a doctorate in instructional systems from Florida State University, and an undergraduate degree in computer science from the University of West Florida.

Miguel Buendia Gómez, PhD, is currently director of the Master's Programs in Adult Education at the Eduardo Mondlane University (Mozambique). Miguel has extensive experience and expertise in distance education in Mozambique and other developing countries. In this capacity he is currently involved in the establishment of a National Institute of Distance Education in Mozambique. Miguel holds a PhD in philosophy and history of education from University of Sao Paolo (Brazil).

Margaret Crawford lives in Iowa where she holds various leadership positions, teaches computer applications, and works as an information specialist. She is the co-editor of the *Proceedings*, a yearly publication of the

Association for Educational Communications and Technology. In addition, she is a copy editor for *Distance Learning* magazine. Margaret holds a degree in instructional technology.

Sensu Curabay, PhD, is currently associate professor at Anadolu University (Turkey). Her research interests are focused on the intersection between women's issues, media, and distance education. Sensu holds a doctoral degree in media and planning from Anadolu University.

Bob Day, PhD, is a consultant in information and communication technologies (ICTs) for international development projects. Bob's interests are multidisciplinary, involving the interdependence of innovation systems, knowledge ecologies, sustainable development, open learning, and the wide variety of potential benefits that ICTs can provide across all these factors. In these contexts, he contributes to national, regional and international initiatives aimed at poverty eradication and socioeconomic development with particular focus on the poorest communities in Sub-Saharan Africa. Bob moved to South Africa 29 years ago, after obtaining his PhD in applied physics at the University of London. He has held executive and senior positions in several organizations, and is chairman of the board of SchoolNet South Africa, and chairman of the Advisory Council of the National Science Festival, SciFest.

Emine Demiray, PhD, is associate professor at Anadolu University (Turkey). She has a strong interest in studying the intersection between women's issues and media, distance education, and family. She holds a doctoral degree from Anadolu University.

Ugur Demiray, PhD, is a professor at Anadolu University (Turkey). His research interests include distance education and scholarly online journalism. Ugur has written a variety of articles for national and international journals. He is currently a member of the editorial board of various distance education journals, and is the editor-in-chief for the *Turkish Online Journal of Distance Education*. He holds a doctoral degree from Anadolu University (Turkey).

Tony Dodds, is a consultant for international development projects involving open and distance learning. From 1996 to 2001, Tony served as the director of the Centre for External Studies of the University of Namibia. Prior to that, Tony served as director of the International Extension College in Cambridge (United Kingdom) for 25 years. During that time he helped to set up the Mauritius College of the Air and the Correspondence and Open Studies Unit of the University of Lagos (Nigeria).

He received an honorary degree from the Open University in the United Kingdom in acknowledgement of his contributions in distance education.

Kristen Gagnon is an instructor in the Department of Instructional Technology and Research at Florida Atlantic University. She holds a master's degree in instructional technology. Prior to completing her master's, Kristen was a mathematics instructor at the International Technical Institute in Florida. Kristen graduated with honors in business management from Florida State University. Her undergraduate internship thesis was nominated for the Baker Undergraduate Research Award from Florida State University. She plans for a future dedicated to improving the process of education.

Andrea Hope is the associate academic vice-president of the Hong Kong Shue Yan College in Hong Kong. Prior to her appointment to her current position, Andrea served as a higher education specialist for the Commonwealth of Learning, in British Columbia, Canada. Based on her international experience to date, Andrea has a particular interest in quality assurance in face-to-face instruction and distance education for higher learning.

Deb LaPointe, PhD, is the assistant director for education at the Health Sciences Library and Informatics Center and professor in the Organizational Learning and Instructional Technologies program at the University of New Mexico. She has designed and taught distance education courses in a variety of formats. She has worked with organizations and learners in Taiwan, Mainland China, and Australia and continues to research peer interaction in online learning environments. Deb received her doctorate in organizational learning and instructional technology (with a focus on distance education) from the University of New Mexico. Her dissertation received the William Rainey Harper dissertation award.

Frederic Michael Litto, PhD, served as professor of communications in the School of Communications and Arts of the University of São Paulo (Brazil) from 1971 to 2003. He was the founder and scientific coordinator of the university's research laboratory "The School of the Future," which he continues to direct. He is president of the Brazilian Association for Distance Education, and a member of a variety of editorial boards. Frederic serves on a working group of the World Bank, creating a new area of financing for distance learning projects in rural and isolated communities. In addition he is a consultant to the Commonwealth of Learning in a training project in Mozambique.

François Marchessou, PhD, is director of Maison des Pays du Cône Sud, an exchange center between a number of Latin American countries and France. In this capacity he is extensively involved in overseas projects in educational technology and distance education. François is also active in international consulting work. From 1974 till 2002, François served as director of the Department of Educational Technology of the University of Poitiers (France). During that time, he was closely involved in the development of distance education in a variety of settings. Francois studied in France and the United States.

Jeffrey S. Sievert is an assistant in research for the Learning Systems Institute at Florida State University working on projects sponsored by the U.S. Navy. He is currently leading a project task to identify, assess, and support learner attributes important for online success. He holds an master of science degree in instructional systems from FSU and is pursuing a doctorate in the same field. His research interests include training complex cognitive skills in traditional and distance learning environments.

Michael Simonson, PhD, is a program professor in the Instructional Technology and Distance Education program at Nova Southeastern University. He has authored four major textbooks dealing with distance education, instructional technology, instructional computing, and instructional media. He has won the award for most outstanding research in the field of distance education presented by the United States Distance Learning Association. Mike serves as editor for several journals related to instructional technology and distance education. Mike has considerable experience working with domestic and international businesses and industries, especially on projects related to instructional technology and distance education. He holds a PhD in instructional systems from the University of Iowa.

Meira van der Spa is currently employed as a marketing and communications representative at the Agrotechnology and Food Sciences Group of Wageningen University and Research Center (The Netherlands). In addition, she is affiliated with the Learning Development Institute, participating as a researcher and an editor. Meira holds a degree in Latin American studies from the University of Utrecht (The Netherlands) and, a postgraduate certificate in journalism. Her areas of interest include journalism, management, literature, editing, teaching and horse-riding.

Jan Visser, PhD, is president and senior researcher at the Learning Development Institute. He has prime responsibility for the Meaning of Learning and The Scientific Mind focus areas of the organization. He is also UNESCO's former director for Learning Without Frontiers. A theoretical physicist by original vocation and training, he strayed into many other areas, including filmmaking and instructional design, while broadening his interests and activities beyond the study of nature, developing a career that lasted more than 3 decades in international development, working around the globe. Jan is also a musician (who builds his own instruments) and an avid walker.

Lya Visser, PhD, is director of training at the Learning Development Institute. She has rich experience in learning and working in distance education environments, and has explored distance education and e-learning themes and issues on different continents and in a variety of exciting circumstances. Her professional interest and background is in the development of effective learning systems. Her research and publication interests are in the areas of student support, critical thinking and motivation and communication. Lya holds a doctoral degree in educational science and technology from the University of Twente, The Netherlands.

Yusra Laila Visser, PhD, is assistant professor in instructional technology at Wayne State University. She has taught courses covering a variety of topics, including instructional design, distance education, technology integration, computer courseware, instructional program development, and curriculum webs. Yusra serves on the board of directors of the Learning Development Institute. Previously, she served as assistant professor at Florida Atlantic University, as instructional designer for the Office for Distance and Distributed Learning at Florida State University, and as a program associate for international instructional technology projects at Education Development Center. Yusra holds a doctorate in instructional systems from Florida State University. Her research, writing, and presentations have focused on Web-based distance education, attitudes toward the sciences and science education, and the effectiveness of various instructional strategies.

Muriel Visser-Valfrey, holds a PhD in mass communication from Florida State University. She has worked extensively in education, health and rural development in sub-Saharan Africa. Muriel has both personal (as a student) and professional experience in distance education. Part of Muriel's secondary education as well as her Master's degree (in distance education) were completed at a distance. In addition, Muriel provided support to Mozambique's second upgrading course for teachers through distance education in the late 1990's. Residing in France, Muriel works as a consultant and part-time researcher for the Learning Development

Institute, concentrating on issues related to HIV/AIDS awareness and education in Southern Africa.

Lixun Wang, PhD, works as a lecturer in the Hong Kong Institute of Education. In addition, he is leading two research projects at the Hong Kong Institute of Education, one on corpus linguistics, and one on online learning. Previously he worked as a research associate for the Open University of Hong Kong. He has also developed a variety of Web sites for online learning purposes. Lixun's academic interests include distance education, online learning, computer-assisted language learning, applied linguistics and computational linguistics. He has an extensive publishing record. Lixun earned his doctoral degree in computational linguistics from the University of Birmingham.

Paul G. West is an education specialist and coordinates knowledge management activities at the Commonwealth of Learning (COL). In this capacity he works with the COL Knowledge Finder, which indexes over 1 million documents from the Global Distance Education Network and other sources. Previously, Paul was responsible for establishing the African Digital Library, a fully Web-based library that provides free access to over 8,000 full-text eBooks.

Steve Wheeler, PhD, is a senior lecturer in information and communication technologies (ICTs) and education at the University of Plymouth (United Kingdom). His research interests include distance education, technology supported learning, e-learning, telematics, individual differences in learning, collaborative learning, problem based learning, and creativity. He is on the editorial board of, among others, the *Quarterly Review of Distance Education* and editor of the recent volume titled *Toward the Virtual University: International Online Perspectives*. He is author of more than 50 journal articles and book chapters. Steve is a graduate of the British Open University and his PhD investigated the psychological effects of tutor-student separation.

Brent Wilson, PhD, is professor and coordinator of the Information and Learning Technologies program at the University of Colorado at Denver. Active in the Association for Educational Communications and Technology and other professional organizations, Brent serves on editorial boards for a number of journals. Current research interests relate to the following questions: How to help instructional designers create good instruction? How to help students, teachers, and workers make good use of learning resources? How to encourage best practices relating to educational technology? How to strengthen the instructional-design profession by improved sharing among practitioners and by grounding practice in a broader theory base?

Weiyuan Zhang, PhD, is research fellow at the Centre for Research in Distance & Adult Learning at the Open University of Hong Kong (China). He has 18 years experience in educational research at East China Normal University, the University of Victoria, the University of Edinburgh, the University of Hong Kong, and the Open University of Hong Kong. He is a recipient of 11 institutional, national, regional, and international awards in open and distance education. Weiyuan has published the *English-Chinese Dictionary in Open and Distance Education*. In addition, he has published several books, and over 100 articles in scholarly journals and conference proceedings. He has been on the editorial board of a number of journals.

CPSIA information can be obtained at www.ICGtesting.com
Printed in the USA
LVOW031034291011

252572LV00002B/1/A